The MEAT Hook

The Pete Carroll
A sausage for winners
$12⁹⁹/lb

The

MEAT HOOK

MEAT BOOK

The
MEAT HOOK
MEAT BOOK

Buy, Butcher, and Cook
Your Way to Better Meat

Tom Mylan

ARTISAN
NEW YORK

To our customers and friends,
past, present, and future.

CONTENTS

FOREWORD
by Annaliese Griffin, editor in chief, Brooklyn Based

When I met Tom in 2003, he was fond of saying that he had moved to New York City to watch the world burn down. In actuality, he started rebuilding even before the flames went out. When The Meat Hook opened in the fall of 2009, just six weeks after we got married, the expertise and relationships that it took to turn a cavernous bowling-alley-supply shop with filthy carpet and drop ceilings into a living, breathing butcher shop had been years in the making. You can't understand The Meat Hook without understanding the backstory and the gang of weirdos who continue to make Brooklyn the most exciting place in the country to live, work, and eat.

The Meat Hook and The Brooklyn Kitchen, a kitchen-supply shop, cooking school, and food-nerd power center, are two separate businesses housed in the same huge building in Williamsburg, Brooklyn. They opened together on a shoestring budget that was cobbled together with incredible resourcefulness during the depths of the recession post—housing bubble burst. The fact that they didn't just survive but have actually flourished isn't simply a matter of luck—it's evidence of a fundamental shift in the way we eat, and in what we think businesses can and should do for the communities they serve.

Though Brooklyn is full of young businesses, very few of the people behind them started out with entrepreneurial ambitions. Many of us grew up in the nineties, when selling out was the worst sin you could commit and no one wanted to be "The Man." We all wanted to be artists and musicians and writers. So how do you get from the cavalier nihilism of watching the world burn down to owning a business that is based on the earnest concept that supporting local farmers is better for the animals, the farmers, the customers, and the world? If there's one person who promoted the idea that owning a business could be a creative pursuit and a positive force in the world, it's cheesemaker Mateo Kehler. In fact, it's fair to place a certain amount of blame for the rise of jam operations, pickle concerns, and $9 candy bars squarely on his shoulders—that's what an inspiring motherfucker he is.

When I say that he is a cheese wizard, I mean in fact that Mateo actually resembles a wizard. He has these insane eyebrows that sprout out about three inches from his face. Also, his cheese is excellent. In the late 1990s he spent time in South Asia working on economic development projects, and then decided to start Jasper Hill Farm, and eventually The Cellars at Jasper Hill, in Greensboro, Vermont, with his brother, Andy, as a way to use the principles he learned in the Third World to improve the depressed dairy economy there. When he wants to talk to you about economics and liberation and changing the world, it gets real heavy real fast. Tom and I met Mateo not long after we met each other, when we were both working at the cheese counter at Dean & DeLuca. Jasper Hill was just starting to sell cheese in the city, and Mateo called every week to ask us what we thought of their cheeses. As Tom and I moved from job to job and both started writing

about food, we stayed in touch with the Kehlers. By that time, Tom was working at Marlow & Sons, a farm-to-table restaurant in Williamsburg that also had a small store where you could get coffee and buy local honey and Tom's homemade hot sauce and bitters. It was one of the first spots to truly lose its mind over all things made in Brooklyn, and Tom was the buyer. Journalists from *The New York Times* and *Saveur* would call him weekly for the scoop on the new, cool artisan thing. At the same time, he was aging a prosciutto in our apartment. For a year, I would wake up every morning to see the hoof-on hind leg of a pastured hog hanging across our loft apartment in an old sewing factory. Tom always had projects lined up on top of the refrigerator: Green walnut liquor. Hot sauce. Tom started a blog called Grocery Guy and we both wrote for it obsessively, documenting every meal, every project. I had also become an editor and partner at Brooklyn Based, a small media company covering the increasingly insane Brooklyn food scene.

We started organizing a sort of combination artisan showcase, flea market, and party called The UnFancy Food Show once each summer as a way to call attention to all the people we knew in the city and beyond who were growing and making delicious things. At the second UnFancy, in 2008, Mateo spent the entire afternoon proselytizing about his cheese to the customers and about the power of capitalism to the other vendors. Mateo's message was this: playing at making something delicious is fine if you want a hobby, but starting a business gives you economic power that can be transformative, and to waste that is, well, fucking stupid.

That was when The Meat Hook became a twinkle in Tom's eye. The previous winter, he had become a butcher in the crazy space of just a few months. While organic pickles and local jams and ethically sourced chocolate were all fantastically abundant, it was beginning to seem more and more that what really mattered was meat.

Marlow & Sons and Diner were the first two restaurants in Brooklyn to embrace the idea that buying locally raised animals of known provenance was the most ethical and delicious way of eating meat. The two restaurants, located next door to each other in South Williamsburg, had been the first places to really catch hold in a long-ignored neighborhood. Owners Andrew Tarlow and Mark Firth (Mark has since left the partnership to move to the Berkshires to farm and open his own place) took a real chance opening there, a few doors down from a Hasidic funeral home in the shadow of the Williamsburg Bridge. Andrew and Mark promoted Tom from buyer and manager of their tiny general store at Marlow to butcher in the fall of 2007.

Marlow and Diner had been buying meat from Fleisher's Grass-Fed and Organic Meats in Kingston, New York, but Josh and Jessica Applestone, the owners, decided that the economics only worked out for everyone if the restaurants would take whole animals rather than nearly-ready-to-fire cuts. That necessitated having an in-house butcher. Tom became that person, after spending long weeks that fall riding the bus up to Kingston to apprentice at Fleisher's.

A year later, in late 2008, Marlow & Daughters, New York City's first locally sourced butcher shop, opened with Tom at the helm. Inspired by the success of Daughters, and the fact that people really would seek out meat that had been properly raised by local farmers, Tom and the two other butchers at Daughters, Brent Young and Ben Turley, started thinking about opening their own place. Less than a year later, The Meat Hook opened.

In the buildup to the opening of Daughters, Brent and Ben had arrived from Richmond, Virginia, where they'd been working at a butcher shop and in restaurants. Brent had heard through whatever whiskey-saturated grapevine runs between kitchens in Brooklyn and Virginia that Diner and Marlow & Sons were hiring and that they needed someone with experience breaking down whole animals. Pretty soon, Brent was working on the line at Diner and as Tom's backstop in the tiny metal box—a walk-in refrigerator, and not a particularly large one—that served as his butcher station. Until Brent came on, Tom had been spending ten hours a day, six days a week, in the box. At minimum.

All the while, he'd been teaching pig butchering classes at The Brooklyn Kitchen, then located in a space not far from the restaurants. The classes were a strong indicator, even more so than picklemania, that the world had lost its goddamn mind when it came to food. There was a months-long waiting list for the opportunity to crowd around a table for an hour and a half while Tom sweated and broke down a pig, talking about the cuts and how and why you would use them, where the pig came from, and how it was raised. Harry Rosenblum and Taylor Erkkinen, the couple who owned The Brooklyn Kitchen, became our friends. Over bourbon and pulled pork, it became clear that they had been talking about a business similar to one that had been floated over our kitchen table: a combination store and event space, where customers could both buy high-quality ingredients and learn how to use them. A place to put on big dinners and host book parties. The butcher shop Tom and Brent and Ben wanted to open would anchor it, but it would be so much more. Harry and Taylor found a space; they handled the build-out and begged and borrowed to finance the whole project. A weird old bowling-alley-supply store was transformed into a combination kitchenware shop, cooking school, and butcher shop.

The first year was awful.

There were tears. There were fights. There were frantic phone calls and raised voices and long hours and lots and lots of whiskey. Brent and Ben and Tom worked twelve-hour days, six days a week. Harry and Taylor moved their existing business to the new location while managing construction, dealing with finances, and caring for Moxie, their infant daughter. I handled publicity and marketing while working three editorial jobs and smoothing ruffled feathers and soothing disgruntled employees.

Now The Meat Hook is the embodiment of what Mateo was talking about way back when. While the Brooklyn food scene has been mocked for its twee artisan goods, what Tom and Brent and Ben have built is not about offering the world an unnecessary luxury. It's about offering farmers in New York State an opportunity to distinguish themselves in the marketplace, to sell people properly raised meat from animals that never see a feedlot and that add to the tilth of the soil and the health of the world. It's about offering customers the option of knowing where their meat comes from and how those animals lived. It's a choice that not that many people have, and it's one that Meat Hook customers, and everyone attached to the shop in any way, feel passionately about.

In our food-obsessed world, glossy magazine spreads, gross-out food safari shows, and underground meat-fests provide ample opportunity to see just exactly how the sausage gets made. While *The Meat Hook Meat Book* illuminates any remaining sausage-making mysteries, it also offers a rare peek at how a butcher shop gets made, at how a twenty-first-century business gets made. There are a lot of other books on butchering and butcher shops out there now, and that is a good thing. When Tom began his journey, there were almost none, and he and Brent and Ben and everyone else in the world of The Meat Hook, many of whom you'll meet in the pages to come, are happy to have played their part in bringing back the grand tradition of the local butcher. This book is not intended to be the last word on butchering, but rather one personal, crazed, and, hopefully, useful version of what butchering can be.

INTRODUCTION

The way our society thinks about meat has changed a lot in recent years. A decade ago, I was a vegetarian, because it seemed to me that not eating meat was the only alternative to eating meat that was raised under unethical conditions and pumped full of synthetic hormones and antibiotics. I had never heard of a farmers' market, and I didn't know that there were still people raising animals on family farms; I was like most Americans at the time. Since then, through the hard work of countless journalists, farmers, and chefs, we're no longer ignorant about a better way to do meat in this country.

One of the most unexpected elements of this movement is the huge interest in butchering. When I was tasked with finding well-raised local meat for the restaurant I was working for in 2006, I never suspected that just a few years later meat and butchering would become my entire life. In a similar way, people's interest in where their meat comes from has led them back into the butcher shop after decades of shopping at the supermarket. Supermarkets are places to buy things, but a butcher shop is a place to ask questions, to learn how to cook unfamiliar cuts, and, most important, to get exactly what you want, not just what has been put out for sale.

What is it that makes a butcher shop so different from anywhere else? A good butcher is equal parts marketplace, community center, and neighborhood bar, where regulars shop, gossip, and run into each other—not unlike the barbershops and drugstores of Norman Rockwell's America. It has recently become fashionable to promote a butcher shop specializing in grass-fed, pastured, local products as some sort of exclusive, boutique lifestyle "experience," but fashion is a cheap commodity with a shelf life measured in weeks or months. A real butcher is an institution and a fixture of the community, as essential and emotionally nourishing as a church pew, stoop, or front porch and as utilitarian as a corner store or gas station.

Our desire at The Meat Hook to provide a home away from home for our customers comes from being part of a community of Brooklynites framed by the backdrop of an increasingly fractured rural and suburban landscape marked by sprawl, anonymous megamarts, and chain restaurants. It is our hope that The Meat Hook becomes part of the fabric of our customers' lives, providing one of the few places in the wilderness of anonymity where everyone truly knows your name.

Partners
TOM, BRENT, AND BEN

How did three guys with liberal arts degrees from three different parts of the country end up owning a butcher shop in Brooklyn, New York? It's a long story. A really long story. A story better told at 3 a.m. at a picnic table in the backyard of a bar when you're really, really drunk, so I'm not going to go into it here.

Who are we?

Brent Young is a Pittsburgh native with a penchant for all things smothered with coleslaw and French fries. After a less than satisfying attempt at making a go of an advanced English literature degree, Brent returned to his longtime vocation of working in food. He eventually landed a job at a butcher shop in Richmond, Virginia, where he was living and playing in bands that toured church-basement venues in off-brand college towns east of the Mississippi. In 2008, he heard the siren song of Brooklyn and packed it up in Richmond to come work with me. Things then quickly spiraled out of control.

Our very own Southern auntie, Ben Turley, was born and raised in West Virginia and has what I might call an unhealthy obsession with country hams. Ben is also Brent's best friend, former bandmate, and work wife from their stint as Richmond's most-sought-after line cook duo for dubious restaurants with aspirational names. Although he continued to work at the butcher shop in Richmond when Brent left to go north and find his calling in the big city, it didn't take long for Ben to be convinced by promises of New York butchermania, cold beer, hard work, and low wages to make the trip himself. Once that U-Haul was packed, the *Muppets Take Manhattan* moment of the Meat Hook story began and the inevitability of our unlikely business was assured.

I came to New York in 2003 as a twenty-seven-year-old art school dropout with delusions of grandeur. While I was hell-bent on becoming a respected painter or the writer of the next great American post-postmodern novel, I was also stone broke, and my huge New York City bills needed to get paid. In a burst of laziness combined with necessity, I fell back on what I had always done for money: work in food. I had slaved in pizza kitchens and risen through the ranks at Whole Foods Market from assistant cheese cutter (yes, very funny) to wine buyer. I'd even had a desk job working for a gourmet cookie company (bad idea). But working a food job in New York City was somehow different. It felt like being a part of a big dysfunctional family. The local/farm-to-table movement was just starting to pick up real steam. Restaurants like Momofuku and The Spotted Pig were opening. It started to seem like working in food was becoming cool, which it most assuredly had not been back when I was pounding out pizzas for $2.85 an hour. In 1993, when I got my first job working in a kitchen, restaurant work was for losers. But the more people I met in the business, the more I realized that *this* was what I wanted to do. What I had always done but not considered possible long-term was now a viable career path: food.

Fast-forward a few years, and I found myself working for Caroline Fidanza, the chef at the time at Marlow & Sons and Diner, two restaurants that were key to the farm-to-table movement in New York City. They were among the restaurants that were putting Brooklyn on the culinary map when most critics couldn't be bothered to make the trip over the bridge. I was making big-time under-the-table money writing and editing the *Diner Journal* magazine, visiting farms, and learning how to really cook. I was in heaven. Then came the question, "Do you want to be our butcher?" Once I said yes, my life and the lives of those around me would never be the same. Work days went from eight hours to fourteen hours long. My pay was less. I smelled like blood and had fish scales in my hair at the end of every day, but I loved it. I had, almost by accident, found my calling.

A lot of people say you should never go into business with your friends. Those people are right. However, Ben, Brent, and I are not very good listeners. So we went ahead and did something we weren't qualified for, knew almost nothing about, and had no money to pay for anyway: in the fall of 2009, we opened The Meat Hook.

We were, let's say, willful. We couldn't wait to have the freedom to express all of our infantile creative desires. Brent, with his Pittsburgh background, wanted to make scrapple and sausages with outlandish amounts of cheese in them and stupid names (the Long Dong Bud sausage was named by Brent's dad, Bud, after a brief phone conversation about its ingredients and size). Ben, as West Virginian as a coal miner's lunch box, was lost in a fever dream of making urban country hams and obsessed with getting a proper smoker to perfect our bacon recipe. And me? Well, I was over the moon to finally have a venue where I could start producing all the guilty pleasures of my Southern California teenage stoner years: refried beans with ridiculous amounts of real lard, and chili that was more suited to pouring over a hot dog than eating out of a bowl. I also had the idea of making a sausage that tasted exactly like a bacon cheeseburger. And we all wanted the music at The Meat Hook to be really loud, so loud that now we're half deaf.

It shouldn't have worked. We were too irresponsible to be business owners. Too clueless. Our business plan was written on a bar napkin and we were well on our way to drunkenness when we wrote it. All the numbers were nothing more than wild-assed guesses and hopeful fabrications. We opened The Meat Hook while it was actually still under construction, and our opening staff consisted of three people: us. We worked sick, hungover, and injured, popping ADHD meds and washing them down with energy drinks. I'm not sure how none of us ended up dead, but somehow it worked. We were making money doing exactly what we wanted to do, and nothing else.

Yes, most people say you shouldn't go into business with your friends because you'll end up hating each other, but there is another much more annoying thing that can happen: you can become even better friends by spending every waking moment together, learning way too much about each other and developing the kind of collective language of in-jokes and references that is usually limited to twins, combat units, or those stationed together in remote Arctic research facilities. To our wives, girlfriends, and everyone else who had to deal with us during the first year of The Meat Hook, we apologize.

THE MEAT HOOK MISSION

The existential question of what we will all do with our lives is a pretty hard one to answer. Luckily, through a series of happy accidents, Ben, Brent, and I ended up with the unlikely solution of owning a butcher shop. While we weren't exactly sure how we were going to pull off opening the shop, we did know what we wanted it to be: fun, unpretentious, accessible, and, most important, financially sustainable.

That last bit sounds unromantic, but if you can't make money, all the good feelings and high ideals in the world will not save you. At The Meat Hook, we are in the business of paying our farmers, and to that end, we strive each and every day to simply do it right. From farm visits to pick our animals for the next month's slaughter to chatting up regulars at the counter, everything we do is for the purpose of properly representing our farmers' hard work, deep knowledge, and high-quality animals. We never forget that without them, we'd be just another bunch of jerks selling pork chops. With all that in mind, I hope you will go out of your way to buy meat from farmers' markets and support your own local family-owned butcher shop. Without your support, these farmers and business owners might fade away, but if you choose to spend your money this way, you'll enjoy your meat more, learn new things, and—dare I say it?—do your part to make the world a better place.

CUTTING MEAT AT THE MEAT HOOK
Chaos of Styles

Every culture cuts meat differently. Even in the same country, cuts can vary from region to region, and then, to add to the confusion, they may vary seasonally, reflecting the way people cook in the winter months versus in the summer. No one wants to braise a beef shank or roast a pork shoulder in the middle of August, nor is anyone likely to fire up the grill for a mess of burgers when there's three feet of snow on the ground.

    The way we cut meat at The Meat Hook is in a state of constant evolution. This book reflects the way we cut meat today. But every book we read, YouTube video we watch, and person we interact with can have an impact on what happens at the cutting table. We have been lucky enough to be able to learn from butchers from all over the country and all over the world. The result is that on any given day, we may make cuts of meat familiar to people in Japan, France, Argentina, or Italy (or even Pittsburgh), such as the ones described below.

SECRETO

This is a cut popular in Portugal and parts of Spain. It is the pork version of the flank steak that we seam off the belly. It's great to grill or fry—just don't overcook it, or it will be tough and dry.

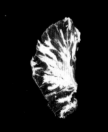

CAMPAGNELLA, OR HEEL

The calf muscle of the rear beef leg is a popular wintertime cut in Italy that is slowly braised (see the recipe on page 78); its name is Italian for "bell" because of its shape.

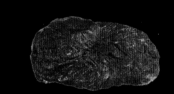

MERLOT STEAK

This is a traditional French cut we learned from our French butcher friend Yves-Marie le Bourdonnec (see page 264). It is simply the campagnella with all of the sinews tediously removed, magically transforming it into a lean and tender grillable cut (see the recipe on page 77).

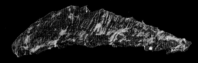

OYSTER STEAK

These tiny steaks are found in the hip socket of the rear beef leg and are similar to skirt and hanger steak in texture and flavor. Watch out! There are only two of these tiny steaks per animal. It's also known as *araignée* ("the spider") in France.

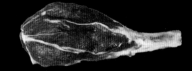

SHOULDER TENDER

Known by many different names, this little buddy is buried in the middle of the beef arm chuck. It's tender, as its name implies, and it makes a great steak for grilling and slicing over a salad.

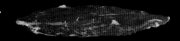

THE PEAR

This is another wonderful tender cut found inside the muscle group we call the top round of the beef leg. It was made famous in Bill Buford's book *Heat*.

THE FOOD-DOLLAR DIAGRAM

The best way to understand the difference between shopping at a local butcher shop and buying meat at the supermarket is to look at how much of every dollar you spend ends up in the hands of the farmer who raised your meat.

When you buy a family pack of steaks at your neighborhood chain store, about 11 cents of each dollar goes to the farmer. Where does the rest go? To multinational corporations, out-of-state distributors, giant packing houses, and all manner of middlemen in the complex supply chain that brought the package in your hands thousands of miles from where it was produced.

At The Meat Hook, 32 cents of every dollar (or almost 300 percent more) goes directly to our farmers, giving them a financial incentive to continue raising local animals properly on pasture. Where does the rest go? To small family-owned slaughterhouses, to local trucking companies that bring the animals from slaughter to our door, and to pay our rent, taxes, and the salaries of the people who make The Meat Hook a place worth shopping at. The important thing here is that the rest of each dollar (well, except the part that goes to federal taxes) stays in our local economy, creating more jobs, hopefully, to serve more people who want to buy local meat.

What can you do if you want to spend less money but use more of what you have to help a farmer? Buy meat in primals (see "Butchering Terms," page 20) from your local farmers' market or meat locker and butcher the meat yourself. The costs farmers have to pay to have meat cut into individual serving sizes and then packaged at the slaughterhouse are ridiculously high, and they have to charge accordingly. Large unbutchered pieces are much more reasonably priced, and you can tailor the cuts you get to what you want to cook, not the other way around.

YOUR NEIGHBORHOOD CHAIN STORE

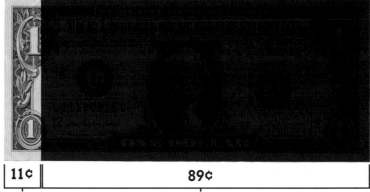

11¢	89¢
FARMER	**MULTINATIONAL CORPORATIONS, OUT-OF-STATE DISTRIBUTORS, GIANT PACKING HOUSES**

THE MEAT HOOK

32¢	68¢
FARMER	**SMALL FAMILY-OWNED SLAUGHTERHOUSES, LOCAL TRUCKING COMPANIES, RENT, TAXES, SALARIES**

So, where to begin on your way to becoming a budding butcher? If you don't already know how to break down a chicken, start there—it's where I started. Cutting up a chicken is a fundamental skill that everyone used to possess, and you should possess it too. Whether you use our unconventional method (see page 170) or follow a video on YouTube, acquiring this skill will give you the basic hand-eye coordination needed to move on to larger stuff like a pork shoulder or even a small lamb.

How far can you go? All the way. With the help of this book and the myriad other resources that have sprung up in the wake of the repopularization of meat and butchering, you can teach yourself to cut up anything you want. Your only limit is how much ambition and freezer space you have. If you can, attend a butchering class if one is offered nearby. Butchering is only as hard as you make it; I butchered my first pig by getting instructions over the phone I held in one hand, with my saw in the other (see page 100). Just make sure you have a plan for what you're going to do with all that meat once you're done!

A word about weights and measures: Some of the recipes in this book are taken directly from our recipes at the shop, and these recipes are measured out in grams. Yes, the metric system! So, for some of the recipes, I did not include measurements by volume, because the recipe wouldn't turn out right. If you're serious about cooking, get a digital scale (see Resources, page 305). You're a grown-up; buy one. The Meat Hook team may not totally have it together in every area, but we're very precise when we need to be, and when making these recipes you need to be precise.

I think of this book as an extension of the idea of the butcher shop: both a place for the home cook to find a recipe for Wednesday night dinner and a resource for a chef to find inspiration and to learn about something new. Whether you read it all the way through like a novel or skim through all the meat cutting and farm stuff until you get to the part about shotgunning beers, none of this is going to be on a test. I've tried to include a little something for everyone here, and it was my goal to present meat in general and well-raised meat in particular in its complete context of farming, slaughtering, butchering, recipes, and cooking—along with a plus-sized dollop of the most important aspect of food: fun and enjoyment with your friends and family.

BUTCHERING TERMS

Here's a glossary to help familiarize you with the words I'll be throwing around in this book. Because it is well nigh impossible to describe one term without using a bunch of other terms you haven't heard yet, you might have to skip around a little here. Don't worry if you don't really get the meanings right away: they will become clear as you work through the book. If a bunch of guys stupid enough to think opening a butcher shop was a good idea can understand them, surely you can too.

BREAKING

In the context of butchering, the term "breaking" is just a tough way to say cutting big pieces of animals into small pieces of animals. This is accomplished with handsaws and knives, not baseball bats, crowbars, or tire irons. I swear.

CARCASS

This is the whole animal post slaughter and evisceration. Beef cattle are usually split into sides to hang and dry-age before they are broken down into quarters or eighths for transport to a butcher shop or restaurant.

CHINE BONE

This is just butcher talk for the spine of a carcass. Maybe butchers made it up because it sounds cool.

CONFORMATION

Conformation is simply what a four-legged carcass looks like. Ideally it should be boxy, thick, and sturdy-looking, not thin, long, and wimpy. Think wrestler, not supermodel.

CONNECTIVE TISSUE

This is a broad catchall term for all the stuff on a carcass that isn't meat, bone, or tendon—all the thin membranes and other weird stuff that literally hold an animal's muscles together but also allow those muscles to move freely enough to do their job. It also, at least in the way I use the term, refers to all the gristly stuff in meat—the tough membranes that run through muscles to anchor them to the bones they move around. Connective tissue is fine if you're slow-cooking a piece of meat, because it will dissolve, but it's bad for hot, fast cooking, which makes the meat really tough and chewy

GRIND

This is how we refer to ground meat of any sort. We might say, "Hey, that grind is looking a little fatty; lean it out" (which means that there's too much fat, so we need to regrind the meat with more lean muscles). Or "Hey, the grind is looking kind of smeary; time to get the plates sharpened" (which means that the grinder blades are dull and they're smooshing the meat through rather than cutting it cleanly, which isn't good). Also that show on MTV with Eric what's-his-face from *The Real World*.

HINDQUARTER/FOREQUARTER

These terms are usually only used with beef. The hind- (rear) and fore- (front) quarters are what you end up with if you cut a side in half at the midpoint, perpendicular to the spine. A whole animal can then be broken down into eighths by cutting those quarters in half. That is how we get our beef so it's easier to carry off the truck.

HOT WEIGHT

This is the weight of the animal carcass right after processing, while it's still, well, hot. It's used to establish how much the animal weighs in a consistent manner so that the person buying the meat and the person selling it can agree on price per pound—which could otherwise be tricky, as a carcass starts losing water weight through evaporation in the slaughterhouse cooler. For example, a side of beef may weigh 15 to 20 percent less after hanging for two weeks. "Hot Weight" would also be a really cool band name.

LOIN

The loin of an animal is the muscle that runs along both sides of the spine from just below the shoulders to just before the hind legs. Those muscles only support the spine and don't do much work, so they are very tender, which is what makes the loin of any critter the most desirable part.

PRIMAL

A primal is basically just a large chunk cut from any animal carcass. The number of primals on any given animal is determined by the size of the animal. Beef are huge, so they have lots of primals, while sheep have only a few. Primals are then trimmed into cuts of meat for sale.

SEAMING

This is a butchering technique where, instead of sawing through muscle and bone in big square chunks with a saw, the butcher uses a smaller boning knife to carefully separate—i.e., "seam out"—the muscles from each other along their seams, where they meet each other with just a tiny bit of connective tissue holding them together. This style of butchery is popular in Asian cultures and in Europe, and it is also used by most game hunters and anyone who can't afford a band saw. About 60 percent of the butchering we do at The Meat Hook involves seaming.

SIDE

This term refers to the halves of a whole animal that has been split down the middle by sawing down the length of the backbone as it hangs at the slaughterhouse after processing (a nice way of saying killed, gutted, and skinned). Typically, beef and market-weight hogs (200 pounds and above hot weight) are cut this way.

MEAT HOOK RULES

While nicking yourself now and again is part and parcel of cutting meat at home or making your living behind a knife, serious injuries can be avoided by following a few simple rules. What follows is a CliffsNotes version of the in-depth safety training we give to all our employees and interns at The Meat Hook. I encourage you to follow these rules at home if you hope to explore meat and butchering for long and you want to keep all of your fingers and toes.

1. NO KNIVES ON THE TABLE

Keep your cutting area clear of any knives that are not in your hand. This seems simple, but I've seen new people screw this up time and time again. A work space cluttered with knives not protected by blade guards or in a hip scabbard is just an accident waiting to happen. In the same way that it is a cardinal sin to put any knife other than a butter knife in a sink full of sudsy water and dirty dishes, leaving a knife anywhere around the meat you're preparing is extremely dangerous and strictly verboten. If you're not using a knife, be a pal and put it away.

2. NEVER CUT ACROSS/TOWARD YOURSELF

This sounds simple, but it's easy to get caught up in the moment, become frustrated, and forget to think about what you're doing. Not that cutting meat is Zen or anything, but . . . it kind of is. The main principle of Zen is to be fully present in the moment. What this means here is that you must always be aware of where your off hand, body, and knife are in relation to one another to prevent injury—or death—in the event that your cut doesn't go according to plan. The easiest and most useful way to think of this is to imagine what would happen if the meat you were cutting were to disappear. Where would that knife end up? If the answer is in your hand, arm, leg, belly, chest, or genitals, rethink your cut and position yourself so you are not in harm's way. Keep calm and carry on.

3. WEAR A CUT-PROOF GLOVE AND A BUTCHER BRA

When learning how to butcher, you will absolutely make mistakes. To make sure those mistakes don't cost you a trip to the emergency room, I strongly encourage you to buy some safety equipment. The cheapest and most practical is a cloth cut-resistant glove (see Resources, page 305), which will prevent 99 percent of possible injuries for the average journeyman meat cutter. If you're really going whole hog (or whole steer, etc.) and planning on doing some serious butchering that requires more than a moderate amount of force, or if you are just a spaz and are always in a hurry, you may want to consider a stainless steel chain-mail apron (see Resources, page 305), which we like to refer to as a butcher bra. This will protect your chest, genitals, and legs from everything short of a speeding bullet. It's also fun to wear under your shirt to parties, where you can encourage people to stab you with a kitchen knife. Not that I've tried this. Ever.

4. SHARPEN YOUR KNIVES

Keeping your knives as sharp as possible at all times goes a long way toward making butchering a pleasant and enjoyable experience. Maintain your knives (see "About Sharpening Knives," page 26) and steel them, at minimum, every five minutes when you are using them. No exceptions! There is nothing more dangerous or tiring than using a dull knife. Cuts require much more force and wrist/arm movement, which, at best, means that you end up with numb hands and wrists or, at worst, carpal tunnel syndrome or a boning knife sticking out of a part of you that you kind of liked. If you simply can't figure out how to keep your knives razor sharp (this was once a real problem for me), seek professional help.

5. WASTE NOT, WANT NOT

Nearly every part of every animal is usable for something, even if you can't eat it. Do your research and figure out how to use all of the meat, bones, and sinew you'll be accruing. The various offal and stock-making sections of this book are an excellent starting point, but certainly not the last word. Use the Internet for something besides LOLCats.

6. WORK CLEAN

That thing about cleanliness and godliness? Totally true. Keeping your work space clean, uncluttered, and organized is the key to success not just in cooking or meat but in life. Your environment influences your thoughts, and your thoughts become your actions. Your actions are literally your life. See where I'm going with this? Yeah, work clean.

7. GET YOUR SHIT TOGETHER

A deeper element of working clean and being organized is, well, really being organized. If you're going to make one of the recipes in this book, first make a list of what you need and take a minute to think about how you're going to make the recipe happen. Think about the ingredients, the pots, pans, herbs, and spices you'll need and get them together, in the order that they'll be needed. Don't wait until you're halfway through making something to realize that you're out of pepper or forgot to preheat the oven. Make a list, check it twice.

8. RELAX; IT'S NOT THE END OF THE WORLD

At some point, you, like every person who puts his pants on one leg at a time, will make a mistake, sometimes a grievous mistake: you will screw up a cut, ruin a piece of meat, and you are going to cut yourself. Accept this. Don't worry about it. These things happen. Repurpose the meat you fucked up and keep your first aid kit stocked and handy.

TOOLS

Whether you're talking the primitive rough-hewn flint knives of our Neanderthal forebears or the sleek stainless blades made from powdered steel and smelted with exotic trace elements, a butcher is only as good as his tools. We at The Meat Hook have a penchant for tools of all kinds: the basic, the functional, and the inexpensive—which is good news for a chef or home cook looking to test the waters of butchering. The large, heavy, and dangerous specialized machines we have at our shop (see page 28) are a lot like a giant collection of rare vinyl records: expensive, even when bought secondhand, and only practical for people who will be using them frequently. So I recommend avoiding the extras unless you have deep pockets and a lot of room for stuff you probably don't really need.

Knives

Knives are at the center of what we do at The Meat Hook. Whereas a typical meat department or butcher shop tends to do most of its work with a band saw, cutting steaks and chops, we rely on our knife kits hanging at our sides. Each knife serves a specific function that makes our job of cutting meat all day, every day easier. If you don't have the time, money, or space for all these knives, don't sweat it—pretty much everything you would ever need to butcher can be done with a $25 boning knife. Anything else is just gravy.

With the exception of a few old carbon-steel blades from the first half of the twentieth century, we tend to avoid the knife-as-fetish-item trap and view our tools as what they are: a means to an end that will be used, ground down, and eventually disposed of. I recommend investing a moderate amount in good-quality knives and using the balance of what you might have spent on fancier knives keeping them sharp, clean, and useful.

BONING KNIFE

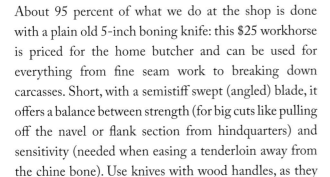

About 95 percent of what we do at the shop is done with a plain old 5-inch boning knife: this $25 workhorse is priced for the home butcher and can be used for everything from fine seam work to breaking down carcasses. Short, with a semistiff swept (angled) blade, it offers a balance between strength (for big cuts like pulling off the navel or flank section from hindquarters) and sensitivity (needed when easing a tenderloin away from the chine bone). Use knives with wood handles, as they can absorb fat and remain stable in your hand, whereas a plastic-handled knife gets dangerously slippery.

BREAKING KNIFE

When we need to make a big, long, deep cut in one fell swoop, we lean on our breaking knife: its 10- to 12-inch-long blade allows us to carve a primal off the animal in one neat cut rather than with several ugly, jagged ones. Styles range from the bull-nosed classic butcher knife to the curved, pointy scimitar, with lots of variations in between. Which one you choose is personal, but keep in mind that scimitar-style knives are more versatile if you plan on breaking carcasses off a hook—and they also look way cooler.

SKINNING KNIFE

At the shop, all of our pigs come from our farmers scalded, scraped, and skin on. A simple and inexpensive skinning knife makes removing the skin from soft, freshly slaughtered pigs a lot more fun than trying to do it with a boning knife. The main difference between a skinning knife and a regular boning knife is the wide rounded tip. Rather than focusing its cutting power at a sharp tip, the round end of the skinning knife spreads it out over a larger area and makes it easier to skin without puncturing the hide.

THE "FRENCH" KNIFE

When our friends from Couteau d'Argent in Paris (see page 264) came to visit, they brought with them a suitcase full of knives we hadn't seen before. Some were short and fat, others long, narrow, and thin. While we were fascinated with all of the foreign shapes and sizes, we ended up stealing the idea of their short, triangular seaming knife for when we need laser-focus accuracy. We couldn't find anyone to buy the knives from in the United States (perhaps we didn't look hard enough), but we'd made a few sketches and handed them over to Jason at Ambrosi Cutlery to craft our own version of these useful small knives (see Resources, page 305). We use

French knives to delicately remove sinews from various cuts and thereby make tender steaks from muscles that would otherwise be tough, stringy, and headed for the hamburger bin.

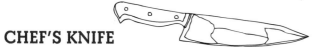

CHEF'S KNIFE

A lot of what we do at the shop involves fancying up the various bits and pieces that we are left with after all the obvious and easy cuts have long since gone into the case. For tasks such as mincing herbs for beef heart marinade, chopping onions for meat sauces, or slicing pig's ears for headcheese, the chef's knife is irreplaceable. I like a knife that is about 10 inches long with a fairly narrow but tall stamped stainless steel blade. Inexpensive but not cheap, chef's knives are the most desirable since they work well, but you won't feel bad when you abuse them or ultimately put them out to pasture after they've been ground down too far.

MEAT HOOK

Obviously I have a certain affinity for meat hooks, and while they inspired our name, they're also indispensable to what we do. We use them to carry large, awkwardly shaped primals off the truck, and they also come in pretty handy as boning hooks, to keep your hands out of the way when taking apart arm chucks on the table.

KNIFE SCABBARD

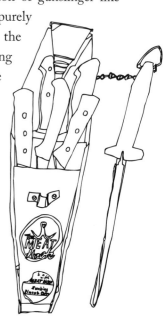

Our knife scabbards have been the source of many a written word in the press, and while they do imbue our crew with a certain perception of gunslinger-like swagger, I can assure you they are purely functional. An invention born in the slaughterhouses and meatpacking centers of America, a knife scabbard keeps knives easily at hand, organized, and, most important, off the cutting table, where they could cause grievous injury. But while scabbards are very useful for professional butchers and look really cool, one is not really necessary if you're just breaking down a chicken at home—but, hey, if you want to wear one, I'm not going to stop you!

ABOUT SHARPENING KNIVES

Don't. Unless you're obsessive and really need a new hobby, leave the sharpening of your knives to the professionals. Find a knife service that will not hollow-grind your knives but instead uses a rotary water stone or similar setup to put a keen, even edge on them.

Avoid any sharpening service that uses a grindstone, as this can and will ruin the temper (hardness) of your knife's edge and will also remove way too much material in the process, which will shorten its useful life significantly.

If in doubt, ask around and see who your local line cooks, butchers, and food nerds use to keep their stuff sharp. If you're totally out of luck where you live, use a mail-order sharpening service (see Resources, page 305) and you'll be set, as long as you can bear to be without your knives for a week or so. Think of it as an excuse to buy more knives!

STEEL

Remember that scene from *Full Metal Jacket* with Vincent D'Onofrio repeating the words, "Without me, my rifle is useless. Without my rifle, I am useless." It's true of the knife and the steel. A knife without a steel is a pointless shiv, and a steel without a knife is only good for poking your friends in the belly button.

A good steel can be had for anywhere from $40 to $250. How much you spend is not nearly as important as how you use it. One of my favorites is a 12-inch steel with four sides: two of medium-cut grooves for bringing up the edge and two of polished steel for honing the edge.

Contrary to common belief, a steel doesn't sharpen. Instead, it actually realigns the microscopic cutting edge of the knife, which becomes distorted when you put it up against hard things like bones or cutting boards.

To properly use a steel, run the edge of the knife down the length of the steel in long, light, even strokes while maintaining a 20-degree angle. After you've done it a thousand or so times, you'll start to develop a feel for where the edge is dull and how to get it sharp. Keep trying! And don't worry if you screw it up the first couple times—just take it by your local butcher shop along with a six-pack of beer, and they'll fix your edge and make fun of you to boot.

CLEAVER

To be blunt, while cleavers inspire romantic visions of the past and an overtly macho image of the "artisan" future, generally I find cleavers a little useless. Obviously, if you don't happen to have a saw of any type at hand, a cleaver, used skillfully, can be a lifesaver. Moreover, a cleaver is capable of truly amazing things that cannot be done with any other piece of butcher's gear. Unfortunately, being able to make this heavy, dangerous instrument do all its tricks requires months, if not years, of practice under the guidance of someone who really knows what he is doing.

If you decide to master the cleaver, choose one that is heavy, thick, and well balanced. I like old carbon steel Dexter-Russell cleavers, which are easy to get on eBay and the like for pennies on the dollar compared to new cleavers, which are inferior in steel, heft, and balance.

A note on using a cleaver: Let the cleaver's weight do the work. Never raise it above chest height. You're there to guide and the cleaver is there to, well, cleave. If you feel as if you have to use more force to get the job done, get a bigger cleaver!

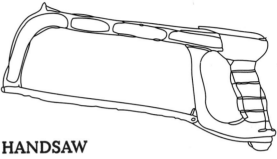

HANDSAW

Any butcher worth his salt can complete almost any task of butchery with nothing more than a boning knife and a small handsaw with the appropriate blade.

A good handsaw should be solidly built, comfortable, and supportive and have a sharp blade of medium-sized teeth set to cut on the forward, or push, stroke. Buy as big a saw as you can afford storage- or moneywise. A longer saw will pay dividends in cleaner cuts and fewer shoulder-wrenching strokes. At The Meat Hook, we use a 30-inch splitter saw, but a purpose-built 19-inch saw is plenty for anyone short of a slaughterhouse.

When you use a saw, make sure that you have used your knife to make as much of the cut as possible, then use the saw to cut through the bone. Try to use a few short, light strokes to create a guide groove for your subsequent full-power strokes. If your saw gets bound up, try changing the angle so that it isn't cutting as much bone all at once.

One last note: Keep your off hand a safe distance away from the saw. If it happens to jump the groove and get into your hand, it will be one of the worst cuts you can get!

Equipment in the Butcher Shop

Here's a tour of the tools we keep at The Meat Hook. Unless you plan on opening your own butcher shop, you won't need most of them.

BAND SAW

Few items in the butcher shop are more useful or terrifying than the band saw. This miracle of the modern age can reduce hours' worth of hand sawing to a few minutes—but it can also remove an appendage (or appendages) of a distracted, untrained, or unlucky user in a matter of a second or less. Such a beast requires the type of reverence and respect given to rabid animals, loaded handguns, and angry badgers. We mostly use our band saw to cut the loins of our animals into more user-friendly chops and steaks. While this can of course be done the old-fashioned way with a handsaw or a cleaver, it's a lot easier and cleaner, as well as quicker, to crosscut them with a band saw.

If you're going to use a band saw, you should learn how from a professional, not a book. Books can't stop you from doing stupid, dangerous things, and they can't always tell you why those things are stupid or dangerous. Books are good for all kinds of things, but training you to use a band saw is not one of them.

That said, books can tell you what to look for in a saw. Brands that I like are Butcher Boy, Hobart, and Biro. I'm sure there are lots of other worthy brands out there, but you can't go wrong with that holy trinity.

Our band saw is a 1971 Biro 3334 with a 124-inch blade that we got for $1,300 (with shipping) from an old butcher shop in Upstate New York that had gone out of business. When we got her, she was filthy and worn out, but a few hours of scrubbing and a few hundred dollars' worth of parts later, she was good as new.

If you're faced with the decision of whether to buy a reconditioned old band saw or a new off-brand saw, go with the classic. Trust me.

MEAT GRINDER

Like a band saw, a meat grinder is a powerful, dangerous, and massively labor-saving device. My advice is to buy a much bigger and more powerful one than you think you'll need. However, "need" is a relative term, so consider what you're planning on doing with it. Is it realistic to think you're going to be making 20-pound batches of sausage with your friends once a month, or are you just going to make enough ground meat for a few burgers every once in a while? Whatever you decide, make sure you buy a grinder that is made of good-quality steel, not plastic. If you don't think you can commit to a full-sized steel grinder, you can always chop your meat the old-fashioned way: with a knife.

When we bought Britney, our 3-hp Hobart grinder, in the late summer of 2009, she was the biggest grinder any of us had ever used, and we could never imagine outgrowing her. But I think we all secretly regret not getting a mammoth 5-hp with a built-in mixer. Sigh.

Whatever the case, your grinder should be either a new or reputably reconditioned name brand (again, we love our Hobart), and buy several sets of good-quality plates and knives—the parts that you mount on the end of the grinder—in various die sizes so you always have a backup, as plates and knives tend to fail and go dull when it's least convenient. The grinder cuts the meat into tiny 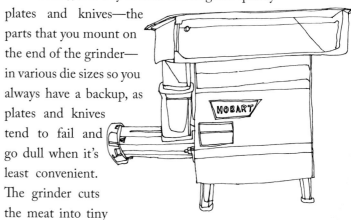 pieces by forcing it through the holes in a plate and then shears them off with a rotating knife (sort of like the way a pair of scissors works).

Make sure to keep the plates and knives as married pairs. Mixing up sets of plates and knives will result in dull cutting surfaces and smeary grind. Last but not least, keep all of your grinder parts (the head, plates, and ring) clean, and refrigerate or freeze them before use to ensure clean, well-minced ground meat.

MIXER

A bright-red custom 60-quart Hobart mixer is the heart and soul of our sausage-making operation. Though it might seem like a piece of equipment you'd be more likely to find in a bakery than in a butcher shop, it performs myriad tasks, from shredding cheese for the bacon cheeseburger dogs to mixing batches of sausage to whipping hot pork and fat into creamy rillettes. During weekday production runs, the rhythmic thump of the mixer is as constant in the shop as Katy Perry is on the stereo, and on the few occasions when the mixer has been out of commission, everything comes to a halt until it's fixed.

Like most of the equipment in our shop, the mixer is an older model that was professionally rebuilt. Rebuilt mixers are not just cheaper—generally they are more heavy-duty than newer models, with bigger bearings and simpler, easier-to-fix wiring. Finding one of these old beauties is certainly more time-consuming than just buying a new one, but I think it's worth it. For the home cook, any reputable mixer will be more than satisfactory for anything you're likely to whip up, but make sure to get one that has the ability to take on powered attachments like a pasta roller and such, as these can make your life a lot easier.

SAUSAGE STUFFER

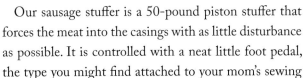

Many butcher shops that make their own sausage simply attach a stuffing attachment to their grinder head and call it a day. While that is fine for most folks, we are obsessed with our sausage, and the chance of the sausage mixture getting overworked into a crumbly mess as it is pushed out by the grinder screw is a chance we're not willing to take.

Our sausage stuffer is a 50-pound piston stuffer that forces the meat into the casings with as little disturbance as possible. It is controlled with a neat little foot pedal, the type you might find attached to your mom's sewing machine.

When buying a stuffer for your home, make sure that you get a good one. They're not inexpensive, and the price difference between a used high-quality stuffer and a brand-new Chinese-made item may make the cheaper one seem too tempting, but trust me on this and spend a little more. Whatever you do, don't attempt to use the stuffer attachment for a home stand mixer—these are a pain in the ass to use and will heat up and overwork your meat mixture. If you're in a bind you can always cut the top off a plastic water bottle and use it as a stuffing horn, pushing the meat into the casings with your fingers. I've had to do this more times than I can believe. At The Meat Hook, we rent out sausage stuffers by the day—maybe a cookware shop or butcher shop near you does too, so ask around. Small piston stuffers are also relatively inexpensive now (see Resources, page 305).

BUTCHER BLOCK

Oh, the butcher block! What a romantic image: a massive, well-worn monolith of wood and iron with an old-timey cleaver unceremoniously stuck into it for safekeeping. Well, butchers rarely use cleavers anymore, and as cool as the idea of the butcher block is, ours is only used at the counter as a showpiece, where we line up orders and cut boneless steaks. All of the real cutting is done on our three large butcher tables.

Our tables, which we get from John Boos Blocks in Effingham, Illinois, are huge custom-built jobs with 4-inch-thick hard maple tops. While they lack a bit of the charm of the old-school chopping blocks, they are infinitely more useful. If you get one, make sure that it's as big as possible. Space on the table fills up more quickly than you think!

For home butchering, you can get by with a regular cutting board if you're just cutting up something small, but a good-sized countertop butcher block made of thick maple or other hardwood is best for butchering anything larger than a rabbit or chicken. If you're considering redoing part or all of your kitchen setup, I would highly recommend putting in hardwood butcher block countertops as your work surface. They're beautiful, relatively inexpensive, durable, and, most important, easy on the blades of your knives, unlike granite or stainless steel.

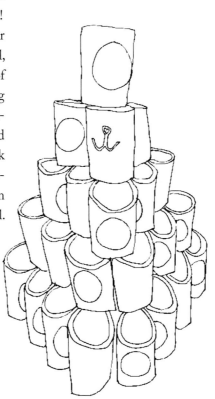

BEEF

Whether you're a butcher, a chef, or a home cook, beef is the main event. The cult of the pig notwithstanding, when it comes to cutting meat, there is nothing that compares to a beef carcass. Learning to cut up a pig can be achieved in a matter of weeks, but mastering the art of beef butchering is a lifelong process.

With a mythic history ranging from the iconic cowpuncher on the prairie to President Eisenhower grilling T-bones in khaki shorts, no other animal we eat is as large in terms of size or cultural significance as the majestic *Bos taurus*. The question "What is good beef?" fills our minds with so many different connotations, from childhood memories to pop-culture references and current food activism, that we might have an easier time answering the question "What is it to be human?" If our humanity is to be judged in part by how good the beef we eat is, it is my sincere hope that we at The Meat Hook are doing our best to improve the quality and character of both.

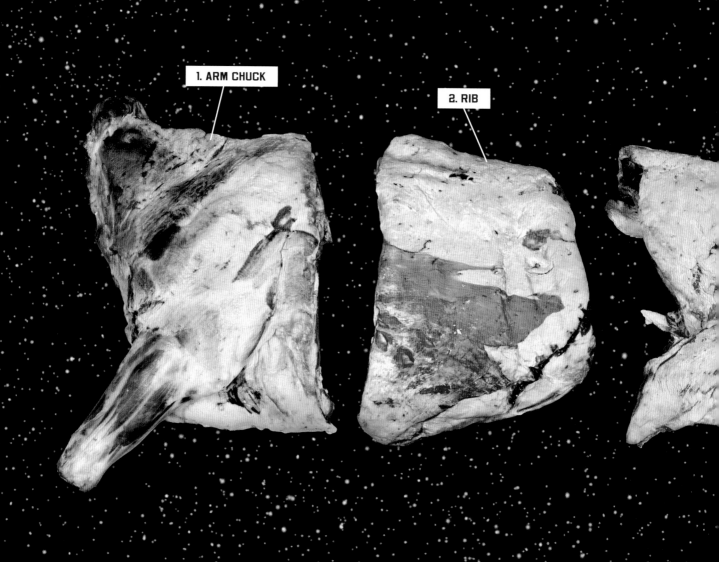

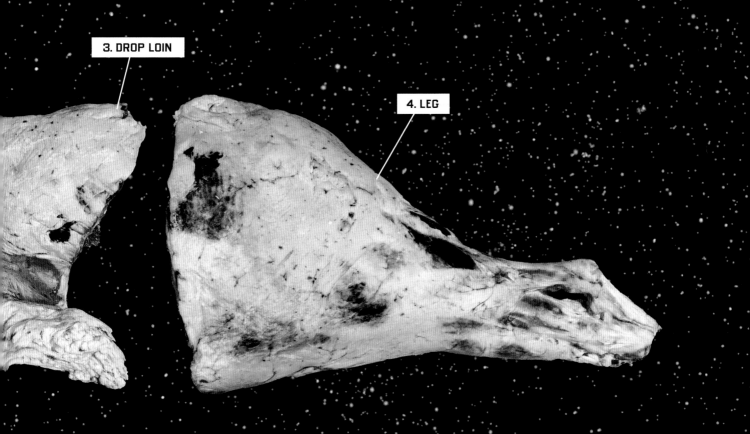

3. DROP LOIN

4. LEG

1 2 3 4

SIDE OF BEEF

HOW WE BUY BEEF

Type the word "beef" into any search engine and you'll be confronted with countless links to horror stories about industrially produced beef and its environmental, economic, and health-related issues. While I do encourage you, as a consumer, to educate yourself about what you buy and put into your body, I don't want to waste too much time talking about what other people are doing wrong. Instead, let me explain how to do things right.

Cattle are truly remarkable. If treated right and managed properly, they can magically transform a few acres of lush spring grass into some of the most profound food you can eat, all the while nourishing and improving the land on which they graze. Although that might sound easy if you tilt your head back and dream of a shiny-coated bovine quietly munching on grass, it is definitely not.

Of all the animals that pass from our coolers to the tables of our customers, we pay the most attention to our supply of beef. The reason for this has little to do with its historical significance and everything to do with cold, hard pragmatism. Quite simply, beef carcasses are four to five times bigger than anything else we bring into the shop and represent at least 50 percent of our active cutting time.

If we got, forgive the pun, "a bum steer" from one of our farms, we would be screwed for the better part of a week, until we dealt with a low-quality animal that we wouldn't dare sell to our customers. To avoid such a situation requires a lot of skill and knowledge, but the first and most important skill any butcher worth the salt on his cleaving block needs is how to read a carcass—that is, how to examine a hanging side of beef to ensure it is of good quality.

Every year, we close The Meat Hook for a few days, rent a big old church van, and cram all of our employees, interns, and sometimes even a few regular customers into it to take a road trip to some of our farms and slaughter facilities. A big part of the ritual is dropping off bottles of whiskey and cases of beer for the farmers and slaughterhouse owners to help engender another year's worth of goodwill. One of the perks of that ritual is that they allow us to bring our entire clown car of farm trippers into the cooler to look at the carcasses and teach everyone how to judge the good from the bad. While it might not be likely that you'll ever buy a side of beef hanging on a hook rail in a slaughterhouse cooler, we would like to invite you to take a look with us and, hopefully, help you think differently about where your meat comes from. A lot of really important stuff happens between the time a steer is on pasture and when it becomes a steak on your dinner plate.

READING A CARCASS

A side of beef can tell you a lot. Reading the inspection stamp can tell you what slaughterhouse it was killed at (provided that you have an index of slaughterhouse numbers or have committed that information to memory). The kill tag can tell you the day it was killed, how much it weighed, the "hot weight" (its dressed weight immediately after slaughter), and even the farm it came from.

Fine. Reading is easy. What can the animal itself tell you? The cartilage buttons on the tops of the feather bones of the chine (the backbone) will tell you the animal's rough age (the longer, the younger and vice versa) and the curve of the pelvic bone, or aitch bone, will tell you whether the animal was female (slightly curved) or male (very curved). While you're looking, how big are the knobs of kidney fat? They should be full, thick, and slightly crumbly, not thin or floppy.

Looking at the outside of the animal can tell you how well it was fed if you examine its "cover," the layer of fat on the outside of the carcass. Ideally, you don't want to see any muscles coming through the fat. This is important, because beef have to put on at least three-quarters of a pound a day of muscle, bone, and fat to even be worth considering for anything but grinding into burgers.

Another good sign of quality is the thickness of the plate (the rib cage below the rib loin—aka short ribs). Generally, a thick plate means the animal was well fed and mature, and the meat will be delicious. While you're looking at the plate, take a peek at the eye of the rib loin. It should be dazzling with many layers of fat between the muscles and a large triangular piece of fat where the loin transitions into the ribs. A superb animal will have a thick, psychedelic spiderweb of fat throughout the lean section of the eye, which will ensure mind-blowing steaks. Above all, the meat should be a deep, rich red. Light red or pink means the animal was too young, and dark spots of blood are signs of the dreaded "dark cutter," a chronically stressed animal that underwent a prolonged adrenaline response.

One final consideration is the conformation, or what the carcass looks like as a whole. It should be square, blocky, and butch looking. An angular, willowy carcass is a sure sign of a stinker.

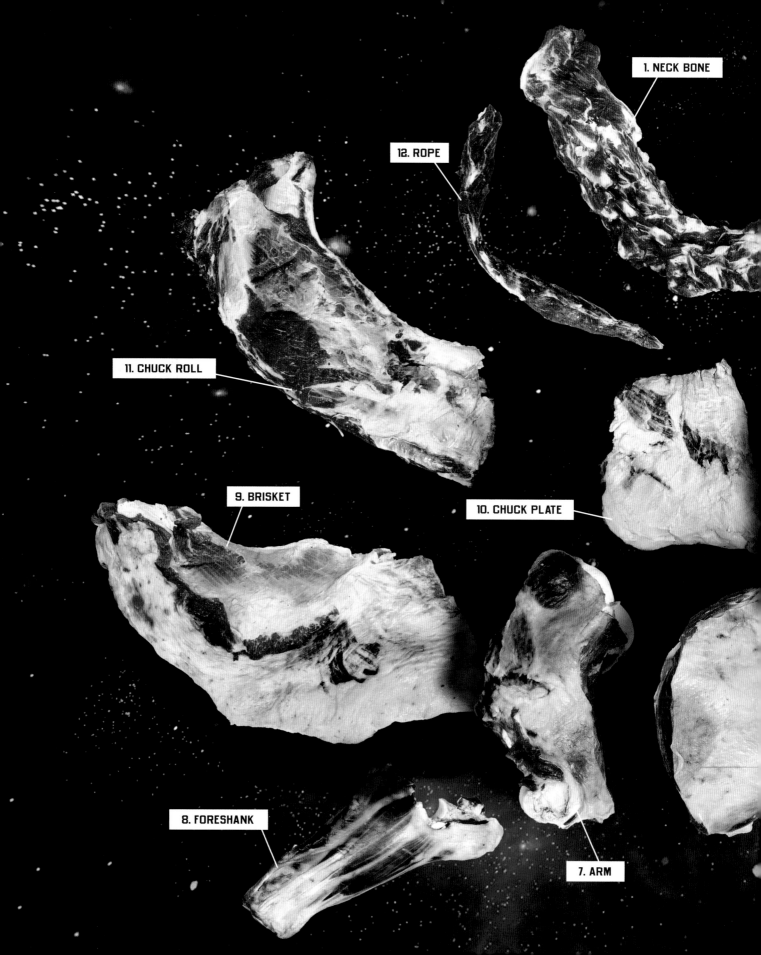

1. NECK BONE

12. ROPE

11. CHUCK ROLL

9. BRISKET

10. CHUCK PLATE

8. FORESHANK

7. ARM

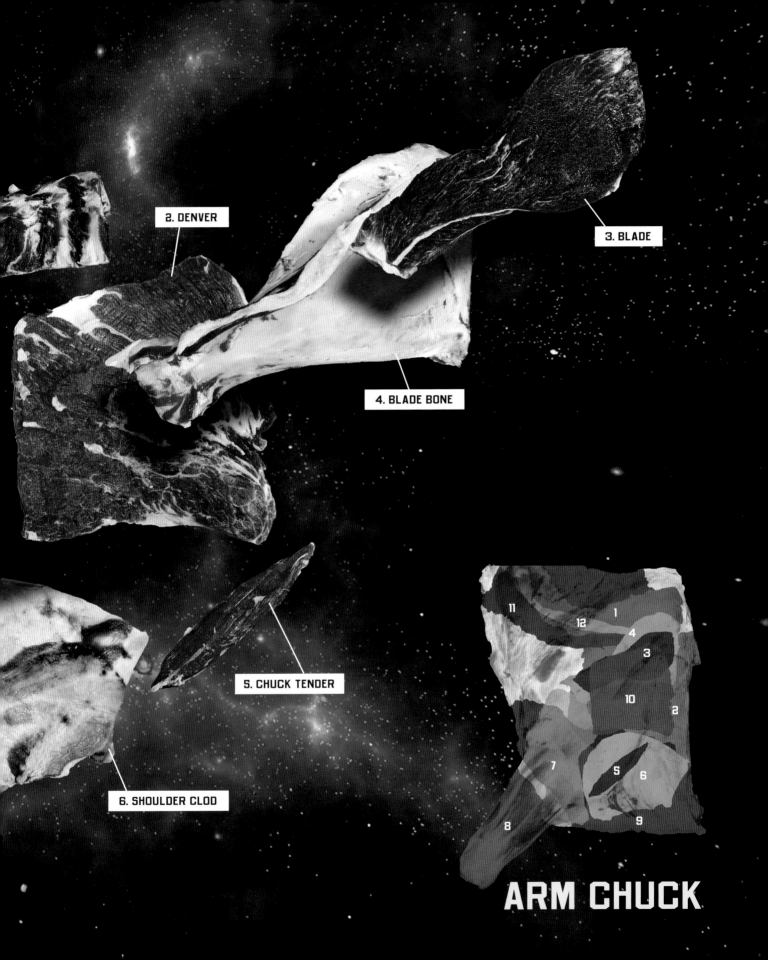

2. DENVER

3. BLADE

4. BLADE BONE

5. CHUCK TENDER

6. SHOULDER CLOD

ARM CHUCK

ARM CHUCK

The arm chuck is the least understood and most underappreciated of the beef primals. It is the most complicated and difficult primal to cut, and it is typically thought of as tough and only good for grinding into hamburger meat. The truth is that if you know what you're looking for, the arm chuck can be a treasure trove of unsung but ultrabeefy steaks and other oddball grillables. And it is the home of the king of barbecue cuts: the brisket.

CHUCK ROLL

The chuck roll is really two different cuts—the first third on the loin end has more in common with the rib eye than it does with the rest of this cut. Steaks from here have a perfect balance of fat, tenderness, and flavor. The rest of the chuck roll, as the eye of the loin disappears and the muscles of the neck and shoulder take over, is better suited for slow-roasting whole, so the muscles, silverskin, and collagen sheaths have adequate time to break down.

BRISKET

Brisket is fatty and loaded with collagen, making it ideally suited to being smoked for the better part of a day, cured, or simmered.

CHUCK PLATE

Leaner and more tender than the ribs found farther down the animal, the chuck plate can be cut and grilled like a steak. It is a favorite for Japanese yakiniku barbecue.

FORESHANK

Tough and lean but loaded with connective tissue, this cut is perfect for a velvety ragout or stew, as long as you have around eight hours to kill.

SHOULDER CLOD

A little-known staple of Texas barbecue and where you'll find the delicious flatiron steak, the shoulder clod, located in the center of the shoulder, is essentially the deltoid muscle of the animal.

BLADE

The beef shoulder blade is typically lumped in with the chine and chuck roll and cut into thin steaks called 7-bones, but it also houses the two paleron steaks, on either side of the beef. Lean and tender with a fine grain, these are great for panfrying.

HIDDEN STEAKS OF THE ARM CHUCK

There are a lot of steaks hidden within the beast that is the arm chuck. It's a shame that in this country, most of these steaks get ground into hamburger.

FLATIRON

Lean, tender, and flavorful, if odd-shaped, flatiron steaks from the clod heart, or center of the shoulder clod, make great panfried steaks. They are too lean for grilling beyond medium-rare.

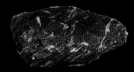

BLADE

The paleron is tender and well marbled, with a fine texture not unlike that of tenderloin. Unfortunately, there are only two of these steaks per animal.

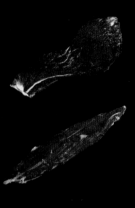

CHUCK TENDER

This boat-tail-shaped cut off the top of the shoulder clod is lean and flavorful and a good choice for when you want an inexpensive but nice steak on a Wednesday night.

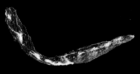

ROPE

Little known in the United States, this French cut is fabricated by seaming out all of the sinews that form the small muscle running up the inside of the chine of the arm chuck. It's delicious and tender when cooked in a hot pan with some oil and butter, but good luck finding it!

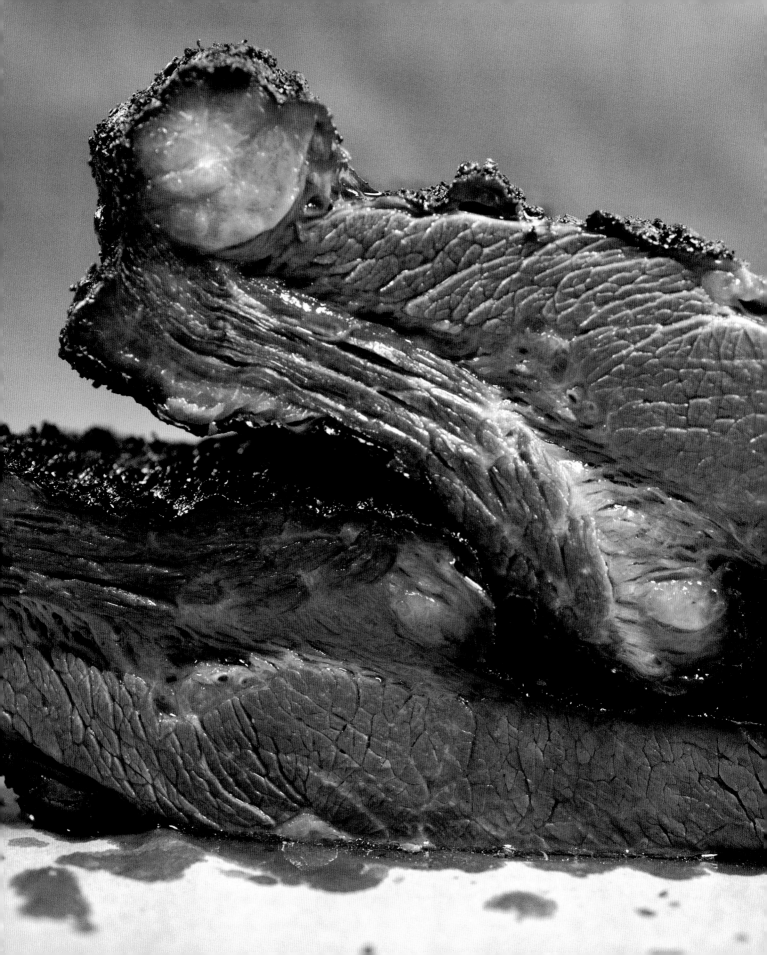

MEAT HOOK PASTRAMI

This pastrami recipe grew out of a vague description of the methods and ingredients in *The Food Lover's Companion*. I had eaten lots of pastrami, but I had never really thought about how it was made until we were faced with a mounting surplus of briskets and had precious little to do with them. It took countless experiments and wild guesses and, literally, years of tinkering to come up with this recipe.

Like a number of recipes in this book, making pastrami is not for the uncommitted. There are no shortcuts, and if you make this you will be living with pastrami for several weeks. There really is no point in trying to do a smaller amount than a whole brisket: it's just not going to come out right. And don't try to half-ass anything here by using preground spices! The recipe will not work, and you'll blame me. Do pastrami right, or don't do it.

The good news is that once you master this recipe and the various steps and techniques involved, you can pretty much pastrami-cure just about anything, from salmon to lamb neck.   SERVES 10 TO 14

1. To make the cure, grind together the peppercorns, coriander seeds, red pepper flakes, and cinnamon stick in a coffee or spice grinder, working in batches and making sure not to overload the grinder.

2. Next, combine all of the ground spices with the kosher salt and curing salt in a bowl, wearing your gloves. Be very thorough. Add the minced garlic and white wine, adding just enough wine to make the mixture a nice paste that will stick to the brisket.

3. Get your brisket and your tub together. With your gloves on, place the brisket in the tub and start smearing on the cure until the whole brisket is coated in a ¼-inch-or-so-thick layer of cure. Refrigerate any remaining cure in a covered container to pastrami-cure something else later.

4. Now you wait: Let the brisket hang out covered in the tub on the bottom shelf of your refrigerator for 2 weeks. During this time, you want to keep anything particularly stinky out of there, lest it taint the flavor of the brisket. You may find it helpful to wrap the whole thing tightly in plastic wrap to keep creepy smells away if you can't bear to be without washed-rind cheese for that long. No matter what, you must flip the brisket over every day.

Recipe continues

FOR THE CURE
1½ cups black peppercorns
1 cup coriander seeds
½ cup crushed red pepper flakes
1 cinnamon stick, broken into
    small pieces
2 cups kosher salt
½ teaspoon pink curing salt
    (see Note and Resources, page 305)
3 garlic cloves, chopped very fine
About 2 cups dry white wine
1 brisket, approximately 8 pounds,
    moderately trimmed

SPECIAL EQUIPMENT
Spice or coffee grinder
Disposable gloves
Food-safe plastic tub the size of
    your brisket
Smoker (see "Smokers," page 284)

5. Again, there is no half-assing this recipe, so you *must* smoke the brisket in a real smoker. I find that about 8 hours at 220°F in a cheap offset smoker (see "Smokers," page 284) is about right. The internal temperature of the meat should be at least 160°F.

6. At this point, you can serve the brisket, chill it and slice it cold later for sandwiches, or (my favorite) steam or braise it (whole) in an inch or two of water in a covered roasting pan for 2 hours; serve it with plenty of rye bread, kraut, and spicy mustard. If you don't get around to eating all of it, you can wrap it tightly in plastic wrap or aluminum foil and refrigerate it for up to a week, but it will be getting drier and less delicious each and every day, so you should eat it sooner rather than later.

Note: Curing salt is what fixes the meat's color and makes pastrami pink. If you choose to omit it for health reasons, use sea salt instead of the kosher salt to get the same preservative effect.

BURGER TIME!

In the last few years, America has been besieged by burger hype. Restaurants charging $15 or more for the simple pleasure of a good hamburger and meat purveyors touting their proprietary blends of different cuts of beef, cuts that should never be ground into burger, are the rule now instead of the exception. I'm just going to go ahead and call bullshit on the whole thing.

There are a lot of factors that go into making a good burger, but using a fancy cut of beef is not one of them, in our experience. In fact, what you really need for a truly tasty burger are tougher, cheaper, harder-working muscles, because they have more myoglobin, the thing that makes red meat red and is one of the biggest factors in delivering a bold bovine flavor. The other main factor is fat, and lots of it. For our burgers, we like to see at least 20 percent fat, ideally 30 percent, for maximum juiciness. Don't believe the hype: when it comes to burgers, cheaper meat is better.

Fat Kid Blend

In response to the growing hysteria over custom-blend burgers, we started doing our own Meat Hook burger blends that took the craze to its logical conclusion: the Fat Kid Blend. We typically produce different iterations of our gimmick blend during the summer months, when the shop is busy as hell and we're scrambling to find new and absurd things to put in the case to satisfy the meat-greedy throngs of Brooklynites looking to grill.

Here are a few of them.

Fat Kid Classic: Lean leg or chuck meat ground with bacon bits made from the ends of our house bacon. Meaty, smoky, and slightly sweet—perfect for bachelor parties or chili mac. We normally grind a ratio of about 4:1 lean beef to bacon bits, but if you feel like more bacon, who are we to say no?

Fat Kid Blend, W.o.W. Edition: Like the Fat Kid Classic but with sharp cheddar cheese and sour-cream-and-onion-flavored potato chips mixed in. If you're an antisocial stoner agoraphobe, this is for you. Fire up the Xbox and dig in!

Hypertension Blend: This bad idea was a collaboration with Noah Bernamoff from Mile End Deli. Grind 2 parts lean beef with 1 part smoked meat or pastrami ends. Salty. Smoky. Makes you feel insane.

FAT KID BURGER

This is a deadly simple recipe that almost needs no explanation. It's gross, indulgent, and shameful. Have fun secretly eating this beast of a burger. **MAKES 2 BURGERS**

1. Start by heating up your skillet over medium heat or your grill to medium heat.

2. Next, form your Fat Kid Classic Blend into 2 burgers (8 ounces each), by hand or using a burger press. If doing it by hand, make sure to make the patties thinner in the middle so they won't hump up as they cook. Yes, you can add salt and pepper to these burgers, but if you ground enough bacon bits into the blend, you shouldn't have to.

3. Plop these guys in the pan or onto the grill. (If in the pan, no oil is necessary, as they will quickly start to produce more than enough of their own rendered fat.) Start flipping them after 1 to 2 minutes and flip them every minute thereafter. Make sure to move them as necessary to keep them from being scorched by flare-ups if using a grill—there will be a lot of them!

4. Once the patties have shrunk by about 20 percent, 5 to 7 minutes, place 2 slices of the cheese on each of them, cover them, and allow 45 seconds to 1 minute to melt the cheese.

5. Once the cheese has melted, immediately place the burgers on the potato rolls, top with 2 Funyuns each, and serve. You disgust me.

1 pound Fat Kid Classic Blend (page 43)
Kosher salt and freshly ground
    black pepper (optional)
4 slices American cheese
2 potato rolls (not toasted)
4 Funyuns or similar fried onion
    snack food (in a pinch, canned
    French-fried onions will work)

OPTIONAL EQUIPMENT
Burger press (see Resources, page 305)

MEAT HOOK CHILI

Making chili is not neuroscience. It's just a combination of dried chiles, spices, onions, garlic, and good meat. If it's late summer and you're lucky enough to have a farmer who raises flavorful, ripe red chile peppers, you can fire-roast the skins off them, seed them, and make a puree of them, though you might want to add some dried ones for depth of flavor and an earthy finish. **SERVES 10**

10 dried guajillo chiles
2 pounds ground beef
2 pounds ground pork
1 pound ground lamb
Olive oil
3 large yellow onions, roughly chopped
1 head garlic, separated into cloves, peeled, and chopped, or to taste
Two 16-ounce cans whole tomatoes
Three 12-ounce cans hominy
1 cup or so toasted cumin seeds, finely ground
¼ cup cayenne pepper, or to taste
Salt and freshly ground black pepper
Cheap beer or beef stock if needed
White wine vinegar or cider vinegar if needed
Sour cream, shredded cheese, onions, scallions, and saltines for serving

SPECIAL EQUIPMENT
Immersion blender

1. Let's start with the most important part: the dried chiles. Take your chiles, pull off the stems, and shake out the seeds. If you're both anal and want a milder chili, you can slice open the chiles and remove the white veins too.

2. Once you have your deseeded chiles, you want to boil water equivalent to the volume of the chiles (about 4 cups) in a saucepan and then turn off the heat. Make sure that the pan has a lid, or when you add the chiles you'll pepper-spray your kitchen with the spicy steam that will result. Add the chiles, punch them down, and put on the lid. Basically, you want to wait until the pan has cooled to the point where you can touch the sides with your hand (45 minutes or so).

3. Now puree the whole thing with an immersion blender until it's smooth. This might be a good time to run the paste through a China cap (fine strainer) to get any bigger pieces out, but if you're not trying to impress anyone with your flawless French Laundry chef skills, skip it.

4. Next, you want to brown your meat in a large pot, the pot you're going to be simmering your chili in. Brown over medium heat until, well, brown. I like to sauté the diced onions and garlic separately in some olive oil in a large sauté pan, then add them to the meat, but I don't think it matters that much.

5. Now add your chile paste, tomatoes, hominy, most of the cumin, the cayenne, and salt and pepper to taste to the combination of meat and onions. After it simmers over low heat for a while, say 45 minutes, taste it and correct the seasoning. Usually I find that it needs more garlic, heat (cayenne), cumin, and/or salt.

6. Your chili should simmer for another hour.

7. Now it's time to hit the pot with the immersion blender, making sure to break up all the clumps of meat and catch any stray tomatoes. This may take a while! You're shooting for Hormel consistency here. Now give the chili a taste. Is it too thick? Add beer or stock. Too fatty? Add some white wine vinegar or cider vinegar.

8. Serve with sour cream, shredded cheese, onions, scallions, and saltines.

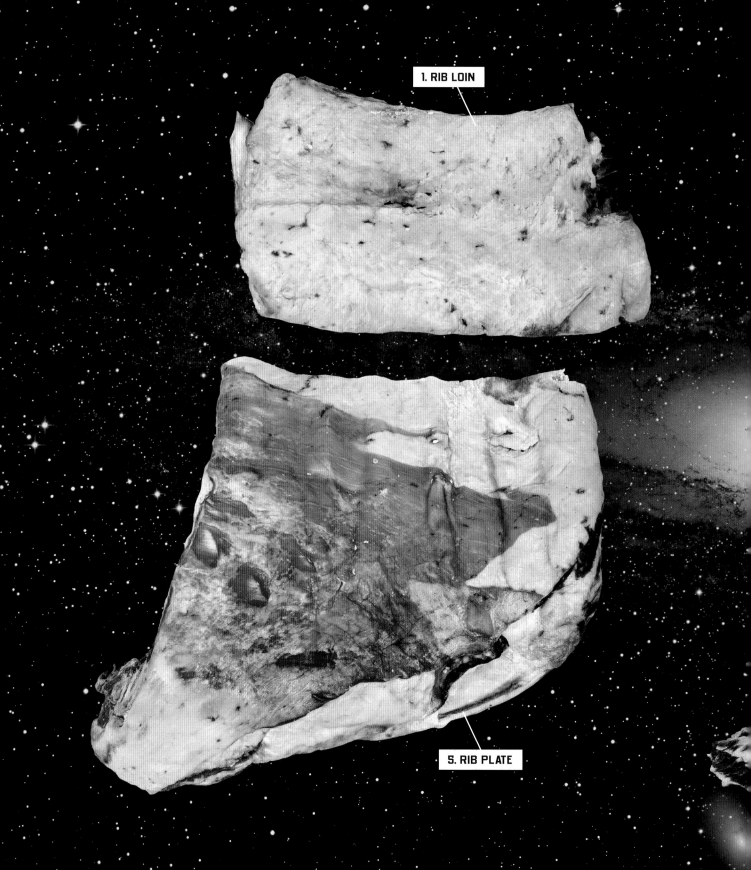

1. RIB LOIN

5. RIB PLATE

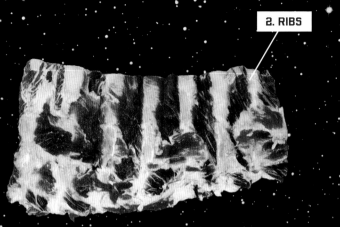

2. RIBS

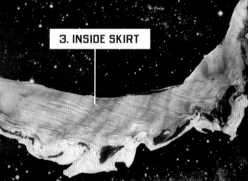

3. INSIDE SKIRT

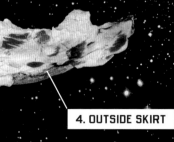

4. OUTSIDE SKIRT

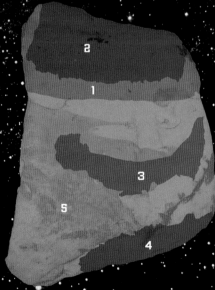

2

1

3

5

4

RIB

RIB

Most beef primals have at least a few cuts on them that are less than ideal. Cuts to be dealt with, to be ground up, braised, or cured. Not so with the rib section; it yields beefy skirt steaks, rich short ribs, and what many people consider to be the best steak on the animal: the rib steak.

RIB LOIN

The rib loin is home to the rib eye, côte de bœuf, prime rib, and all things fatty, beefy, and steamy. The shoulder end contains more fat and more of the delicious muscles from the shoulder, while the loin end is leaner but more tender.

RIB PLATE

Few parts of the animal are as deeply flavored or as versatile as the rib plate, yielding cuts ranging from thin short ribs for Korean kalbi to Argentinean asado to Jewish flanken to English-cut short ribs. The rib plate can be grilled, braised, roasted, cured, smoked, or even made into beef bacon.

SKIRT STEAKS

The two skirt steaks on each side of the animal are separated by just a few inches on the inside of the rib section, and are made up of the inside and outside skirt. The inside skirt, or diaphragm muscle, is located along the side of the rib cage. It is plump and covered with a thin layer of papery skin. The skin is usually removed in the United States, but it does a great job of keeping in the juices if grilled whole in the style of Argentinean asado. The outside skirt, which is rarely seen here, is wider and thinner and must be carefully teased off the bottom of the rib plate and trimmed of membranes. It makes a great bar steak, balancing flavorful, striated meat and streaks of luscious fat.

HOW TO TIE A ROAST

The purpose of tying a roast is to make the piece of meat you're cooking more uniform in shape and thus allow it to cook more evenly. How many times you tie your roast is up to you. A few loops of twine will keep the roast firmly in shape while cooking, but you may want to tie it more for presentation's sake or because you have control issues.

To begin, cut enough lengths of cotton butcher's string (12 inches long each) to tie your roast every 2 inches or so. Always start tying a roast in the middle and work out from there to keep everything snug, even, and looking good. An easy beginner's knot to use is the surgeon's knot.

To tie a surgeon's knot, run the piece of string under the piece of meat evenly so there are equal lengths of string on either side. Next, cross the ends and run one end under the other three times and pull both ends of the string to snug the knot. Snug is the key word here. Using too much pressure will cause meat to stick out between the string. To finish the knot, tie one regular old knot

THE RENO ROLL

Growing up in the northern Nevada casino boomtown of Reno, I developed a deep and abiding love for all things prime rib.

Unlike traditional prime rib, which is cooked on the bone and then sliced off, the Reno-style version of my youth was generally boneless, with a big, fatty flap of plate wrapped around the meat exposed by removing the ribs and chine bone.

This clever technique not only made it easier to season, roast, and slice, it also allowed the portion size, which was all-important in the hotel-casino restaurant game, to be larger without using more of the precious loin meat. While it may have been born of shrewd food costing and deceptive advertising, it also yielded a prime rib with thick, buttery layers of slow-roasted beef fat that I came to prefer to the meat itself.

Before you get all excited about making a Reno roll, you must be willing to abide by the preparation methods. There are no shortcuts here, and refusing to follow the program will result in your spending a small fortune on meat and then screwing it up. You cannot make this dish for two. You cannot cook it hotter, or faster. You will need patience, time, and a bunch of people to eat this thing. Good luck!

SERVES 8 TO 12

One 5- to 10-pound dry-aged loin with at least 5 inches of the fatty "tail" of short rib attached
2 to 3 cups coarse sea salt
1 cup cracked black peppercorns

SPECIAL EQUIPMENT
Nonreactive food-safe container the size of your rib loin
Butcher's twine
Digital probe or instant-read thermometer

1. First, you need the meat. Take this book to your butcher and annoy him with the pictures of what you want, as shown here. Cut the rib loin with an extra generous helping of the "tail" of short rib plate attached. How much rib loin is up to you but it must be *at least* 5 pounds, or about 3 bones long, for the recipe to work.

2. Now the rib loin must be carefully deboned, hugging every curve and contour of the skeletal structure. Once the butcher has done this and you have your meat, go ahead and take the spareribs home as well, and use them to make Dinosaur Ribs (page 55).

3. OK, put your rib loin in a large nonreactive food-safe container. Rub the entirety of it down with generous amounts of coarse sea salt and the cracked pepper. Don't skimp here—really lay it on in a nice even coat.

4. Now you're going to want to refer to "How to Tie a Roast," opposite, and follow those directions to tie up the loin snugly, being sure to wrap the tail around the open face of the loin that was exposed by the removal of the ribs. Tying the loin

may require a good bit of force and perhaps two full-grown persons if the loin has been dry-aged (as it should have been). This extra effort is worth it.

5. Congratulations! The tough part is over. Now all you have to do is let the loin sit for 4 to 5 days in your odor-free refrigerator in that food-safe container, covered with plastic wrap if the container doesn't have a lid. Bust out a new box of baking soda, and refrain from putting any leftover Indian food away for the duration of the salting period, so your meat won't taste like anything but beef. Dry-aged beef can drink in aromas and get real weird real fast. Trust me—don't stink up the fridge.

6. What is happening during this rest period, and why do you have to wait so long to fire up the oven and crack open the bottles of Silver Oak 1995? Well, unexcitingly, osmosis. Your huge rib loin needs some time to redistribute all that salt from the outside to the inside. Ever heard the old adage "Good meat loves salt"? Well, this is good meat and it really needs the salt, and the time to assimilate it, to taste its best.

7. It's here! Today is the day to eat like a king (or a pit boss). Start early and remove your loin from its frosty repose first thing in the morning. Let it sit out somewhere at room temperature where it can coexist peacefully with its surroundings. (Have your pets stay with a friend today, because there is no way they will leave this thing alone.) It's best if you can let the meat sit out for at least 3 hours before you put it in the oven, but if it's not completely room temp by the time you're ready, don't freak out—it'll be fine.

8. Six to 8 hours before you plan on serving the loin (depending on how huge it is), place it in a roasting pan and preheat your oven to about as hot as it can get without smoking (at my house, that's around 450°F). Place the room-temperature loin in the oven and roast until it is nicely browned, about 30 minutes.

9. Next, drop the heat to as low as your oven will go, 150° to 175°F, and continue cooking, turning the roasting pan 180 degrees every hour or so to ensure that it's cooking evenly. Stay loose with the timing of your meal and have plenty of fine red wine and a few snacks on hand to avoid the desire to rush things along. Start checking the temperature at hour 4, mostly for your own peace of mind, then check every 20 to 30 minutes thereafter. A digital-probe thermometer is best for this, so you don't have to keep opening the oven door. When the beast has reached an internal temperature of 125° to 135°F in the middle, pull it out of the oven and let it rest, covered with foil, for about 30 minutes.

10. Pop the corks, dress the Caesar salads, and top the baked potatoes—you're ready to eat! Slice the loin onto a nice serving platter into as many pieces as you have hungry guests. If everything turned out right, the fat will be buttery, the meat a nice medium-rare, and all of it worth the wait. Good job. Drink a toast to your admirable patience!

DINOSAUR RIBS

Dinosaur ribs are like bacon, **truffles, and foie gras in places where they don't belong**—they are a gimmick, but a gimmick that never gets old.

We started making dinosaur ribs the summer after we opened. We'd signed on for an ill-conceived waterfront-concert concession stand selling hot dogs, barbecue sandwiches, and anything else we had lying around that we thought drunk people would eat.

So, we decided to foist these ridiculous arm-length ribs off on intoxicated Weezer fans and the wasted faithful of Faith No More.

You can certainly make the ribs in the oven, but if you're going to bother cooking something so cartoonish, you may want to go all out and spring for a cheap offset smoker. Ask your butcher for a square-cut whole rib plate. If he doesn't know what you're talking about, call around and find someone who speaks your language.　**SERVES 7 OR 8**

1. To fabricate the ribs, take a bullnose butcher knife or large chef's knife and cut the riblets off the bottom of the ribs at the joint where they meet.

2. Next, cut all the way through the space between the ribs with your knife, making sure that each rib has meat on it. Place the ribs in a large nonreactive food-safe container.

3. To make the marinade, combine the salt, brown sugar, soy sauce, pineapple juice, black pepper, lemon zest and juice, and bonito flakes and mix well in a medium bowl, using your hands to squish any lumps of sugar. Pour the mixture evenly all over the ribs and rub it in. Cover and refrigerate overnight. Set an alarm to wake up as early as you think you can.

4. When the alarm goes off, remove the ribs from the refrigerator and place them out at room temperature somewhere where they are unlikely to be molested by man or beast. Go back to bed.

5. When you wake up again, fire up your smoker or oven. You can cook the ribs at 220°F for 12 hours or at 250°F for 8 hours, depending on how early you got out of bed and what time you want to eat.

6. Put the ribs in (if using an oven, wrap them in foil first), sit back, and settle in for a day of lazily poking at the ribs. When the ribs are tender but not quite falling off the bone, they are ready.

7. Serve with the barbecue sauce, cold beer, and loud music.

1 square-cut beef rib plate, 8 to 10 pounds

FOR THE MARINADE
1 cup kosher salt
1 cup packed light brown sugar
1 cup soy sauce
One 6- to 8-ounce can pineapple juice
2 tablespoons freshly ground black
　pepper
Grated zest and juice of 1 lemon
2 teaspoons bonito flakes
　(see Resources, page 305)
MH Barbecue Sauce (recipe follows)

SPECIAL EQUIPMENT
Butcher knife or large chef's knife
Nonreactive food-safe container large
　enough to hold the ribs
Aluminum foil or a smoker (see
　"Smokers," page 284)

MH BARBECUE SAUCE

Why buy when you can make your own?

MAKES 3 CUPS
2 cups ketchup
1 cup water
1/2 cup cider vinegar
1/3 cup light brown sugar
1/3 cup granulated sugar
1 tablespoon freshly ground
　black pepper
1 tablespoon onion powder
1 tablespoon mustard powder,
　such as Colman's
1 tablespoon fresh lemon juice
1 tablespoon Worcestershire sauce

Combine all the ingredients in a nonreactive saucepan, bring to a simmer, and simmer gently for 1 1/2 hours. Remove from the heat and let cool for 45 minutes.

Stored in an airtight container in the refrigerator, the sauce will keep for up to 1 month. Freezing is not encouraged.

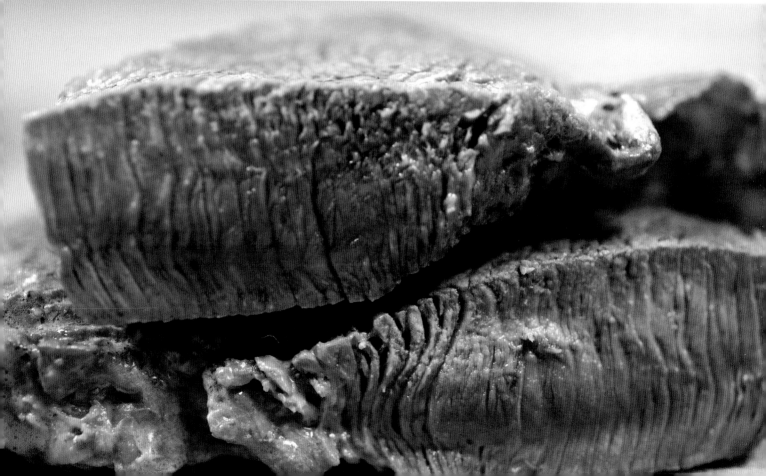

RESTING STEAKS IN FAT

While the details are a little sketchy as to who first figured out that resting a steak submerged in warm fat is the best way to make sure the juices stay inside where they belong, we came by this technique from the collective genius of chef Dennis Spina and sous-chef Homer Murray of the Roebling Tea Room, in Williamsburg, Brooklyn.

How does it work? When the steaks are completely immersed in fat, the juices have nowhere to go, so instead of leaking out of the meat and onto the cutting board, plate, or what-have-you, they stay inside the steaks until the fibers of the meat have recovered from the stressful act of cooking. Once the meat takes a few deep breaths, counts backward from ten, and finds itself again, the juices will be redistributed throughout the muscle fibers, and you can remove your rested, perfectly cooked, and extra-juicy steaks from the fat! Here's how to do it.

1. Place your fat in a deep ovenproof container, such as a roasting pan, roughly the size of the steaks you're grilling. Place in a low oven (200° to 250°F) until the fat is 100° to 110°F (it should take 10 to 15 minutes). Remove from the oven.

2. Meanwhile, grill your steaks to about a half step less done than you want them (i.e., for medium-rare, cook them to the edge of rare/medium-rare). Once your steaks are done to that point, pull them off the grill, place them in the fat, and let them rest for 3 minutes.

3. Remove the steaks, shake off as much liquid fat as possible, and slice and serve as fast as possible, to prevent the fat from becoming solid as it cools. Pack up the leftover fat in an airtight container and refrigerate until next time. It will keep for about 3 months, but it will get saltier over time as it takes on some salinity from the steaks. This is a good thing.

2 pounds unsalted butter, duck fat, or rendered beef suet
Steaks (almost any thicker cut will benefit from this treatment), about 1 pound each

SPECIAL EQUIPMENT
Instant-read thermometer

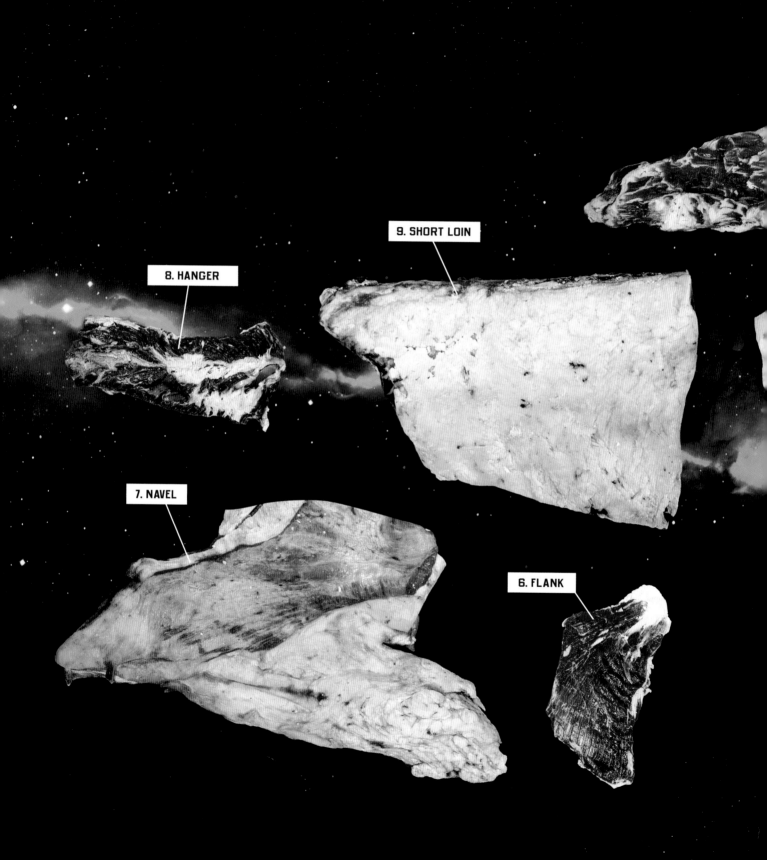

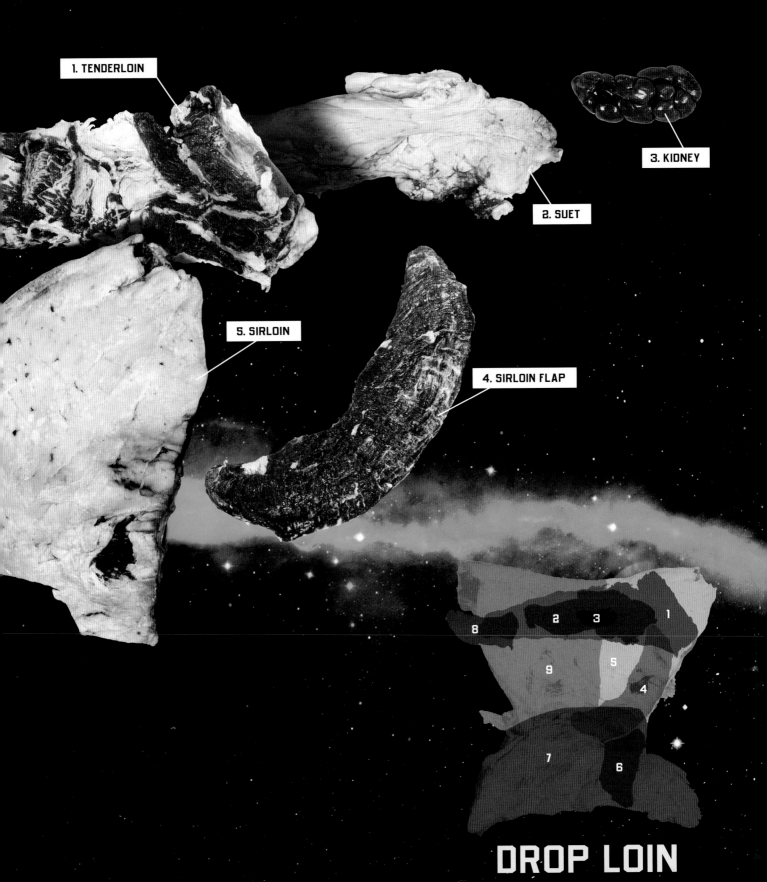

1. TENDERLOIN

2. SUET

3. KIDNEY

4. SIRLOIN FLAP

5. SIRLOIN

DROP LOIN

DROP LOIN

The drop loin is the Cadillac of primal cuts. Every part of it is good, and all steaks, from the treasured pittance of hanger to the overpriced tenderloin, the flank, New York strip, porterhouse, sirloin, and T-bone all hail from this most money of the money cuts.

Its unlikely name comes from the fact that when you saw through the aitchbone (pelvic bone) to free the drop loin from the hindquarters, it is all too easy to literally drop it on the ground if you don't have a meat hook dug into it ready to take its weight once it has been cut clear. This is a common occurrence that is nevertheless extremely frowned upon in the meat-cutting circles that deal with whole beef.

HANGER

Hanger is the best steak on the animal, according to anybody who actually knows anything about beef. Unfortunately, it is also the rarest in terms of its relation to the rest of the animal. Out of one whole beef (600 to 950 pounds hot weight), there will be two good-sized portions of hanger, assuming that the splitter at the slaughterhouse didn't accidentally cut it to shreds with a boom saw. It's tender, with a revelatory flavor and perfect texture—beef doesn't get better than the hanger.

SHORT LOIN

The short loin is not one cut but many. It can be parsed into T-bones and porterhouses that will make even the most humble man feel like a Cuban-cigar-puffing fat cat or, alternatively, it can be separated into tenderloin and New York strip, for more restrained dining. It's the most-sought-after cut and, pound for pound, the most expensive. If artificial meat is ever grown in a lab, this will surely be the first to be replicated.

SIRLOIN

The sirloin is the workingman's steak. Relatively lean, tender, and flavorful, it is the best compromise between tougher meat loaded with bold taste and easy-to-masticate loin meat. Other less lauded cuts from the sirloin include the culotte, or French-cut steak, as well as the little known but amazing tri-tip steak, which surrounds the more popular top sirloin commonly found in middle-of-the-road steak houses.

FLANK

Flank steak is the best marinating cut for the grill right after skirt steak. Relatively lean, it was the first of many cuts marketed under the vague catchall "London broil." Flank is a great choice for casual grilling, but make sure you cut it thinly across the grain for tenderness.

SIRLOIN FLAP

This is a real stealth cut from around the bottom of the sirloin. Beefy with deep striations, the sirloin flap is best cut into "faux hanger" by cutting it across the grain into smallish hangeroid-looking steaks and then marinated to help tenderize it. Sometimes it's referred to by its French name, *bavette*, to make it sound all fancy and to get a few extra dollars per pound out of the easily impressed consumer.

KINDERHOOK FARM

Kinderhook Farm is a 100-percent grass-fed beef supplier, located on some two thousand acres outside Chatham, New York. Lee Rainney and his team have been producing the best grass-fed beef in the region since 2005, and they have been our number one beef producer from day one.

All of their herd of 425 Black Angus, Black Baldie, and Red Devon cattle are born on the farm and raised exclusively on pasture and hay harvested from their lush fields. To ensure fat, happy cows, Lee rotates his herds to new pastures of sweet fresh grass daily. And, unlike many other grass-fed beef farmers, he allows his beef to mature to 26 to 28 months old, providing key extra months of grazing to ensure a carcass that rivals any grain-finished beef in fat, marbling, tenderness, and flavor.

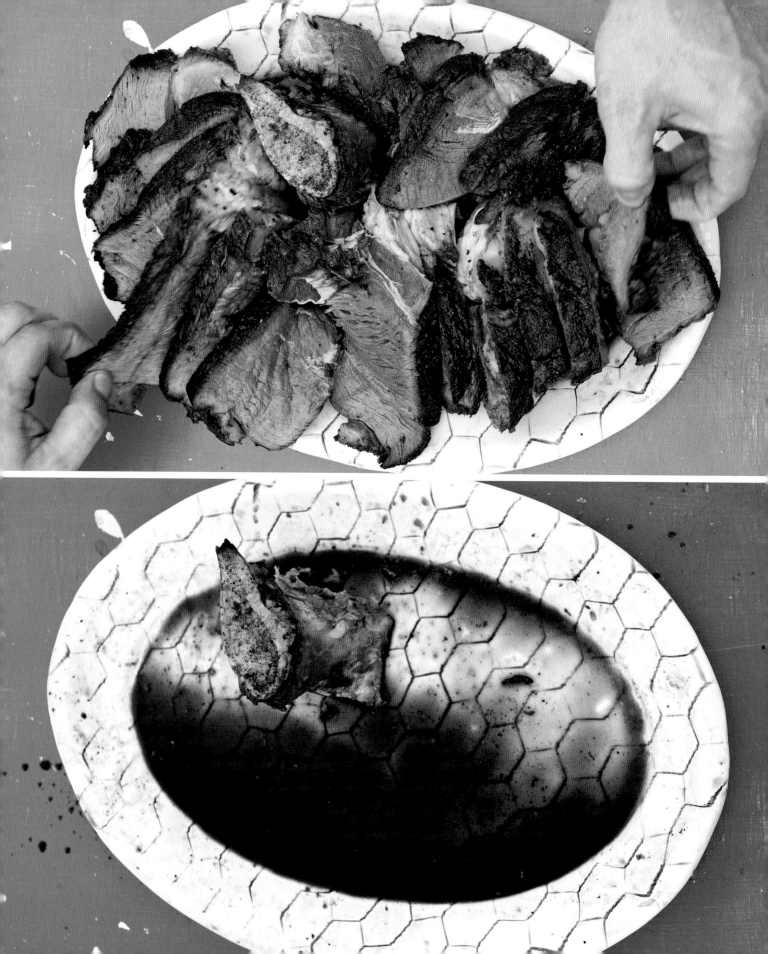

THE MAN STEAK

The Man Steak is The Meat Hook's reification of the grand pinbone steak of times of yore. It was once a common cut among butchers who aged whole drop loins in their cold boxes and cut the massive multiperson steaks for men who truly appreciated their beef. But the age of Cryovacked box beef has seen the whole sirloin fall out of favor in deference to the now ubiquitous top sirloin, which is the boneless heart of the Man Steak.

Comprised of the sirloin with all of its various muscles intact (including the tenderloin), the Man Steak is a thing to behold. With a typical specimen weighing in at more than five pounds, it is not for the faint of heart. It takes steady nerves and an iron constitution to see it through the lengthy grilling process. Take heart, intrepid grillmaster! Because of its mass and thickness, the Man Steak suffers neglect better than any normal steak, allowing margins of error to be measured in minutes rather than seconds. And its sheer size invokes a sense of theater that will bowl over even the most snobbish of steak connoisseurs no matter how overcooked it may be.

We hope we inspire a new generation of butchers and home cooks to dust off this lost page of American beef history and enjoy the last bit of the drop loin in the way it should truly be experienced.

To cook a Man Steak, you must first find a butcher who can cut you a pinbone or flat-bone sirloin steak. This is harder than you might think, so call around before you go. Have the butcher cut the steak at least 2 inches thick, but 3 inches is better. **SERVES 6 TO 10**

One 2- to 3-inch-thick pinbone sirloin, 3 to 5 pounds
Kosher salt and freshly ground black pepper

SPECIAL EQUIPMENT
Instant-read thermometer

1. At least 2 hours before you plan to grill it, salt and pepper your monster of a steak aggressively, then let it sit out. Please don't ignore this step or the steak will cook unevenly.

2. Now, fire up your grill so that you have nice, even medium heat.

3. Lay the steak in the center of your grill and flip it every 2 to 3 minutes for about 15 minutes before you start checking it with a digital instant-read thermometer. You're shooting for 125° to 135°F. The thicker the steak, the longer this will take; just be patient and bask in the aura of grilling the biggest steak in the world. Rest the steak for 5 minutes before slicing and serving. Ideally, the Man Steak is served with nothing else at all.

MARROW BUTTER

The simple pleasure of a great porterhouse, **T-bone,** or sirloin steak in its elemental perfection is undeniable. However, that is not to say that you cannot improve on it with a bit of clever engineering and a soul full of thrift. Exhibit A: bone-marrow butter.

The butter is a creation that goes back to my old stomping grounds, Williamsburg's South Side, where we made our bones (pardon the pun, please) as cooks and butchers before we opened The Meat Hook. Marrowbones were a rare commodity to be revered, extended, and savored. The idea of this recipe was to somehow make the sublime pleasure of roasted marrow available as a more than occasional treat. Naturally, being that we were working just down the road from the lauded Peter Luger Steak House, with its internationally famous porterhouse steak drenched in hot melted butter, we turned to butter.   **MAKES 1½ POUNDS**

1 pound unsalted butter, softened
3 whole femur marrowbones, about
   3 pounds, at room temperature
Salt and freshly ground black pepper
½ cup finely minced shallots
½ cup finely minced chives
¼ cup finely chopped parsley

SPECIAL EQUIPMENT
Stand mixer

1. While the butter is softening, preheat your oven to 375°F.

2. Give the ends of the marrowbones a good rub of salt and pepper and place in a suitable baking dish.

3. Put the marrowbones in the oven for 10 to 12 minutes, until fully cooked but with just a kiss of pink in their centers. Allow the bones to cool enough to be handled.

4. Now scrape out the goodness inside the bones with a slender knife or the handle of a spoon, making sure to get every last bit of roasted marrow into the bowl of your mixer. Add the butter and all the remaining ingredients, including a few good three-finger pinches of salt and pepper, and begin mixing slowly. Once the marrow and herbs are well blended, taste the butter and adjust the seasoning accordingly; it should be pleasantly salty.

5. To use, smear a small amount of room-temperature marrow butter on a resting steak just before serving, and freak out. It'll taste that good. Leftover marrow butter can be frozen for weeks, if not months, until needed. Smear it on some good bread in the absence of a suitable piece of grilled red meat.

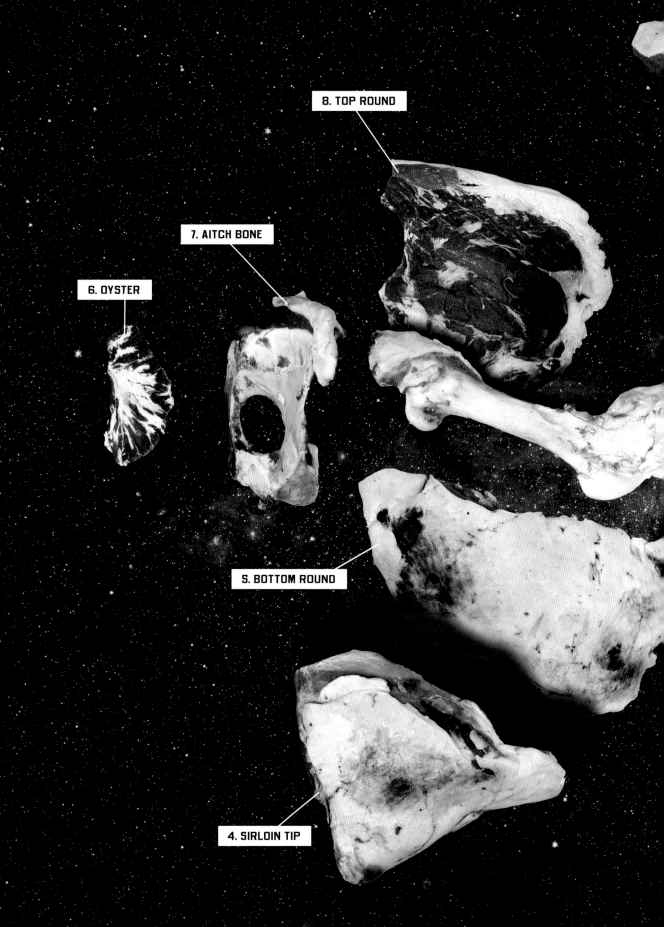

8. TOP ROUND

7. AITCH BONE

6. OYSTER

5. BOTTOM ROUND

4. SIRLOIN TIP

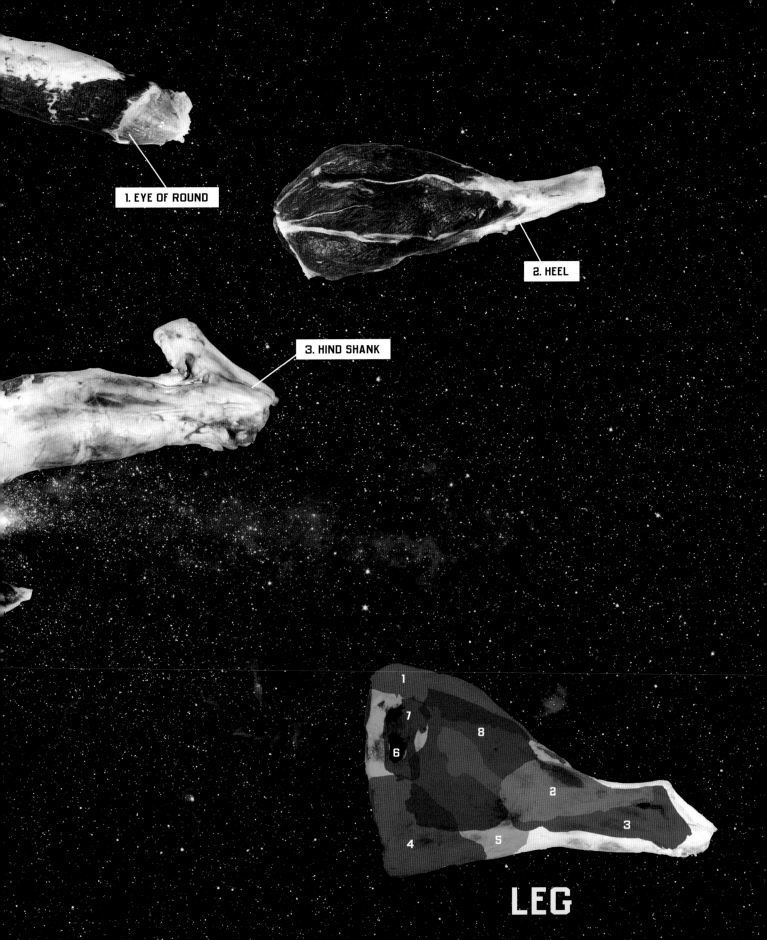

1. EYE OF ROUND

2. HEEL

3. HIND SHANK

LEG

LEG

The beef leg, or round as it is sometimes called, is a true thing of beauty and the single most satisfying of all pieces of beef to the butcher. Its noble mass and nearly equine aspect are at once graceful and awe-inspiring, conjuring up images of both savage precolonial feasts and the elegant dining rooms of Industrial Revolution steamship dinners, which gave this grandiose cut its nickname "steamship round."

Often maligned as lean and tough, the leg remains an impressive exaltation of all that beef can be. These days the leg meat is usually minced up for lean ground beef or sold as cube steak, but its charms do not elude the savvy butcher. The bottom round is prized as a beef roast and the top round clamored for by chefs who know just how desirable its lean but flavorful meat is as tartare or carpaccio.

TOP ROUND

The biggest muscle of the beef leg, top round is great left whole and cooked as a delicious slow-roasted British-style roast beef or steaked out by cutting it across the grain to make classic London broil.

The top round is made up of several different muscles:

- The cap can be rolled for a roast or marinated and grilled like skirt steak, depending on how you're feeling and the time of year.

- The soft side is a tender nugget on one side of the top round, sometimes called "the pear." It can be cut into nice little cheap bistro steaks and seared in a pan.

- The main body of the top round can be further seamed out into two more cuts, but they're more or less the same texture- and flavorwise. This cut makes prime carpaccio, tartare, or Cannibal Sandwiches (page 73) and is really best eaten raw, though it can make a good steak with the judicious application of a Jaccard knife or other meat tenderizing tool.

BOTTOM ROUND

Also known as the silver side or inside round, the bottom round is occasionally sliced and foisted off on the unsuspecting consumer as London broil. But the bottom round is too full of bouncy collagen to make a good grilling item or much of a raw beef dish. It excels, however, in the role of deli-style roast beef, partially cured and then slowly roasted and sliced thin.

EYE OF ROUND

Roast beef for two! The eye of round, or pope's eye, has a neat little fat cap that makes it the perfect amount for an intimate dinner without massive amounts of leftovers.

SIRLOIN TIP

We've been known to sell (and occasionally serve) a whole sirloin tip, to be cooked on the massive femur bone, or cannon bone, for a truly over-the-top dinner. Alternatively, the sirloin tip can be seamed out into cute small roasts or well chilled and sliced thin for Fighting-Cock Jerky (page 75).

HIND SHANK

Shank is the middle portion of the front or rear leg of a steer. It's tough, full of sinews, and extremely lean. To enjoy shank, you have to know what you're getting into: it cannot be grilled, roasted, or cooked in any sort of timely fashion. If you're in a hurry, leave the velvety goodness that is the beef shank behind.

However, if you have a day to while away as your kitchen slowly fills with the perfume of grass-fed beef, read on. Shank is in its element when cooked in a Dutch oven or slow cooker for a minimum of 8 hours at 275°F or longer (see The Campagnella, page 78). Long, slow cooking allows the prodigious amount of connective tissue to melt into the braise, releasing the rich shreds of meat from the bone and forming a lip-smacking sauce or stew thick with collagenous insanity.

OTHER BITS

The beef leg is a complicated part of its anatomy, and there are a few other pieces worth mentioning too, though they are, unfortunately, usually ground up or discarded.

The heel is one cut that is equally at home in a pot as a braise or seamed out of its silverskin and connective tissue and grilled as a steak (see Grilled Heel, page 77).

The oyster, or spider steak as it is sometimes called, is a tender and nicely fatty little morsel found on the inside of the aitchbone, just opposite the hip socket. While it weighs in at less than 6 ounces, it is a classic butcher's cut that is a perfect choice for light summer meals, with a bottle of chilled rosé or a Schlitz tall boy.

CANNIBAL SANDWICHES

When Brent was young and his mom was out with her friends for the night, dinner with his dad meant one of three things: (1) Happy Meals, (2) fancy-pants hamburgers, or (3) Cannibal Sandwiches. The Cannibal Sandwich, if it isn't clear from the pictures, is like a hamburger, only *completely raw*. The recipe closely resembles making hamburgers but doesn't waste time with all of that cooking. It includes raw egg too, so as with much else in this book, proceed at your own risk!   **MAKES 3 SANDWICHES**

1 shallot, minced
1 teaspoon capers, chopped
4 cornichons, chopped
1 teaspoon red wine vinegar
1¹/₂ pounds freshly ground top round
Kosher salt and freshly ground
    black pepper
1 large egg yolk
Hot sauce, such as Texas Pete
Worcestershire sauce
3 brioche rolls, split, or potato rolls
1 red onion, thinly sliced
A big handful of arugula
Dijon mustard

1. In a medium bowl, combine the shallots, capers, cornichons, and vinegar, add the top round, and mix well. Season aggressively with salt and pepper. Add the egg yolk, a dash of hot sauce, and a splash of Worcestershire sauce and mix to combine.

2. Form the meat into 3 equal burgers. Place each patty on a roll and top with sliced red onion, arugula, and a little Dijon. Close the sandwiches and enjoy.

FIGHTING-COCK JERKY

James Lum, or the Jizzler as he was sometimes known, was our resident jerky specialist. A real Cinderella story, James, a Virginia native, started as a dishwasher and porter and quickly worked his way up to be our principal beef cutter and resident expert on everything jerky. As of this writing, he's gone on to open his own butcher shop in Charlottesville. I think I might be tearing up, I'm so proud.

Few people would speak of beef jerky in the same breath as fine charcuterie, yet the two do have something in common. Making jerky is a talent that you are either born with or you're not. You either get it or you don't, and no amount of reading or practice will make you much better at it. James was born with it; I hope you were too.

This is a spicy version of our basic jerky that is jazzed up with Sriracha sauce. It is from the kitchen vernacular for Sriracha—"cock sauce"—from its rooster label, that this jerky gets its name. The weights are in grams, so bust out your digital scale. **MAKES ONE MEDIUM-SIZED PAPER GROCERY BAG OF JERKY**

80 grams brown sugar
80 grams kosher salt
20 grams freshly ground black pepper
25 grams garlic powder
8 to 9 pounds sirloin tips,
    sliced ¼ inch thick
160 grams Worcestershire sauce
160 grams Sriracha sauce
5 grams soy sauce

SPECIAL EQUIPMENT
Large nonreactive food-safe container
Dehydrator with racks

1. Combine the dry ingredients in a small bowl and mix well. Put the sirloin tips in a large nonreactive food-safe container and rub all over with the spice mixture.

2. Combine the Worcestershire, Sriracha, and soy sauce in a bowl and mix well, then toss the sirloin tips with the mixture. Cover with plastic wrap and refrigerate overnight.

3. Spread the meat out on the dehydrator racks. The slices should not be touching each other or folded over on themselves, or they will not dehydrate properly.

4. Dry the sirloin at 125°F for 5 to 6 hours; the time will vary depending on the humidity. Check the meat after 3 hours and then every subsequent hour until done. It will be very dark brown, shiny, and slightly flexible when ready.

5. The jerky will keep at room temperature for 1 month in a paper bag.

GRILLED HEEL

The heel is a true pinch hitter. **If you have the skill and patience, you can seam out all the silverskin and cook the resulting pieces of steak in a pan or on the grill, or you can leave the heel as is and braise it with red wine, tomatoes, and winter vegetables—see The Campagnella, page 78.**

The heel may be hard to come by at your typical grocery store or megamart. To find it, head to your nearest old-school butcher shop, specialty market, or Chinatown meat shop. SERVES 2

1 heel of beef, about 4 pounds
Olive oil or unsalted butter
Kosher salt and freshly ground
   black pepper

SPECIAL EQUIPMENT
Very sharp 5-inch boning knife
One well-rested mind

1. If the heel still has the tendon attached (see page 71), cut it off at the base of the heel and freeze it for Sichuan-Style Beef Tendon (page 83) or to include in Basic Brown Stock (page 243).

2. Next, using your boning knife, remove all of the exterior silverskin and connective tissue. Then, following the seams of the remaining thin ribbons of silverskin, cut into the body of the heel with the tip of your knife, slowly and without rushing it or getting frustrated (see "well-rested mind," above!). Nick away at the meat clinging to the tendon filaments until you have one large steak. Season liberally with salt and pepper.

3. Place the steak in a very hot pan or on a hot grill and sear it for about 2 minutes on each side, or cook it on a cooler part of the grill, or over medium heat in a pan, taking care not to go much past medium-rare, 3 to 4 minutes per side. Enjoy with a Tuscan kale Caesar salad and good red wine.

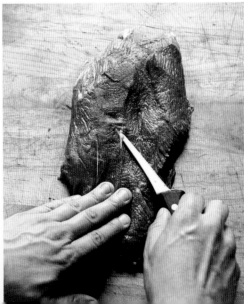

THE CAMPAGNELLA

In Italian, *campagnella* means bell, and this cut is roughly bell shaped—well, sort of, anyway . . . and who are we to question the Italians? All you really need to understand is that this cut is cheap and delicious, and this recipe takes your food dollar a long way, as, with pasta involved, one Campagnella can easily feed six people.

This recipe also works beautifully with crosscut beef shank, but you'll need to double it due to the mass of bone in the shank. **SERVES 6**

3 tablespoons olive oil

1/2 heel of beef, hopefully with tendon, about 2 pounds

1 head garlic, peeled and roughly chopped

2 cups mirepoix (2/3 cup each roughly chopped celery, onions, and carrots)

1/4 cup Italian red wine, such as Sangiovese

About 3 cups Basic Brown Stock (page 243)

One 28-ounce can San Marzano tomatoes, undrained

Kosher salt and freshly ground black pepper

2 pounds rigatoni or other large dried pasta shape

1 teaspoon anchovy paste and/or minced oil-cured olives (optional)

1. Let the olive oil get hot in a Dutch oven over high heat, then brown the heel on all sides, 2 to 3 minutes per side. Set the meat aside on a plate.

2. Add the chopped garlic and mirepoix to the pot and cook over medium heat until browned, about 20 minutes.

3. Preheat the oven to 275°F.

4. Add the wine to the pot and stir to deglaze it. Return the meat to the pot, then add enough stock to come three-quarters of the way up the sides of the meat.

5. Toss in the tomatoes, season with salt and pepper, cover, and place in the oven to cook overnight or all day (about 8 hours); keep the pot covered so that the outer muscles, which are leaner, don't dry out.

6. Meanwhile, when you're almost ready to eat, fill a large pot with 8 quarts water, add 1/4 cup salt, and bring to a boil. Cook your pasta according to the directions on the box minus a minute or two to give the pasta a toothier, more al dente texture; drain.

7. Break up the meat into the sauce with a spoon, then taste and adjust the seasoning. Add the pasta and toss well. Allow to sit for a minute to let the pasta soak up some of the meaty juices. For an added umami blast, hit the dish with the anchovy paste (or toss in some minced olives).

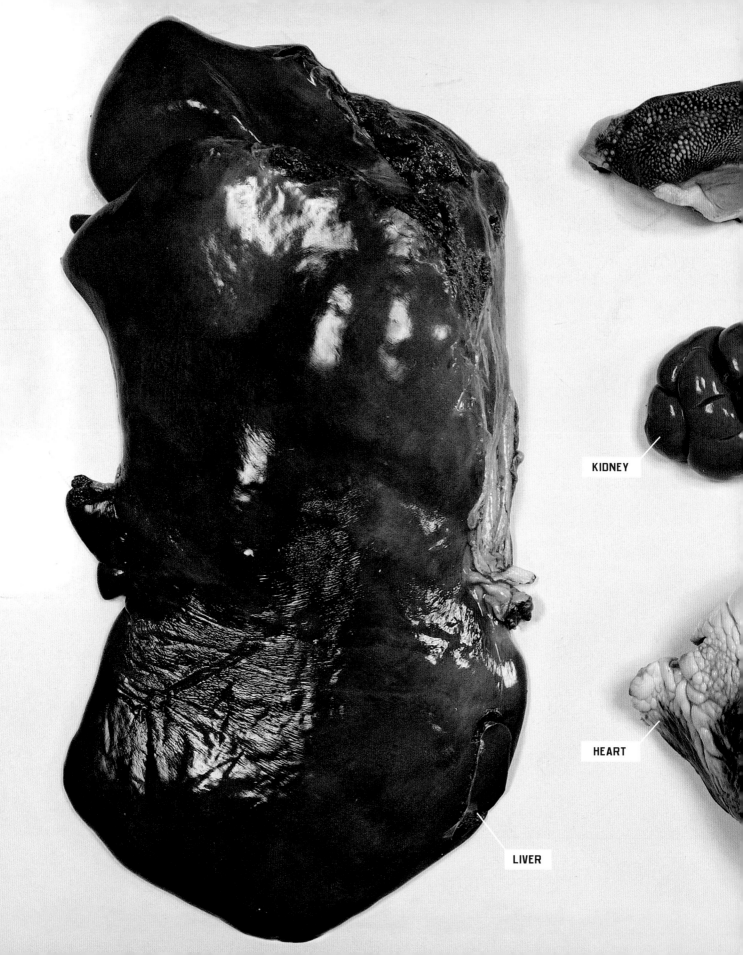

KIDNEY

HEART

LIVER

TONGUE

SUET

BEEF OFFAL

Pigs and sheep seem to rule the offal roost in most of today's avant-garde cookbooks; I'd beg to differ. Sure, beef offal is more difficult to master, because of its larger format and stronger flavor, but it's also more rewarding to know that you have gone beyond the canon of well-worn classics and solidly into the realm of the unknown, be it silverskin, tendon, kidney, tongue, or heart. It's a good place to be.

SICHUAN-STYLE BEEF TENDON

Beef tendons, like pig's feet and veal knuckles, are an easy way to add body to any stock or broth, but they are also delicious in their own right. We've found a few ways to make use of the usually discarded bits of the beef carcass.

Since they are completely composed of collagen fibers, tendons aren't really meat per se, but they're still mighty fine. The rub is that uncooked, they have a texture not unlike that of vulcanized rubber tire. To break them down to a chewable form, they need to be simmered or braised at a low heat (under 300°F) for several hours.

I enjoyed this dish at a Sichuan place in Chinatown one afternoon while playing hooky from the incessant demolition, painting, sanding, and repainting that was the DIY clusterfuck of getting the Meat Hook space ready for prime time. It's not complicated and it is really good—but people who can't handle weird textures or a lot of heat should probably leave this recipe alone. **SERVES 2 AS AN APPETIZER**

2 beef tendons, from the hind shank (about 1/2 pound)
Kosher salt
1/2 cup peanut oil
3 garlic cloves
1 coin-sized slice unpeeled fresh ginger
1 teaspoon Sichuan peppercorns

SPECIAL EQUIPMENT
Chef's knife or cleaver

1. Fill a medium saucepan with 8 cups of water, add the tendons and salt to taste, and bring to a bare simmer over low heat. Let simmer, uncovered, for 3 to 4 hours, depending on how toothsome you like your tendon. Longer = softer; shorter = more bite.

2. Meanwhile, in a small saucepan, combine the peanut oil with the garlic cloves, ginger, and Sichuan peppercorns and bring to a simmer over medium heat. Once the oil has simmered for 15 to 20 minutes, remove from the heat and set aside to infuse.

3. When the beef tendons are done, drain and chill in a bowl of cold water for 20 minutes; drain again.

4. Using a sharp chef's knife or a Chinese vegetable cleaver, thinly slice the tendons lengthwise. If you can't get them superthin, don't worry—they'll still taste good. Transfer to a bowl.

5. Strain the peanut oil and toss with the tendons. Serve chilled or at room temperature—it's up to you. Serve with rice, along with plenty of water and ice-cold Tsingtao.

ENGLISH WHITE PUDDING
with Leeks

Cooking with beef suet, the girthy knob of fat that hangs inside the drop loin around the kidneys, is a challenge. Sure, you can render it for frying or perhaps grind it into ground beef for some extra fat, but there seemed to be no easy solution for the problem of what to do with all the suet we found ourselves with.

As it turns out, anytime you're faced with an insurmountable amount of nettlesome offal, you need only look as far as the cuisine of the British Isles to figure out how to dispose of it. As maligned as British cuisine is, the English excel at turning completely useless things into filling, if not always delicious, food. This happens to be one of the simplest and tastiest inventions from the lexicon of their peasant fare. **MAKES ABOUT 35 LINKS**

3 cups (2$\frac{1}{2}$ pounds) rolled oats

6 cups whole milk

2$\frac{1}{2}$ pounds beef suet, ground

5 large eggs

2 large leeks, white and pale green parts, finely chopped

100 grams kosher salt

20 grams freshly ground black pepper

1 to 2 lengths hog casings (see Resources, page 305), rinsed and soaked

SPECIAL EQUIPMENT
Disposable gloves

Sausage stuffer

Digital probe or instant-read thermometer

1. The day before you're going to cook, mix the rolled oats with the milk in a large stainless steel bowl; set aside in your refrigerator to soak for at least 12 hours.

2. With gloved hands, take your soaked oats (the milk should be completely absorbed), ground suet, and the rest of the ingredients (except for the pork casings) and mix well in a large bowl for 5 minutes. Immediately load the mixture into your sausage stuffer and fill the casings tightly, twisting them into 6-inch-long links. Set aside on a baking sheet to dry overnight in the refrigerator (see Garlic Sausage, page 157).

3. The next morning, fill a stockpot two-thirds full with water and heat it over high heat until it reaches 180°F (check with a digital probe or instant-read thermometer). Lower the heat to medium-low and add enough of the links to bring the water level to within 3 inches of the top. Poach the links until they are white and firm, 20 to 30 minutes, then *carefully* transfer them to an ice bath to chill (you have to be very gentle, as the tender casings can burst and spew molten suet all over you and everything in your kitchen if you don't watch out!). Add the next batch of links to the hot water, and continue until all the links are poached and chilled.

4. Drain the links. To store them, cut them into links, put them in Ziploc bags, and freeze—or give them away to hungry Anglophiles. They'll keep in the freezer for 2 to 3 months, but we've never had them around that long! To serve, fry over medium heat for 5 minutes a side; they go great with fried eggs.

TAIKI'S TONGUE STEAKS

We first met Taiki Otsuka one summer afternoon **during the months leading up to opening The Meat Hook.**

Taiki, the manager and only full-time employee at Japan Premium Beef on Great Jones Street, was behind the tiny counter serving Wagyu beef (the heavily marbled beef breed that is commonly, if incorrectly, known as Kobe beef in the United States) to an older French lady. We sampled some hanger, flank, and tri-tip. Before we knew it, we were exchanging cards and arranging to have a drink.

That fateful interaction and the night of sake and sashimi that followed led us to hire one of the most amazing characters who would ever charm our customers in broken English. I don't have space here to even begin to describe the grand hallucinatory saga of The Life of Taiki Otsuka.

What I can say is that Taiki is now back in Japan dealing in the rarified world of certified A5 Wagyu semen and dairy cattle genetics. Before he left us, he taught us a thing or two about eating, among other things, raw chicken and beef sashimi, and this recipe for grilled beef tongue. **SERVES 2 TO 3**

1 beef tongue, 2 to 3 pounds
2 tablespoons peanut oil
1/2 cup soy sauce
1/2 teaspoon grated fresh ginger

SPECIAL EQUIPMENT
5-inch boning knife

1. Use a chef's knife to separate the tough tip from the thick rear third of the tongue. Reserve the tip for another use.

2. Run the blade of your boning knife just under the skin of the tongue, being careful to remove any of the sharkskin-like taste buds or hard cartilage buttons on the bottom.

3. Slice the peeled tongue across the grain into 1/2-inch-thick steaks.

4. Now get your cast-iron pan hot over high heat and add the oil. This would be a good time to mix the soy and ginger together in a dish for the dipping sauce.

5. Notice how incredibly marbled these steaks are? Yep, all that white marbling is luscious beef fat, which makes these little morsels pound for pound the most insane steaks on the animal. Toss a few of the medallions at a time into the hot pan (avoid crowding) and sear them just long enough to brown, 1 to 2 minutes on each side. Serve right away, with the dipping sauce.

SILVERSKIN STEW

Silverskin stew, made with those **shiny connective membranes that are usually thrown away**, was one of Taiki Otsuka's favorite dishes (see page 87). To obtain this lovely bit of beef bycatch, you may need to ply your local butcher with a six-pack or two, but it is worth the hassle (both yours and his).

Instead of with scallions, you could garnish each bowl of stew with a few thin slices of lean beef or a raw egg.   **SERVES 2**

2 quarts Basic Brown Stock (page 243)
1/2 cup mirin or sake
3 tablespoons soy sauce
1/2 pound beef silverskin
2 eggs
1 cup chopped scallions

1. In a large saucepan, bring the stock, mirin, and soy sauce to a simmer over low heat. Add the silverskin and cook for 45 minutes to 1 hour, giving it a stir every so often until the silverskin is plump and pale in color.

2. Ladle the stew into bowls, drop in the raw eggs, and top with the scallions. Serve with nigori sake.

GRILLED BEEF HEART

I'll be honest with you here: a lot of offal, no matter how well pre-pared, is OK at best and god-awful at worst. But beef heart, unlike liver, or lungs, is actually good, as long as you follow a couple of cardinal rules: it must be marinated (or it is likely to be tough, rub-bery, and underseasoned) and it must be grilled to medium-rare (*see* tough and rubbery).

This recipe is really the best, easiest, and most reliable offal recipe you can tackle. Just pay attention to the fact that you *must* marinate it for 24 hours before grilling, and your reward will be the most profoundly satisfying steak of your life.   SERVES 3 OR 4

1 beef heart, trimmed, 1$\frac{1}{2}$ to 2 pounds

FOR THE MARINADE
$\frac{1}{2}$ cup olive oil
$\frac{1}{4}$ cup red wine vinegar
1 rosemary sprig, roughly chopped
1 to 2 garlic cloves, minced
1 tablespoon crushed red pepper flakes
Kosher salt and freshly ground black
    pepper to taste

SPECIAL EQUIPMENT
5-inch boning knife or a paring knife

1. Trim off the collar of the beef heart. Then, using a sharp boning or paring knife, remove all the membranes, inside and out. Cut the beef heart into steaks (there should be 3 or 4 steaks) and place in a Ziploc bag.

2. To make the marinade, mix together all the ingredients in a small bowl. Pour into the Ziploc bag, seal the bag, and let the beef heart marinate overnight in your refrigerator—or for several days, if you forget about your little beef heart project and get lured into drinking cheap Canadian beer and playing game after game of Big Buck Hunter.

3. When you're ready to eat, fire up the grill or broiler—either way, you need high heat here. (You can cook beef heart in a pan, but I don't recommend it.)

4. When your cooking appurtenance is hot, toss on the heart steaks and give them a good sear on both sides, 2 to 3 minutes each. Then move them to a cool portion of the grill or move them onto a plate and place in a warm oven to finish, 2 to 3 minutes more. Let the steaks rest at room temperature for 5 minutes.

5. Slice the steaks into $\frac{1}{3}$-inch-wide strips, and serve with a simple salad.

EDOARDO'S FRIED BEEF KIDNEY

Edoardo Mantelli has been a friend of The Meat Hook from the beginning. My relationship with him started years ago—I served him and his business partner coffee at Marlow & Sons every morning. Our friendship evolved as Marlow & Daughters opened and he started his restaurant, Saraghina, in Bed-Stuy. We went from regulars and friends to peers in a matter of months, as we both took our leaps into the world of owning food establishments in Brooklyn.

What to do with all those beef kidneys had always been a problem for me. I hated to throw them out, but I was damned if I could think of anything more constructive to do with them than grind them into our dog food. We polled our more adventurous customers to see if they had any ideas on uses for kidneys and came up with zilch, until a chance conversation one afternoon with Edoardo. He leaped at the chance to fool with the bottom-of-the-barrel offal we offered him for the taking. What he gave us is an old family recipe from his native Italy. When you make this, be sure your beef kidney is as fresh as possible (or it may fill your home with the unmistakable aroma of a minor-league baseball stadium urinal).   **SERVES 2**

1. Pull off any membranes or fat on the outside of the kidney. Using a chef's knife, slice it crosswise into ½-inch-thick medallions.

2. Toss the medallions with the vinegar in a bowl and set aside. Mix together the flour with a few good pinches each of salt and pepper in a shallow bowl.

3. Heat the oven to 250°F.

4. Drain the medallions, rinse in cold water, and pat dry with paper towels. Dredge each one in the seasoned flour and arrange on a plate to await frying.

5. Heat a few good-sized glugs of olive oil in a large cast-iron skillet over medium-high heat. Fry the medallions a few at a time until nice and brown, about 2 minutes a side. Keep the finished batches warm in the oven. Serve with a medium-bodied Italian red wine, like Nero d'Avola.

1 fresh beef kidney, 1 to 2 pounds
   (weight varies)
1 cup red wine vinegar
1 cup all-purpose flour
Kosher salt and freshly ground black
   pepper
Olive oil for frying

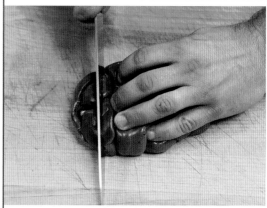
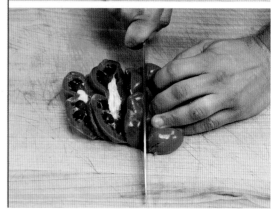

In late winter 2010, we were given the opportunity to be part of our fellow Brooklyn restaurant friends' bid to take over the derelict WPA snack bars along Rockaway Beach in Queens. Brent decided to assume the mantle of the project. Rippers, the result of our partnership with our soul mates at Roberta's, is hard to describe. It is as much about the grass-roots, for-the-people future of the outer boroughs as it is an exercise in childhood nostalgia. Rockaway was abandoned to urban decay around the same time that Brent and I were having our first exposure to MTV's The Grind beach party episodes. Rippers is the unintelligible and yet strangely familiar result—like finding a pair of acid-washed jeans and a Day-Glo tank top in your luggage that you're sure you didn't pack.

**"Stoned to the bone, I'm a hardcore ripper."
—Brandon Hoy**

By Brent Young

I was alive in 1989, but I hardly got to live the glamorous life that was shown on my family's 28-inch console television. And by glamorous life, I mean the one that MTV presented to me each spring and summer. My hometown of Pittsburgh, Pennsylvania, barely offered me spring-break shenanigans. Eric Nies, prompting babes in string bikinis to dance to Crystal Waters, was nowhere to be found; my dad didn't own an '86 Corvette; and I wasn't friends with David Lee Roth.

Little did I know that my adolescent dreams would manifest themselves in the year 2010. A good friend, Andrew Field, was running a little taco shack out at Rockaway Beach, aptly called Rockaway Taco. The place made its name serving the best fish tacos in New York City, in one of the strangest neighborhoods around. Andrew approached the Meat Hook team and other neighborhood food friends about opening businesses at the beach, in the old WPA concession stands. Beach shack business? Yes, please.

We and our Roberta's friends began scheming about how to re-create that 1989 Daytona Beach vibe. Before I go on, you should know a couple things about our friends from Roberta's.

These dudes have made the most ambitious restaurant that Brooklyn has ever seen. When I say "restaurant," I mean pizzeria, radio station, clubhouse, tiki bar, and tasting room. The owners, Brandon Hoy, Chris Parachini, and Carlo Mirarchi, are all insane in their own right. The first time we hung out with Brandon, he convinced Tom and Ben and me to buy a one-fifth share of a sailboat (see page 186). The first time I really hung out with Chris, he taught me how to sail said boat, and we almost got run over by a cargo ship. Carlo fueled our intern sessions with gasoline-extract pisco, and then went on to open Blanca, the most highly sought-after tasting room in New York City.

So, we decided to open a burger shack with these dudes and call it Rippers.

This couldn't have been more of a hood rat project to begin with. The shack really was a shack, with room only for a hot line and a couple coolers for beers. The building hadn't been occupied for over fifteen years.

We painted the ceiling pink with sealant, liked the way it looked, and kept it fluorescent. We had our friend Steiner paint the walls. With some tape and spray paint, he created what looked like futuristic neon Pendleton-inspired Mondrian-style graffiti. What we were able to offer the community turned out to be highly sought after. Real, honest food. Properly sourced burgers, homemade hot dogs, fresh juice, and killer fries. We opened for breakfast that first year, and ladies on the boardwalk would stop, almost in tears with excitement over the fact that they could actually get a cup of coffee after their morning walk for the first time in thirty years. We also provided a great place to get *insanely* drunk, dance your face off, or listen to surf-punk.

Start-up was a bitch, as it always is, but by the following summer, we'd really hit our stride. That stride was named Domenic Boero, my current roommate and one of my best friends. Dom ran the ship at Rippers the way only a California kid could, like a drunken banshee more concerned with skating than with worrying about tomorrow. We had created the perfect job for our sixteen-year-old selves. Babes, burgers, and beer. We started the summer with a tattoo contest, which ended quickly after Dom started spending every paycheck on tattoos. No regrets. He put together a crew that insisted that you have a good time. No excuses.

It was a great summer. But after the summer, Rockaway was subject to the natural disaster that was Hurricane Sandy. After the storm, there wasn't much left that looked like a town. It was as if a bomb had gone off, or every home had been hit with a bulldozer. But with the tragedy came an outpouring of help and goodwill from other Brooklyn communities, eager to do what the city or FEMA could never do. There's still an unbelievable amount of rebuilding to be done, but we're in it for the long haul.

So with the paint drying on the walls, the new concrete boardwalk setting out front, and welders spraying sparks to create a shade structure, we opened the doors on a sunny Memorial Day 2013, under pressure from Mayor Bloomberg. We had burgers and cold beers, and the community felt normal for the first time in more than six months. Locals came out to Rippers and got ripped, and all shared tales

of their horrific winter, but with summer on the horizon, everyone was smiling and optimistic. That optimism for community development proved true and the crowds flooded to the beach. The heat hit quick that summer, and everyone rushed away from the asphalt to the minor respite of the beach. We had to redesign and update the restaurant every week for the first month to accommodate the crowds. Every weekend the crowds grew bigger, and on the Fourth of July, the other concession stands at 96th and 106th were finally able to open too. The real construction projects continued: dredging sand and rebuilding the beaches. The majority of the actual Rockaways looked like a Beijing construction project, with cranes, barges, and bulldozers built like Transformers. To our amazement, this somehow did not deter New Yorkers from turning out. Each weekend the parties got bigger; we saw more international passports at the bar, and laughed at foreigners' attempts to pronounce "Narragansett." (You can't blame them; it's $3 a beer.) The community continues to brace for the next storm, but for the sunny months, we put the thought out of our minds and enjoy life in NYC.

Rippers is a business, but to a community of surf bums, it has become a way of life. While this might be the proper place for a dumb "perfect slider" recipe, I'd rather give you my favorite Rippers indulgence, a good old-fashioned New York City–style piña colada.

RIPPERS PIÑA COLADAS
MAKES TWO 16-OUNCE DRINKS (BECAUSE YOU SHOULD NEVER DRINK ALONE)

4 ounces pineapple juice
4 ounces Coco Lopez
4 ounces light rum
4 ounces dark rum
4 cups ice cubes
2 maraschino cherries

SPECIAL EQUIPMENT
Heavy-duty blender

Pour the pineapple juice, Coco Lopez, rum, and ice into a blender and blend until smooth. Pour into two glasses (tiki glasses are a good choice). Top each drink with a cherry. Cocktail umbrellas are optional but recommended.

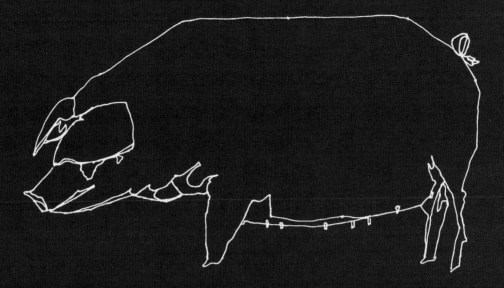

PORK

If there's anyone who doesn't understand the luscious pleasures of pork in all of its various forms, from chicharrón to chop to belly to jowl, they've either been a vegetarian for the past twenty years or have been living under a rock. The last decade has belonged to the pig, thanks to the efforts of people like Fergus Henderson and David Chang.

Through the hard work of countless visionary farmers, meat men, and chefs, the quality of pork has skyrocketed over the last ten years or so, with scores of breeds rescued from near extinction for their creamy fat and marbled loins. What was once something of a sentimental hobby for history-obsessed farmers and backyard agrarians has swung into the mainstream. Where the only real alternative to industrial white pork was once Berkshire, a breed that never really went away, now there seems to be a new breed coming out of the woodwork every six months or so and being touted as the new "It" pig.

Perhaps the best part about pigs is that they're one of the easiest and most forgiving animals to raise out of doors and they can be fed nearly anything (I mean whey, old tomatoes, and rotten pumpkins—not plastic bags and cardboard) and still taste pretty damned good. Combine that with a pig's fairly fast growth cycle, six to nine months from piglet to porker, and it makes pigs one of the best ways for new or veteran farmers to get into the pasture-raised meat business. And properly raised pork may be the gateway animal for vegetarians looking at eating meat again.

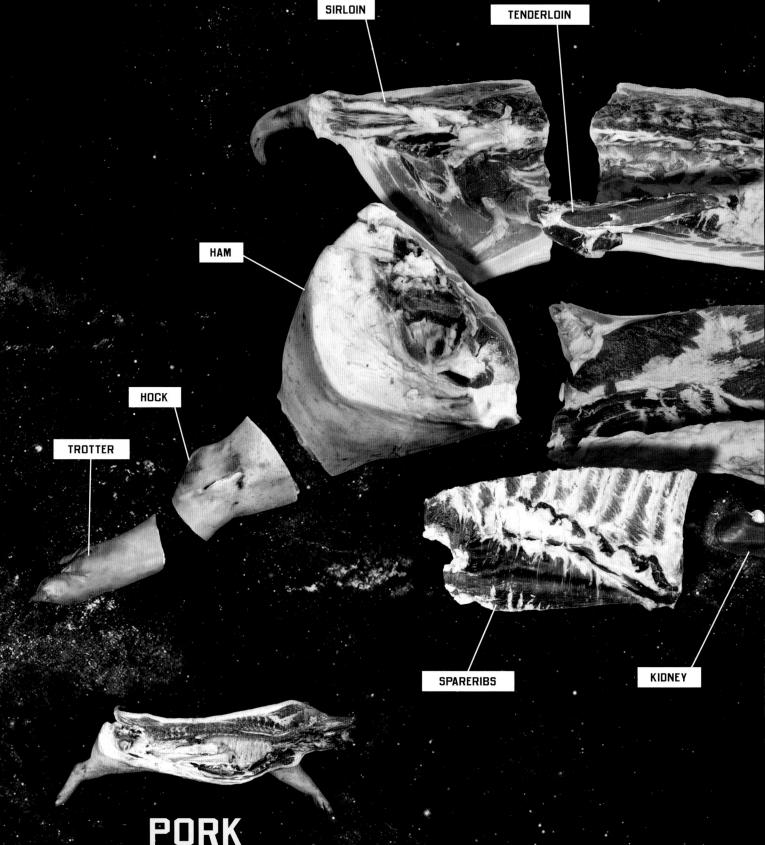

SIRLOIN

TENDERLOIN

HAM

HOCK

TROTTER

SPARERIBS

KIDNEY

PORK

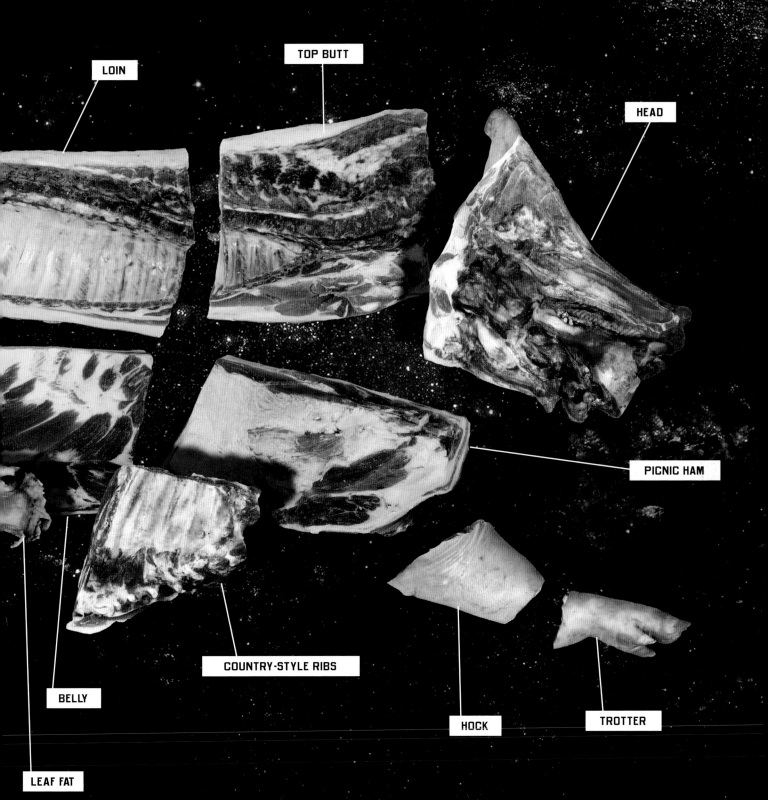

LOIN

TOP BUTT

HEAD

PICNIC HAM

COUNTRY-STYLE RIBS

BELLY

HOCK

TROTTER

LEAF FAT

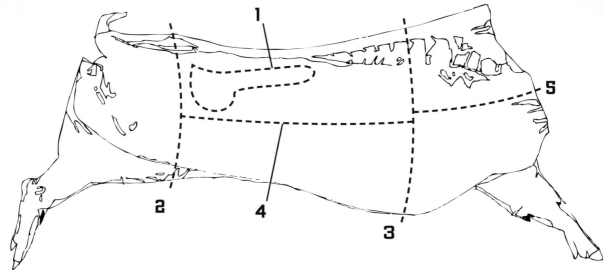

PIG TO PORK IN FIVE EASY CUTS

Even though I have my early pig-butchering classes to thank for much of my success as a butcher and, in a lot of ways, the success of The Meat Hook, I do have to come out and just say it: butchering a pig is not difficult.

When I butchered my first pig, I had a saw in one hand and a phone in the other, getting step-by-step instructions from Josh Applestone at Fleisher's. I had never cut up anything more imposing than a chicken before, but the pig turned out pretty well, all things considered. With that in mind, I present you with this easy five-cut tutorial that will enable you to take a side of pork and reduce it to its basic primals for easier handling and storage. I am in no way suggesting that there is nothing more to be done after these five cuts; quite the contrary. It is after these cuts are made that the *real* butchering starts, and that can't be learned from a book, or even a video. What happens next is something people can devote their entire lives to—who knows, after butchering that first pig, you might want to spend the rest of your life doing it.

Word of advice: Although butchering a pig can be easy, you're probably going to screw things up more than a few times. I've butchered several thousand pigs at this point and I still screw up now and again. Don't beat yourself up about it; just learn from your mistakes. The pork will taste great no matter what awkward shape it might have been cut into.

Note: If you are not confident with your knife skills, wear cut-proof gloves to prevent injuries. Disposable gloves provide a slight defense but are not nearly as safe as wearing real cut-proof gloves (see Resources, page 305).

1 side of pork, preferably around
   100 pounds hanging weight
   (see Resources, page 305)

SPECIAL EQUIPMENT
Cut-proof gloves or disposable gloves
   (see Note)
5-inch boning knife
Handsaw with a bone-cutting blade
10- to 12-inch breaking knife

1. Before you start making your best "I'm a butcher" face and find yourself posing with a pig head and a cigarette dangling out of your mouth, you have to dress the part. You need, first and foremost, some clothes that you absolutely do not care about, because in the end, they'll be bloody and smelling like a dead pig. The stuff you normally wear on laundry day is a good start: old jeans and a T-shirt are just about right. Next you'll need a long, full-coverage apron. I go with a classic white apron, but if yours is acid-wash denim with flaming chile peppers all over it, the pig absolutely will not care.

2. Next you need a space to butcher on that is about 7 feet long and at least 3 feet wide. The surface should be clean and dry, of course, but it should also be one that you will not feel bad about putting some gouges into, as you inevitably will. I think one of the most perfect places to cut up a pig is a wooden picnic table in the shade on a cool fall afternoon. You can buy enough large, cheap plastic cutting boards to cover the table-top or surface, if you'd like. Don't do this job in your garage if it stinks like motor oil and car exhaust, please—the smells may permeate the meat and make it taste like your garage.

3. Another thing to consider is where, exactly, you are going to put this pig once you've sawn and cut it into its respective parts. Do you have enough freezer paper, rubber bands, and tape at the ready to pack it up? Can you and your friends eat all that meat in the next 2 to 3 months before it gets freezer burn? I'm sure you'll figure all this out, so let's get on with the butchering.

4. First, use your boning knife to remove the tenderloin. (If you want the tenderloin to remain part of the loin end of the chops so you can have pork porterhouses, skip this step.) Run the tip of your knife down the inside of the chine bone, hugging it close to the bone and then running it up along the sirloin bone. Once the tenderloin is free from the chine and sirloin bone, you can pretty much just pull it off with your hands.

5. With your saw, cut between the last two vertebrae before the sirloin. One or two pushes with the saw should about do it. You just need to get through the bone—do not saw through the meat. To finish the cut, go straight down with your breaking knife and curve around the flank part of the end of the belly, making sure to get all the way down to the cutting surface.

6. Next, count five ribs down from the front of the shoulder. Be careful: the first rib is really small and doesn't really look like a rib. Trust me, it is. Once you've counted down to between the fifth and sixth ribs, mark between them with a shallow knife cut and switch to your saw. Unlike the previous cut, this one will be made in the middle of the vertebrae, as cutting between them will send your saw into the rib bone after the chine, and that's no good. Once you have sawn through the chine, finish the cut with your butcher knife, again taking it down to the board.

7. Now, take the freed shoulder (unless you want to try your hand at Trotter-on Porchetta, page 105) and, with your mind's eye, draw a line parallel to the line of the animal just below the lowest dip of the chine, where the neck comes into the shoulder. Saw through the ribs along this line until you've made it through all the bones. Now cut down to the board through this cut, going over the shoulder blade/arm bone in the middle. Saw through the blade/arm junction (later, if you get tricky, you can just cut through the joint with the knife) and then finish with the knife.

8. The last cut will be about a hand's width off the chine bone parallel with the chine through the ribs to separate the belly and spareribs from the loin. I usually sketch a line with the tip of my knife and then make the cut with the saw, starting at the shoulder end of the ribs and sawing toward the loin end. Once you clear the ribs, finish the cut with your boning knife.

PORK CUTS

As I said on the previous pages, breaking down a pig isn't rocket science. One side of pork broken down into five smaller cuts will yield these familiar pieces (and by-products).

SHOULDER

Pork shoulder is a real cornucopia. The shoulders of most animals are kind of considered garbage meat, to be made into sausage or stew, but a pork shoulder is prized for everything from huge flavorful chops to roast pork, pulled pork, porchetta, and country-style spareribs.

Most cut charts in the United States show the shoulder portioned into three sections: the butt, picnic, and shank. But in other parts of the world, it's cut up into so many different shapes and areas that the diagrams on the cut charts of Italy and Portugal for pork shoulder look more like gerrymandered congressional districts than parts of a pig's anatomy. The lesson to be learned here is that pork shoulder is as much or as little as you choose to make it.

LOIN

The loins of most animals are really the glamour girls of all the cuts, but for some reason this seems much less true with the pork loin. All pork is almost equal in the minds of diners, and I have seen as much enthusiasm for a pulled pork sandwich made from the shoulder or a platter of juicy bacon as I have for a big old pork chop. That said, the pork loin *is* something special. Whether you're roasting a joint rubbed with herbs and garlic, with Frenched rib bones and crispy, bubbling fat, or grilling up a cartoonish giant chop, there are few things that can be as satisfying and homey and consumed with such delight.

When the time comes for you to satisfy your cravings for pork loin, it's worth noting that all pork chops are not the same. By this I don't mean breeds or whatnot, I mean which end of the loin they come from. The shoulder end is made up of shoulder muscles with more layers of fat, while the loin end (the end closest to the rear leg and sirloin) is leaner, has a smaller eye, and is a little more tender. Many recipes call for center-cut pork chops, but for cooking purposes, I generally lump them in with the shoulder end, because they have ribs and are more like the shoulder end than the loin end.

What does that have to do with anything? A lot. If I'm roasting or panfrying pork chops, I generally use chops from the shoulder end, with all of that glorious fat

BRUCE CONOVER, SIR WILLIAM ANGUS

When we first opened The Meat Hook, I'm ashamed to admit, we got all of our pigs through a middleman. The pigs were decent quality and properly raised, but compared to some of the pigs I'd cut up before, they were solidly mediocre. Not good. Enter Bruce Conover of Sir William Angus, who raises truly amazing 100 percent Berkshire hogs, and is one of the sweetest guys you'll ever meet. I had cut some of his pigs back in my early days of butchering and really missed the creamy texture of the fat on his hogs and the quality of the meat. A few phone calls and a month or so later, we were taking all the hogs he could spare, and by the end of that year, pretty much every Berkshire he raised.

that, through careful cooking, can be rendered out and enjoyed. For grilling, I choose chops from the loin end, since they are leaner and will cause fewer out-of-control, pork-chop-ruining grease fires. Also, because grilling uses higher heat, it won't allow the fat of a shoulder chop to be properly rendered for full enjoyment.

When selecting a pork loin or chops, you should look for a nice layer of dense, white, creamy fat and meat nearly the color of beef. Most heritage-breed pigs tend to lean that way, and it's worth the time and expense to find these by hook or by crook. Stay away from pork that looks dried out or weepy. Neither of these things is good.

RIBS

Aside from bacon, ribs are the cut of pork that most provokes longing, fantasies, and anticipation. Unlike bacon, ribs are something that we eat at restaurants more often than we make them at home. They're a lowbrow special event of sorts, whether you're going to a real-deal backwoods barbecue place, a Chinese banquet, or a big chain restaurant with a million NASCAR tchotchkes all over the walls. I'll admit that I rarely eat pork ribs unless it's for breakfast on Saturdays. At the shop, we put them in to smoke the night before and pull them out first thing in the morning when we get in. I defy anyone, even if it's before you've had your first cup of coffee, to deny the smell of brown-sugar-and-salt-cured ribs, straight out of the smoker.

It will serve you well to know that not all pork ribs are the same. Here's the rundown.

Spareribs

These are the most common form of ribs. They're cut right off the pork belly and they should have about half an inch of meat on them on top.

St. Louis–Style Spareribs

These are just plain old spareribs but with the cartilaginous riblets cut off, to make them symmetrical so they cook a little more evenly—or that's the theory anyway. I wonder what happens to all those riblets?

Baby Back Ribs

Baby backs are the direct result of America's insatiable lust for boneless pork loin and boneless chops. They come from the same ribs as spareribs, but they are taken from where the ribs meet the chine bone in the area of the loin. They're smaller and narrower than spareribs and because the meat (loin) on them is more tender, they cook faster. Crap. Now I have that Chili's jingle stuck in my head!

Country-Style Ribs

These ribs come from the picnic shoulder and are very meaty and fatty. They take longer to cook but end up super juicy and satisfying. They might be my favorite.

BELLY

Pork belly is a cut that people either love or hate. The polarizing nature of the belly is due to its high level of fat in relation to lean meat. The bellies from certain breeds of pigs I have seen often have a ratio of 3:1 fat to meat and that, especially for people of my parents' generation and others still living squarely in the middle of the 1980s, is a deal breaker.

I also think the aversion that some have to pork fat is really the fault of bad pork. Pork from properly raised good breeds has great, creamy fat that starts to melt when touched with a warm hand; crappy pork from the grocery store can be almost hard and rubbery with fat that rather than melting away into an unctuous mass, becomes tough and chewy. And I almost always get a slight whiff of urine from bad pork, what my wife calls the "torture meat smell."

HAM

When people say the word "ham," almost everybody pictures some sort of pale pink, cured, usually cubic-shaped pork product. But a ham is actually the rear leg of the pig, and in many parts of the world, it is almost a religion. In Spain, hand-sliced cured ham, or jamón, is as common as Coca-Cola, and it tastes a lot better. Italy,

France, Portugal, and, well, almost any place in Europe, have their ham games pretty much nailed. Unfortunately, for most Americans who don't live in the rural South, good air-cured ham is hard to come by. Luckily, there's a bit of a ham resurgence going on these days, and places like La Quercia in Iowa are beginning to make hams that are as good as any in the world. Another American maker of air-cured hams that can give the best of Europe a run for their money is the Edwards family of Surry, Virginia. Their Surryano ham is made from heirloom Berkshire hogs raised on pasture and is aged for more than 400 days.

Whether you cure a pork leg into a country ham or simply make cutlets out of it for schnitzel, I think you'll agree with the Spanish that ham is where it's at. As much as I love turning the rear leg of the pig into prosciutto, there are many other options, like those on page 125.

HEAD

Pig heads can be a problem for a butcher. If you buy only whole animals, the heads start piling up in a serious way once you are getting more than three or four pigs a week. One or two pig heads a week is a cute problem, like having a garden suddenly overgrown with basil. Having seven or ten is a problem like having a public swimming pool full of gremlins. And figuring out ways to use them up is an ongoing challenge for The Meat Hook.

Sure, I suppose we could just throw them away. We've had those weeks where we're constantly in the weeds and never get around to dealing with the heads, and into the trash they go. But the truth is they weigh a lot, and we're paying the same price per pound for the heads as we are for the pork chops, so in a strictly economic sense, let alone the whole nose-to-tail/waste-nothing ethos, we really want to do something with them.

In the struggle to use up pig heads, our shop has separated into two camps: scrapple versus headcheese. The headcheese faction views scrapple as crude and worthy of disdain because it is not technique-driven, merely a pot of slop that simmers away, stinking up the joint. The scrapple fans think that headcheese is overrated, because

so much time and labor are expended on something that, even when done quite well, is ultimately tasty head-meat bits suspended in a (disgusting-textured) gelatin terrine. I fall into the scrapple camp. Unless you're French, you'll like it much better than headcheese for breakfast.

THE OFFAL

Pork offal: it's so good it started a movement. While I'm a bit weary of pork offal by now, it doesn't mean it's not good. Creative and bottom-line-minded chefs like Fergus Henderson of St. John Bar and Restaurant in London took a huge leap not all that long ago by designing menus around the fifth quarter of the pig, which had fallen out of favor during the aspirational second half of the twentieth century. Ballsy chefs like Henderson made it their quest to bring back the food of their youth, what so many of their generation considered peasant food.

As in any truly great food moment, there are bound to be a bunch of coattail riders without the skill to make offal, pork or otherwise, actually taste good. The bright spot is that since the pleasures of the most lowly of animal parts have come roaring back with a vengeance, we should be able to expect a whole generation of cooks, dining in or dining out, who will have grown up with offal as part of their skill set, and a too-good-to-be-forgotten chapter of our culinary history will have been saved from the dust heap.

TROTTER-ON PORCHETTA

When Marlow & Daughters opened, we had a lot of customers freak out over all the options that a real butcher shop offered. One customer in particular wanted something unique for his brother's birthday party, something he couldn't get anywhere else. I had been working on my speed and efficiency at breaking beef shoulders at the time, and I thought that I should apply the same technique to a full pork shoulder, scrape the bones, and tie it back up, keeping the trotter on so you could shake the roast's hand after it was done cooking. *Voilà*. Trotter-on porchetta.   **SERVES ABOUT 20**

1 whole skin-on pork shoulder, including
    the trotter, about 25 pounds
1 cup kosher salt
1/4 cup freshly ground black pepper
2 heads garlic, separated into cloves,
    peeled, and pureed in a food processor

SPECIAL EQUIPMENT
5-inch boning knife
Butcher's twine
Digital probe or instant-read thermometer

1. Using a boning knife, trim the pig's rib bones up to the feather bones, taking the neck and rib bones off as one piece. Set aside.

2. Dig in to find the shoulder blade, and carefully scrape the meat off the scapula; do this working toward the socket. Then crack the socket over your knee and pull out the bone. Don't be a wuss.

3. Scrape all of the bones free of meat and set the scraps aside.

4. In a large bowl, stir the salt, pepper, and pureed garlic together to make a paste. Mix in the meat remnants. Rub the paste into the spots where the bones used to be. Reassemble the shoulder as best you can, then gently roll the shoulder up into itself, allowing the weight of the shoulder and gravity to help keep it in place while you tie it up. Using butcher's twine, make a loop around the center of the porchetta just below the "elbow" of the trotter, tie an overhand butcher's knot, and pull the knot tight.

5. Make another overhand knot, pulling it tight again to lock the knot, and trim the strings almost flush with the knot. Working from the center out, tie the porchetta, using the same knot, every inch until you are about 2 inches from each end. If this is your first time tying up a big roast, it may not be pretty, but it doesn't have to be—it just needs to keep the porchetta together. Place the porchetta in a large roasting pan or on a rimmed baking sheet.

6. Next, figure out how the hell you're going to cook this thing, because it's definitely not going to fit in your oven. So, you're probably going to have to start building a fire pit in your backyard or something . . . maybe I should have mentioned that from the start.

7. Just kidding! You will need to remove all but the bottom rack from your oven, though, as this baby takes up a lot of room. You may have noticed that I haven't mentioned preheating your oven yet—because you shouldn't. Not for any cooking consideration, but because getting this thing into the oven will be a pretty tight fit that may require wrestling it around, and if your oven were hot, you'd most likely burn the hell out of your hands and/or arms.

8. Now that the porchetta is crammed into the oven, you can turn it on to 325°F and slowly cook this thing until it's done, about 8 hours, or until the center of the shoulder reaches 165°F on a digital thermometer. Remove it from the oven and let it rest for 30 minutes before serving.

9. Slice the porchetta and feed twenty of your closest friends.

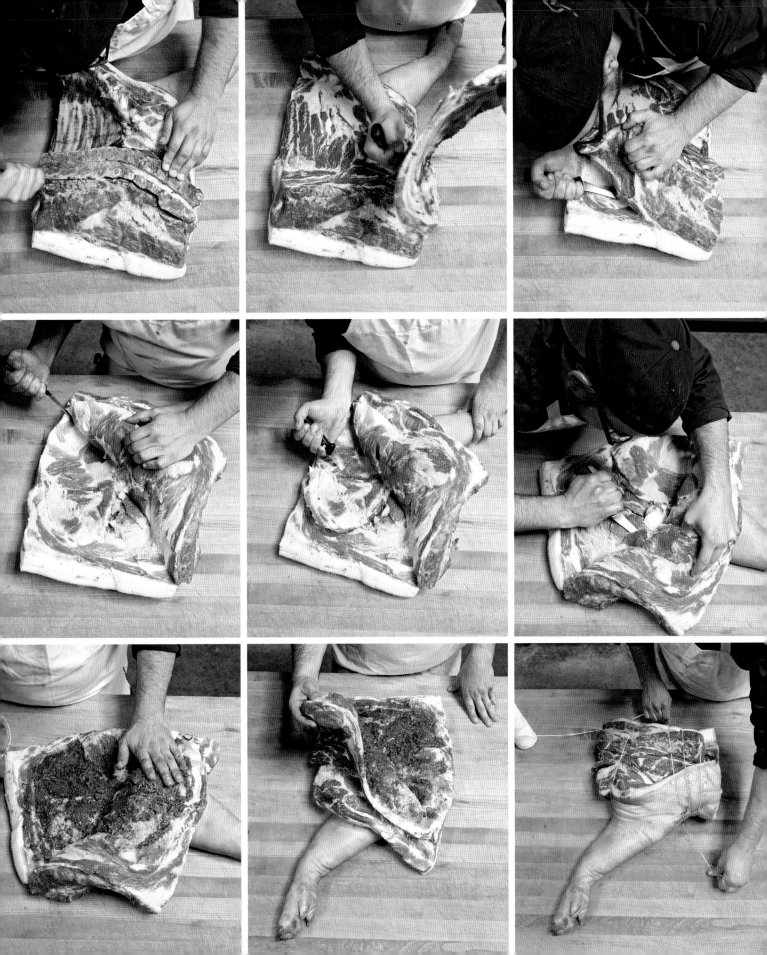

CITY CHICKEN OVER NOODLES ROMANOFF

A popular dish in Rust Belt cities like Pittsburgh and Cleveland, city chicken is not what you might assume—it's not chicken. During the Depression, chicken was more expensive than pork or veal, so chunks of pork or veal were sold to mimic the "luxurious" taste of chicken. Ultimately, pork is much more delicious than chicken, and it's *fried* here. Typically served on a bed of egg noodles, the dish is infinitely better with Betty Crocker's Noodles Romanoff, classic 1960s dried, powdered magic. While the Crocker version has been discontinued, I've managed to muster up a pretty decent replication.   **SERVES 2**

1. Preheat the oven to 350°F.

2. Season the pork all over with salt and pepper. Beat the eggs and milk together in a shallow bowl. Season with salt, pepper, and the lemon pepper. Place the flour on a plate. Put the bread crumbs on another plate. Roll the pork in the flour and shake off the excess. Dip in the egg wash, letting the excess drip off, and then dredge in the bread crumbs. Set on a plate.

3. Bring a large pot of salted water to a boil.

4. In a large skillet, heat the peanut oil over medium heat until hot. Add the chunks of pork and fry, turning occasionally, until crispy and nicely browned on all sides, about 7 minutes. Remove the pork to a paper-towel-lined plate and allow to rest for 10 minutes.

5. Meanwhile, add the egg noodles to the boiling water and cook for 1 to 2 minutes less than it says on the package. While the noodles are boiling, combine the sour cream, 1/4 cup of the Parmesan, the chives, salt, pepper, and garlic in a medium bowl and mix thoroughly.

6. Put the pork chunks on the skewers, set them on a piece of aluminum foil or in a pie pan, and place them in the oven for 10 minutes, to finish cooking.

7. When the noodles are cooked, drain and transfer them to a large bowl. Stir in the butter until melted, then fold in the sour cream mixture, coating the noodles.

8. Divide the noodles between two warm dinner plates and sprinkle with the remaining Parmesan. Place the skewers on the noodles and serve immediately.

FOR THE PORK
1 pound boneless pork shoulder, cut into 1-inch chunks
Kosher salt and freshly ground black pepper
2 eggs
2 tablespoons whole milk
1 tablespoon lemon pepper
1 cup all-purpose flour
1 cup Italian-style seasoned dried bread crumbs
1/4 cup peanut oil

FOR THE NOODLES
8 ounces wide egg noodles
2 cups sour cream
1/2 cup freshly grated Parmesan
1 tablespoon minced chives
1 teaspoon kosher salt
1/4 teaspoon freshly ground black pepper
1 large garlic clove, crushed
2 tablespoons unsalted butter, softened

SPECIAL EQUIPMENT
2 bamboo skewers

THE INEVITABLE PORK CHOP
with Cheddar Grits

Jean Adamson, or "Mean Jean," as she was known back in the day, and I have worked together off and on since I was a fledgling butcher, selling meat to restaurants on the side to make money to pay for my wedding. Her restaurant, Vinegar Hill House, is known internationally for having the single most delicious pork chop in New York . . . if not the world. Somehow I managed to con her into giving me the recipe for this book.   **SERVES 2**

1. You need to start this recipe 2 days ahead of time. You're OK with that? Start by making the brine: Bring 4 cups of water to a simmer in a medium saucepan over high heat. Add all the ingredients and simmer for a few minutes more as you stir, then pour into a bowl and refrigerate overnight.

2. The next morning, transfer the chilled brine to a gallon Ziploc freezer bag (do not strain out the spices), place your shoulder chops in the brine, press out the excess air, and zip to close. Allow the bag to sit in your refrigerator for 12 hours.

3. About 2 hours before you want to eat, start the grits. Combine $2^{1}/_{2}$ cups water and the grits in a medium saucepan and bring to a simmer over low heat, stirring frequently. As the grits continue to cook, they will thicken and you will have to add about $1^{1}/_{2}$ cups more water $^{1}/_{4}$ cup at a time. After about $1^{1}/_{2}$ hours of cooking and stirring, the grits should be almost done. Remove from the heat, cover, and set aside.

4. Remove the chops from the brine, rinse them, and pat dry with a paper towel.

5. Heat a large cast-iron skillet over high heat, then add the oil and heat until hot. Slide the chops into the pan and cook, turning frequently (as the residual sugar from the brine tends to burn quickly), until the chops are browned and close to done, 8 to 10 minutes. Drain off the fat and add the butter to the pan. Baste and continue to flip the chops as the butter foams and starts to brown. Transfer the chops to a rack set over a platter and let rest for 5 minutes, turning them a few times.

6. Meanwhile, remember those grits? Place the pan over medium heat and stir in the butter. When it has completely melted into the grits, add the cheddar and stir that in as well. Add salt to taste.

7. Just when the cheese has melted, portion the grits evenly onto two large dinner plates and sprinkle with a spoonful of the pickled jalapeños. Place the pork chops on top and serve. It's worth all the work. Promise.

FOR THE BRINE
$^{1}/_{2}$ cup sugar
$^{1}/_{2}$ cup kosher salt
20 juniper berries
20 black peppercorns
1 large thyme sprig
1 head garlic, cut horizontally in half

2 double-pork-bone shoulder chops, preferably Red Wattle (see Heritage Foods in Resources, page 305)
2 tablespoons grapeseed or peanut oil
2 tablespoons unsalted butter

FOR THE CHEDDAR GRITS
1 cup coarse grits, preferably Anson Mills (see Resources, page 305)
4 tablespoons unsalted butter
1 cup shredded cheddar cheese
Kosher salt
1 tablespoon roughly chopped drained pickled jalapeños

ROOFTOP RIBS

For most of my life I have not been blessed with access to a real smoker of my own. But cooking with a smoker in a Brooklyn apartment is a tricky thing; more often than not, it will get the FDNY called on you by your neighbors because either (a) they think your house is burning down in a really delicious way, or (b) your smoke is simply bugging the shit out of them.

However, for six years I lived in an apartment with a vast filthy rooftop that was peppered with a large number of grills in various states of disrepair. The roof allowed me the freedom to not have to worry about my neighbors calling the fire department on me, and the plethora of ratty abandoned Webers allowed me to experiment with cobbled-together smoking setups. What follows is my recipe for full-on half-assed ribs using a charcoal grill. Try not to piss off your neighbors when you make this. **SERVES 4**

1 cup kosher salt
2/3 cup packed light brown sugar
2 racks St. Louis–style spareribs
1 cup cider vinegar

SPECIAL EQUIPMENT
Large Weber charcoal barbecue grill, or the like
Nonreactive food-safe container
Wood chunks of your choice
Small spray bottle

1. The day before you plan to be eating your ribs, mix the salt and sugar in a small bowl. Put the ribs in the nonreactive food-safe container and rub the sugar-and-salt mixture all over them. Wrap the ribs in plastic wrap and place on the bottom shelf of the refrigerator.

2. On the day of the main event, build a small charcoal fire off to one side of your grill, as far away as possible from where your smoking is going to go on, preferably directly over the bottom vent. Once the fire has burned to white coals, remove the ribs from the plastic wrap, put them on the grill, cover, and open both the top and bottom vents. Cook for 30 minutes.

3. Fill a small spray bottle with the cider vinegar. Add 2 or 3 wood chunks to the coals and close the top and bottom vents about halfway. Continue adding chunks of wood, keeping the heat going at a nice gentle smoke for about 3 hours. Lightly spray the ribs with the vinegar and flip them every 45 minutes or so. When the ribs are about done, they will start looking done. What does that look like? Uh, like ribs that are done! Seriously. You've eaten ribs—you know what they look like: glossy with glaze and the meat pulling back from the rib tips. When in doubt, cut off a rib and try one. Not tender enough? Give them another 30 to 45 minutes, then try again. Dry? Better luck next time and don't add as much wood/heat. Either way, serve immediately.

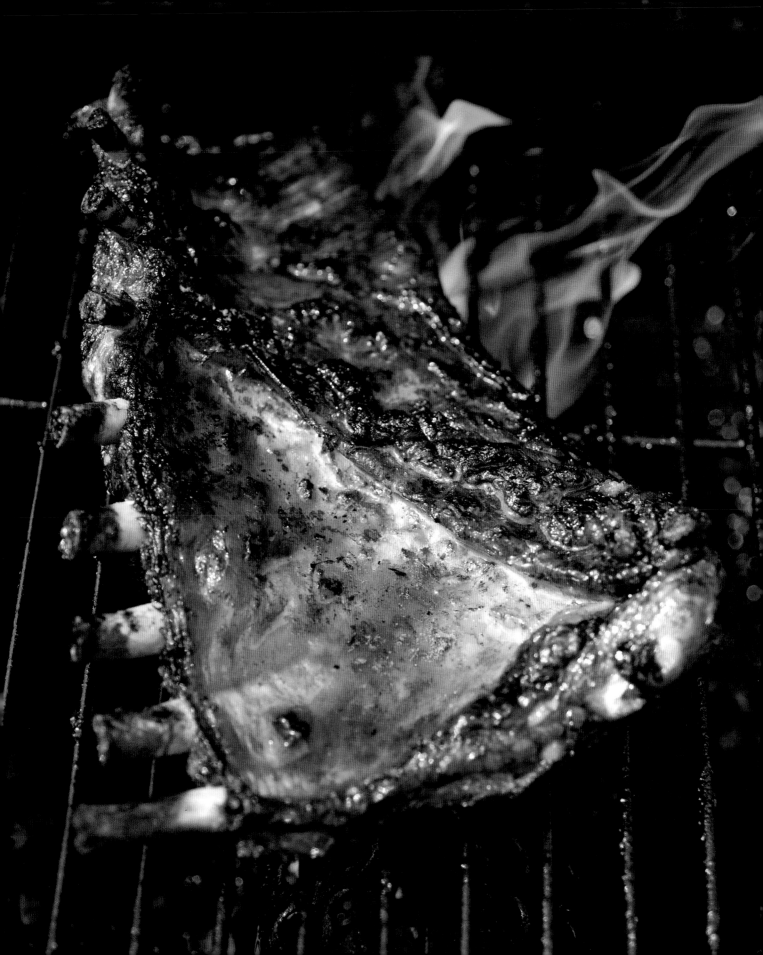

CHINESE BARBECUE PORK

This is a recipe that came together in the basement prep area of Diner back before The Meat Hook was anything to anyone. The name is a little misleading, since this is not Chinese barbecue pork in the true sense of char-siu, which is roasted and basted with a honey-water glaze. It is more of a vaguely Asian version of the French pork belly dish called *rillons*, where the belly is cut into pieces, confited in its own fat, and glazed with the cooking liquid. Whatever the case, it makes a damn good barbecue pork belly, suitable for pork buns, fried rice, or for burning your fingers as you pull chunks of it out of the pan while stuffing your face.   **SERVES 3 OR 4**

1. Preheat the oven to 325°F.

2. Start by taking your chunk of pork belly and, using a long chef's knife or the equivalent, slice it into 1-inch-thick slices as evenly as you can. Use long even strokes and don't press down on the knife—allow the edge to do the work for you: this may take slightly longer, but the cuts will be much more even.

3. In a medium bowl, combine the water, red wine vinegar, sugar, soy sauce, ginger, chiles, peppercorns, star anise, and garlic.

4. Put the pork belly slices in a square cake pan or the like, pour the marinade over them, and cover with aluminum foil. Place in the oven and cook for 1 hour. Then remove the foil and raise the temperature of the oven to 350°F. Cook for about another 40 minutes, giving everything a stir every 8 to 10 minutes or so. What you're doing here is rendering the fat and softening up the pork belly in the first hour, then reducing the braising liquid so it glazes the pork slices and turns them a groovy reddish color at the end. Continue to cook and stir until the pork has the reddish color you're after.

5. Remove the pieces of pork belly using a pair of tongs or a slotted spoon and place them directly into your waiting hot dog buns. Garnish with hoisin and chile sauce, scallions, and cilantro. Eat immediately, over the sink or trash can (no plates or napkins).

2 pounds fresh pork belly

2 cups water

$3/4$ cup red wine vinegar

$3/4$ cup sugar

$3/4$ cup light soy sauce

Four $1/2$-inch-thick slices fresh ginger (unpeeled)

4 dried chiles de árbol

3 black peppercorns

2 star anise

3 garlic cloves

1 package hot dog buns

Hoisin sauce

Chile sauce

2 scallions, thinly sliced

$1/2$ bunch cilantro, leaves and tender stems only, roughly chopped

MAKING BACON

Making good bacon is not that hard, but you have to have patience, time, and, more or less, the right equipment. The process, at least the way we do it at The Meat Hook, is exceedingly simple.

If you have an issue with nitrates, you can replace the curing salt with a slightly larger amount of Sicilian sea salt (see Resources, page 305) to add naturally occurring nitrates. Or, if you omit these salts completely, your bacon will taste fine; it just won't be pink. **MAKES 1 SLAB**

3 pounds kosher salt
2 pounds (4 cups) light or dark brown sugar
A large pinch of pink curing salt (optional; see Resources, page 305)
1 very fresh whole skin-off pork belly, approximately 8 pounds

SPECIAL EQUIPMENT
Nonreactive food-safe container the size of your pork belly
Smoker (see "Smokers," page 284)
Wood chips or chunks

1. Mix the salt, sugar, and pink salt, if using, together in a large bowl, making sure to break up the brown sugar so it has no clumps. Do this quickly before the salt starts to make the brown sugar hard. (I like to break up the brown sugar before I add it to the salt, because otherwise the salt hurts my little fingers.)

2. Next, put the pork belly in a large nonreactive food-safe container and coat it thoroughly on all sides with the sugar-and-salt cure. Do one coat on all sides, shake off the excess, and let the belly sit for 5 minutes. Then reapply the cure and either wrap the belly tightly in plastic wrap or cover the container with plastic wrap.

3. Place the container on the bottom shelf of your fridge. This next part is important: you *must* flip the bacon once a day for the next 7 days. This is somewhat less important if you have tightly wrapped the belly in plastic wrap, but it must be done every day if you didn't—failing to do so will lead to lopsidedly cured bacon.

4. After 7 days, rinse the belly lightly under cold water and pat it dry with paper towels. Place it in a smoker, meat side down, and set the smoker for 170°F, without any wood, chips, or other stuff that causes smoke. (If you have an old-school log-fed smoker, just open the flue all the way to allow the smoke to get out of the smoking chamber.) Run the smoker for about 1 hour, until the exterior of the meat has a dry, somewhat shiny look that says, "Hey, I'm ready to smoke!" This shiny exterior is called the pellicle.

5. Basically, anything you smoke will not take on that beautiful mahogany color from the smoke until the moisture in the outer layer of the meat has evaporated and the proteins on the surface are slightly denatured, or cooked. As this happens, the pellicle will form and the meat will become "sticky," in a molecular sense, enabling the smoke to bond with the pellicle. Failure to achieve a pellicle before you hit it with the smoke will result in a sooty, gray-brown color. Your bacon might taste OK, but it will look like hell.

Recipe continues

6. Now add chips, wood—you know, smoke—to the smoker and lower the temperature to 160°F. I use cherrywood for our bacon at the shop because it imparts a sweet but not wimpy smokiness. If you're trying to flex bold flavors all over the place, feel free to use the magnum-strength smoking woods like hickory, mesquite, or oak, but add them a little later in the process (after 4 hours or so) to prevent the bacon from getting bitter.

7. Smoke the belly for 5 to 6 hours, making sure to give it a turn every hour. The bacon is done when it is firm, not rubbery, with an internal temperature of 155°F. Immediately rinse the belly under hot water to remove any rendered fat, which would make it look less pretty when chilled, and place it in an ice-water bath for 15 minutes.

8. Drain the belly, pat it dry, and wrap it in heavy, breathable paper, such as a large grocery bag. Refrigerate it until it's time to slice and fry. If you're not going to eat all of it over the course of the next 2 weeks, you can wrap chunks of it in wax-lined butcher paper (you can get this from your butcher when you buy the belly) and freeze it for up to a year.

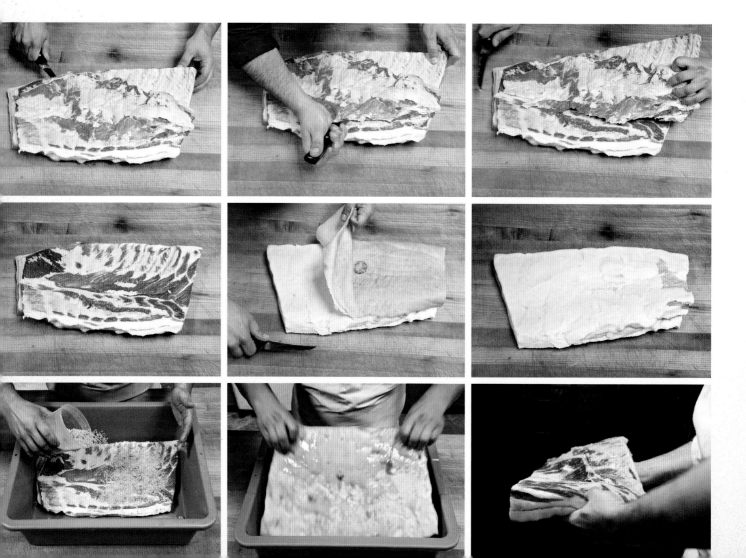

BACONERS AND LARD PIGS

I used to think, like many people, that heritage-breed pigs were static, that from time immemorial breeds remained unchanged while the world around them crashed or soared through the Industrial Revolution, world wars, and global depressions. Pigs seemed like a cute, gentle time capsule from a place where things were simpler, honest, wholesome, and good. Well, that turns out to be a complete lie.

I read a lot of books on livestock, meat, and farming esoterica (I should be a minor stakeholder in some publishing company by now). One unassuming book that I bought on a whim was *The Pig: A British History.* As it turns out, this slim volume completely overturned my ideas about those cute, gentle animals I had been holding up as so pure and practical.

The fact is that British pig breeds, which most of the pork production infrastructure in the United States is based on, are the end product of hundreds of years of breeding trends, show-ring fashions, and pork market tumult; many breeds of British porkers nearly crashed and burned in the late 1800s. Like a harbinger of the intense selective breeding over the past forty years of animals destined for Concentrated Animal Feed Operations (CAFOs), the British had nearly bred their hogs into uselessness by the end of the nineteenth century. Extremely fat hogs became the fashion of the day, and most award-winning show pigs were actually so fat that they could not walk into the show ring under their own power, nor could they breed without a significant amount of help. At the same time the British pigs were getting too fat to breed, the Dutch began to take over the global pork market with their supercharged Landrace breed of pig. These changes in the global pork market nearly put British pork production out of business. This is dark, nearly *Lord of the Rings* kind of stuff, really.

Thankfully, out of the gloom that shrouded British pig breeding at the end of the nineteenth century came a new, utility-based view that hadn't been seen for nearly a hundred years. The breeding stock of the British Isles was saved by the very same thing that we're hoping can save agriculture from the brink of destruction these days: biodiversity. From far-flung islands of the Caribbean, the mountains of Spain, and even China, new blood came in to correct the nearly uncorrectable faults that had been bred into the British pigs. Within a generation, breeds on the brink had been brought back and made hardier, faster-growing, and better tasting. The next time you tuck into that pork chop, pause for a moment to consider how close to doom that heritage pig's ancestors might have come.

BROOKLYN-STYLE COUNTRY HAM

I've been obsessed with curing hams for years, curing them in meat lockers, basements, and even my apartment for almost as long as I have lived in Brooklyn. While classic European hams like serrano and Parma are widely considered the finest in the world, I'm passionate about the uniquely American country ham in all of its salty, smoky glory. I think that the seemingly unsophisticated hams produced by mom-and-pop operations throughout the South, eaten raw and unsoaked, offer a far more complicated and flavor-dense experience than anything from across the Atlantic—and at a fraction of the price. If you'd like to try your hand at getting country, even if you live in the heart of the big city, read on. I think you'll be surprised at how good a ham you made yourself can taste.

Unless you have access to a walk-in refrigerator or have a spare fridge in the garage, you're going to need to start this project in the winter or late fall, when your ham-nurturing space is cool enough to prevent the ham from spoiling before it can cure—under 40°F is what we're talking.

The next step can be the most difficult: getting a high-quality, ultrafresh, skin-on ham. If you don't have a butcher shop that has well-raised local pigs in stock, you're going to have to get creative. The surest way to get what you want is to make friends with a nearby farmer who raises pigs, and the surest way to do this is by giving him a bottle of nice whiskey or whatever else he might be into. The pigs that make the best hams are the most primitive breeds—Ossabaw, Mangalitsa, and the like—but don't get too carried away with being a breed snob; any happy pig is good enough for what you're doing. **MAKES 1 CURED HAM; SERVES 20 OR MORE**

1. Before you buy anything you need to make a country ham, be sure that you really want to do this. Are you willing to creep out your significant other or roommate with a pig leg hanging around the house for at least six months, preferably a whole year? Marriages and friendships have been destroyed by lesser things. Do you have a place to cure and hang the ham? You should have a spot that will be cold enough in the winter months to protect the ham while it cures (45°F or lower), but not so cold (32°F or below) that the ham freezes solid—a perfect way to ruin it—and where it can hang at a moderate temperature through the spring and summer, unperturbed by things like (how to say this?) rats, but still have enough air circulation to allow it to mature properly. A drafty basement or a wine fridge with all the shelves removed is a good option.

2. If you're going to smoke the ham, do you have access, by hook or by crook, to a smoker that can maintain a 70° to 90°F smoke for several days? That's no small feat, as people with smokers tend to need them for things other than providing a hickory-scented home for meat. You may need to buy or build a home smoker and take off a long weekend to tend to the ham nonstop. OK. Are you still game for a yearlong special project? Great.

3. Now that you have your pork, you will need to trim the skin, fat, and meat around the end of the ham with a 5-inch boning knife until it looks smooth, symmetrical, and round, leaving the full thickness of fat. What you're trying to do here is just to remove enough skin and fat so there isn't anything hanging out that will get oversalted. Make sure to save your ham tag, which will have its exact weight on it, so you can determine your curing time.

Recipe continues

1 very fresh skin-on, shank-on ham, about 25 pounds (see headnote)

FOR THE FIRST CURE
3 pounds kosher or coarse salt (5 cups)
1½ pounds brown sugar (3 cups)
1 teaspoon pink curing salt (optional; see Making Bacon, page 119, for more info, and see Resources, page 305)

FOR THE SECOND CURE
1 cup kosher salt
2 cups packed light brown sugar

SPECIAL EQUIPMENT
5-inch boning knife
Large piece of uncoated heavy butcher paper
Wooden wine box or heavy-duty plastic storage box of appropriate size
1 thin cotton pillowcase or a muslin bag (washed with unscented detergent)
Heavy needle with thick cotton thread
Butcher's twine
Up to a year of your time

4. In a small bowl, mix up your first cure of salt, sugar, and pink salt, if using. Rub the mixture into all the nooks and crannies of the ham and the bone, then wrap the ham in heavy butcher paper to keep the cure next to the skin. Place the ham in a wine box or other storage box, put the box in a cool basement or in the refrigerator, and let the waiting begin!

5. Every week or so, unwrap the ham and check on it. Once it has taken on all its cure, rub in the second cure: Mix the salt and brown sugar in a small bowl, rub over the ham, and wrap the ham again; place it back in its cool spot. Keep this routine up for about 2 months—you're shooting for 2¹/₂ days of curing time per pound of pig.

6. After curing, your ham should be nice and firm but not hard as a rock. Scrub it with a clean brush and wash it down with water to get the cure off and to prepare the surface for smoking. Using butcher's twine, tie a tight loop around the shank end of the ham and hang it in your smoker, making sure that there isn't any black fat or grease that will drip on your ham while it smokes. I like to use a mix of hickory and fruitwoods to smoke my hams, but please yourself, keeping in mind that stronger woods like hickory will impart a bitter taste if you oversmoke, so you may want to play it safe with a less forceful type of hardwood the first time around.

7. Every smoker is different, so it may take many hours of cool smoke to get your ham the deep mahogany color you're going for. Don't worry if you have to do the smoking for a few hours a day over the course of several days because you have a job; it'll turn out fine. Ten to 12 hours of smoke time at 120°F is a good amount.

8. Now for some hang time and more waiting. Once you're happy with the color of the smoke the ham has taken on, you'll want to sew it up in a cheap pillowcase, using a heavy needle and cotton thread, or place it in a muslin bag, then hang it in your happy place, whether the basement or your wine fridge. Keep in mind that your ham is going to function as a huge country-ham-scented air freshener, so plan accordingly.

9. Your ham will be cured, mature, and ready to eat in 6 months, but I recommend at least 9 months, if not a full year, before carving into it.

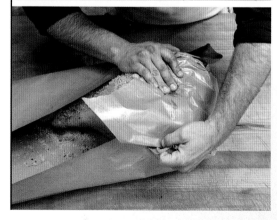

HAM, HAM, HAM

The term "ham" is one of the most misunderstood in all of meatdom. Here's a primer on what's what when it comes to the rear leg of a pig.

FRESH HAM

This is simply the uncured, uncooked, unsmoked, and unsalted rear leg of the pig. Raw. All ham starts out this way before it is turned into any of the things we normally associate with the word. But a fresh ham is a lovely thing to slow-roast for holidays, with the skin on.

COOKED HAMS

Whether they're canned or vacuum-packed in the meat case, these grocery-store hams most Americans are familiar with have been pumped full of a preservative brine to increase their weight and then cooked with steam or smoke and steam. Europeans do make similar hams, like *parma cotto* and *jambon blanc*.

AIR-DRIED HAMS

These are Spanish serrano and Italian parma (prosciutto) types of hams. They are salted for a month and then left to air-dry and mature for 9 to 18 months. They're never cooked—they're treated with salt to remove enough water from the muscles to make them safe to hang.

COUNTRY HAMS

These Southern-style hams are cured for a month or two in a sugar-and-salt cure and then smoked and hung to air-dry for 3 to 18 months. The quality is variable. Spices like peppercorns and red pepper flakes are common. American country hams are a diverse bunch and not all of them are cured with sugar or smoked. Good ham makers take a lot of pride in their often-secret recipes and techniques. (See "The Ham Lady: Nancy Newsom," page 132.)

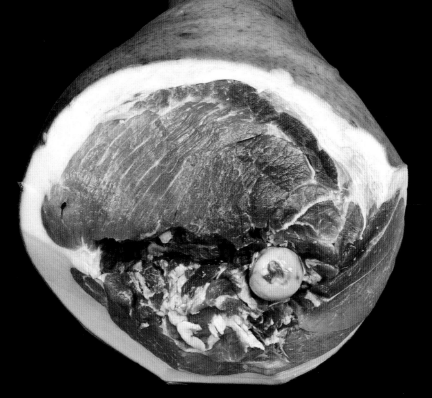

SCRAPPLE

This is the Meat Hook scrapple recipe. Yes, some of it is in grams. Yes, it has to be in grams to turn out right. Buy a scale. **MAKES 2 LOAVES**

1. Soak the head in a large stockpot full of cold water for 2 hours, to pull out the yucky stuff. This doesn't have to be refrigerated unless it's 90°F in your house. And why would you make scrapple in the summer anyway?

2. Remove the head and discard the water and yucky stuff; rinse. Put the head in the clean stockpot, add cold water to cover by 1 inch, bring to a simmer, and simmer gently, uncovered, for 6 hours, or until the meat is falling off the bone. Add more water as it simmers, if needed, to keep the head covered.

3. Pull the head out with tongs or two large spoons and set aside on a rack or tray to cool. Strain the stock through a fine-mesh strainer into a pot, bring to a boil over high heat, and boil until the stock is reduced to 4 cups.

4. Meanwhile, when the head is cool, pull off all the meat, skin, and anything else that doesn't look awful and finely chop, using a chef's knife. Add the head meat, reduced stock, and all the spices to a large pot and bring to a simmer over low heat. Stir in the cornmeal and rye and buckwheat flours a little bit at a time until smooth, then cook, stirring frequently, until the mixture is thick, about 1 hour.

5. Once it's thick, continue cooking, stirring frequently and making sure to scrape the stuff off the bottom of the pot so it doesn't burn (you know, like making polenta). Keep stirring until the mixture is extremely hard to stir, about 2 hours longer. Taste it and add as much salt as you think it needs, then pour or spoon it into the plastic-wrap-lined terrine molds, smooth the tops, and refrigerate overnight.

6. The next morning, slice the scrapple just over 1 inch thick. Place the all-purpose flour in a shallow bowl. Heat a sauté pan over medium heat to melt the butter. Dredge as many slices of scrapple as you like in flour and brown in the butter, turning once, until crispy on both sides, about 3 minutes a side. Serve with a fried egg on top. Scrapple will keep for up to 2 weeks.

$1/2$ pig head, about 8 pounds
8 grams freshly ground black pepper
5 grams freshly ground white pepper
12 grams ground coriander
6 whole cloves, finely ground
5 whole allspice, finely ground
$1/2$ nutmeg, grated
10 grams ground sage
4 grams dried marjoram
10 grams chili powder
3 cups cornmeal
$1/2$ cup rye flour
$1/4$ cup buckwheat flour
Kosher salt
1 cup all-purpose flour for dredging
2 tablespoons unsalted butter

SPECIAL EQUIPMENT
Two 10-by-4-by-4-inch terrine molds

COUNTRY PÂTÉ

This is a cool-guy butchering book, so I'm contractually obligated to give you a pâté recipe. It's actually pretty easy to make. Pâté goes well with mustard, pickles, and toasted rustic bread. You can have your butcher grind the meat for you if you want to make this even easier.   **MAKES 1 LOAF, ABOUT 10 SERVINGS**

1. Preheat the oven to 275°F. Line the terrine mold with the caul fat. Set aside.

2. Combine all the remaining ingredients in a large bowl and mix well with gloved hands. Press the mixture firmly into the lined mold, making sure there are no air pockets.

3. Place the mold in a large deep roasting pan and add enough cold water to the pan to come halfway up the sides of the mold (you're making a water bath). Carefully place the pan in the oven and cook until the center of the terrine registers 150°F, 1½ to 2 hours. Remove the pan from the oven and allow the terrine to cool in the water bath for 2 hours at room temperature.

4. Remove the mold from the water bath and place a baking sheet on top of it. Weight it down with a couple of heavy cans or a cast-iron skillet. Refrigerate the terrine overnight.

5. The next day, remove the weights and the baking sheet. Carefully run a butter knife around the sides of the terrine mold, invert onto a platter, and thump it gently with the back of your hand to release the pâté. Slice and serve it cold, or wrap it tightly in plastic wrap; it will keep for about 2 weeks in the fridge. Do not freeze it, please.

2 pieces pork caul fat (see Resources, page 305) or 1 pound bacon or thinly sliced back fat
2 pounds boneless pork shoulder, ground
½ pound pork liver, ground
1 small shallot, minced
2 grams freshly ground black pepper
1 gram freshly ground white pepper
1 clove, ground fine
2 grams powdered ginger
22 grams kosher salt
1 gram pink curing salt (see Resources, page 305)
1 large egg
2 big pinches finely chopped rosemary
2 big pinches finely chopped thyme

SPECIAL EQUIPMENT
Disposable gloves
One 10-by-4-by-4-inch terrine mold
Digital probe or instant-read thermometer

The Meat Hook Presents

the **BIG** $3

hooker

BIG HOOKERS
A Heart-y Snack

These jerky sticks are the result of (a) my really loving even the crappiest gas-station meat snack and (b) a need to make money from the cascade of beef and pork hearts that comes with whole animals. Inspired by a number of recipes I read in books and online, I cobbled together a fairly decent snack stick. Then the rest of the Meat Hook team took over the recipe and perfected it to the point where we, unfortunately, can't keep these in stock. You will need a dehydrator or a smoker to make this recipe; although an oven will work in a pinch, it's not recommended. You can have the butcher grind the hearts for you.   **MAKES 6 TO 10 STICKS**

1. If you didn't have the butcher grind the hearts for you, grind them through a meat grinder fitted with a small plate. Transfer to a large bowl.

2. Add all the remaining ingredients (except the casings) to the hearts and mix well. Cover and refrigerate for 36 hours.

3. Using a sausage stuffer, stuff the casings with the mixture, making sure to get them as full as possible without bursting. Line the casings up on racks and dehydrate or smoke them at 160°F for 2 hours, then lower the temperature to 135°F and dehydrate or smoke for 10 to 12 hours, or until firm.

4. Cut the sticks into 6 to 10 links with a chef's knife. Allow to air-dry on a baking sheet for at least 1 hour before packaging them up or snacking on them with beer.

5. Big Hookers will keep pretty much indefinitely at room temperature, but they will start to get a little dry after 2 to 3 weeks. If you plan on keeping them longer, store them in a Ziploc bag with the air pressed out before sealing. Do not freeze.

Note: Regular sausage casings are made from the washed and scraped intestines of animals, usually pork or lamb. Collagen casings are made from collagen rendered from animal bones, formed into long tubes, and dried. Yeah, pretty weird, I'll admit, but they're the only option if you want jerky-stick-size casings. They're available online through Butcher-Packer (see Resources, page 305).

3 pounds pork hearts, rinsed of blood and ground
1 pound beef heart, ground
3/4 cup soy sauce
1/4 cup Worcestershire sauce
1 tablespoon Sriracha sauce
10 grams freshly ground black pepper
3 grams ground cumin
60 grams brown sugar
6 grams garlic powder
8 grams kosher salt
2 grams pink curing salt (see Resources, page 305)
Collagen casings (see Note), 3 to 4 lengths

SPECIAL EQUIPMENT
Meat grinder with a fine plate (if you don't have one, have the butcher grind the hearts)
Sausage stuffer with a 1-inch-diameter stuffing horn
Dehydrator or smoker (see "Smokers," page 284)

Ben is The Meat Hook's resident Southern boy, and he has more Southern charm than most. Probably the best example of this was his ability, over the course of an hour-long phone conversation with Nancy Newsom, to convince the producer of America's finest country hams (Nancy has the only American ham in the Spanish Ham Museum in Madrid) to ignore the massive waiting list for her hams and "find" some for us. If a one-hour conversation with a total stranger seems strange, you obviously haven't called a country ham maker recently—they love to talk! If you call Benton's Smoky Mountain Country Hams and get Allan Benton on the phone, you'd better clear your schedule. Anyway, thus began our relationship with Newsom hams and Ben's love affair with Nancy. What follows is less an essay about great country ham and much more of a love letter.

THE HAM LADY: NANCY NEWSOM

By Ben Turley

I first met Nancy Newsom three years ago. I flew to Cincinnati and drove five hours to Princeton, Kentucky (a dry county, yet), to spend a day or two with this woman: the woman who showed me that American ham can be better than any prosciutto or serrano in the world.

I got exactly the opposite out of the experience from what I had expected. I went to Kentucky thinking I would learn all about the singular alchemy Nancy and her family had perfected. No way. Nancy is more protective of her hams than most people are of their children. But if you've ever had her ham, you'll understand why that is. Nancy is one of the last legitimate weathered-ham makers in the United States. Her family has passed down their recipe for literally hundreds of years.

Yes, I did get to see the cinder-block building behind her grandmother's house where she keeps all her hams. She even let me go inside. Can you imagine a basement where mold has been left to grow for ninety years but the smell still makes you hungry?

I don't think Nancy trusted me that first day. I was just another asshole coming from wherever to talk about ham or to steal recipes. I got the feeling there are a lot of these visitors. The second day, though, I left her shop for a few hours. I read for a bit next to a stream that had a plaque letting me know I was on the Trail of Tears, and I fell asleep under a tree. Then I went back to the shop. That was it: when I told Nancy I'd fallen asleep under a tree, she lit up and said, "You're a country boy; you belong here." The rest of that day and the next, I couldn't have paid her to stop talking.

But Nancy still wouldn't tell me too much about her hams. We talked about her relationships, her marriage, her kids, her failings. We talked about my relationships and my failings. She talked and talked, and she gave me the best advice anyone has ever given me. "Stop wasting your time. If you don't know it's good in the first few hours, then walk away. Don't waste your time." We've all heard it before, but with Nancy it carries the weight of experience. She works tirelessly every single day. She doesn't waste her time. I don't think she saw it, but I nearly started crying while she rearranged the smoked hocks.

When I got back to Brooklyn, Tom, Brent, and I sat behind Roebling Tea Room and I told them the very thing she'd told me. I think we sat there quietly for about ten minutes. That's Nancy. I knew I loved her in the first fifteen minutes.

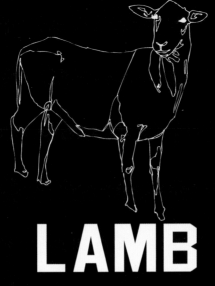

LAMB

Lamb is really the only four-legged animal that comes close to beef when you're talking about flavor, richness, and general meat satisfaction. Like its runner-up, duck, its distinct flavor isn't for everyone. But if you like lamb as much as I do, there isn't anything else that comes close to a slice of rare roast lamb leg or lamb cooked with cumin, garlic, and hot chiles.

I didn't really like lamb when I was growing up. Pretty much all the lamb available where I lived was imported from New Zealand, and whether it actually wasn't good to start with or it just deteriorated on its long trip on a container ship to the West Coast, it didn't appeal to me. I assumed that all lamb was gamy to the point of being almost fishy and as tough as shoe leather. In retrospect, I think that my folks were maybe hunting for a deal and we weren't buying the best lamb available. Whatever the case, my mind was completely changed when, back in 2004, a friend showed up to a sort of *Iron Chef*-ish collective dinner party with a leg of lamb from a farmers' market. Rather than funky and tough, it was as tender as the finest beef and had a distinctive flavor I couldn't get enough of, literally. (Hey, I'm sorry I ate most of your leg of lamb, guy-whose-name-I-forgot-who-brought-it-to-the-party. I owe you one.)

If you think you don't like lamb or feel only lukewarm about it, I'm going to do my part to convince you that all lamb is not created equal and, I hope, to give it a second chance. One of the things I like most about lamb is that its flavor lends itself to some really fantastic big flavors that totally take over other meats or don't completely jibe with them. Cumin, coriander, cinnamon, and resinous and/or potent herbs like rosemary and cilantro are just a few that play really well with lamb, and they could be your gateway to loving it.

Culinary aspects aside, lamb is also a key part of the process of raising and eating sustainable meat. While grass-fed beef need relatively large, flattish pieces of land to graze on, lamb, because of their small size and nimble feet, can graze on rocky hillsides, dry scrubland, and other marginal areas where other ruminants simply can't, which is great because there is a lot of marginal land out there, and raising sheep allows all available grazing areas to be fully used. And because this land tends to be cheaper, it gives a slight economic advantage to anyone who wants to try raising sheep for the first time.

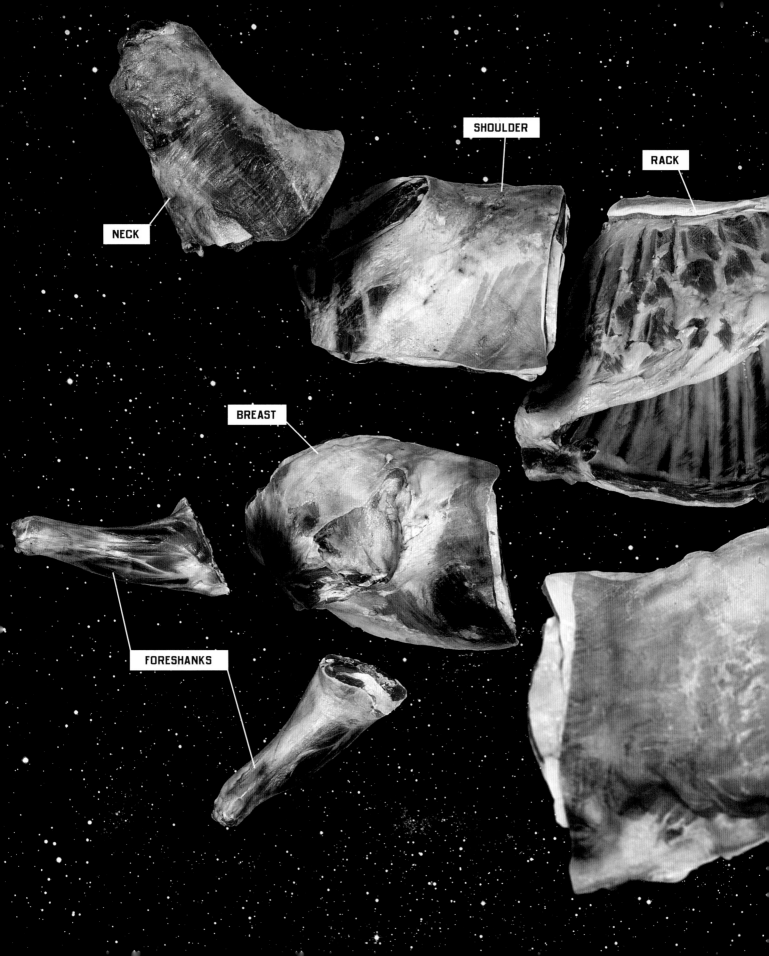

NECK

SHOULDER

RACK

BREAST

FORESHANKS

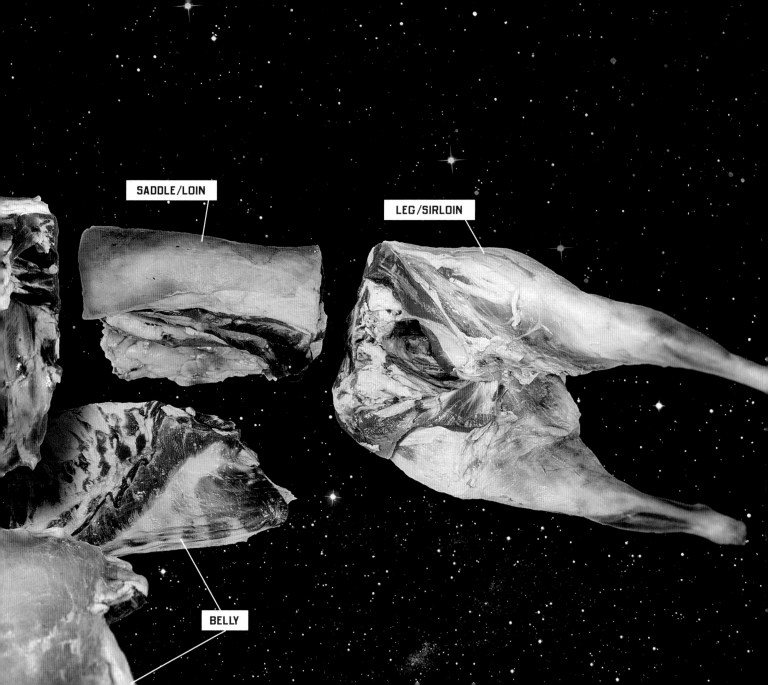

SADDLE/LOIN

LEG/SIRLOIN

BELLY

LAMB CUTS

While breaking down lamb is very similar (if in miniature) to breaking down beef, it is way easier for the beginning butcher (and even the pros) to work with, because it doesn't need to be cut down the middle into sides but can be cut across its entire cross section to make all kinds of groovy double chops and roasts and the like. The result of this crosscutting is a surreal-looking bone-in cut that is as visually appealing as it is delicious. The four basic primals of lamb are as follows.

SHOULDER

The shoulder is the fattiest of all the lamb primals, and it's full of prime braising and barbecue cuts, as well as flavorful and juicy chops for grilling that don't cost a fortune. The shoulder is hugely overlooked by lamb lovers and, because of this, is perfect for the adventurous cook on a budget: the average shoulder cut is easily half or a third the price of a similar cut from the loin, just a few inches away. The shoulder is basically the chuck of the lamb. Boned and rolled, it makes a great roast, especially if your family likes lamb more well done, with multiple layers of nice fat. Cut with a saw into chops, it is the perfect inexpensive alternative to rib chops, and these can be substituted in almost any recipe that calls for them, with a little ingenuity.

Neck

Lamb neck is flavorful and has a nice amount of fat. It can be crosscut and braised like a shank or boned, tied, and roasted, or marinated and grilled.

Breast

At The Meat Hook, we don't cut lamb exactly like everyone else, so our lamb breasts are a little shorter and a little more meaty. That doesn't stop them from being God's gift to barbecue when slow-roasted either whole, like a rack of ribs, or cut into individual ribs.

Foreshank

Unlike most other shanks, the lamb shank, particularly the foreshank of the shoulder, is the perfect size for one person, and it makes a handsome-looking dish to boot. Another plus is that it cooks much more quickly than any other shank.

RACK

The rib loin is the home of rack of lamb, the most expensive and sought after of all the grilling and roasting cuts. I'm going to just put it out there: I don't get it! Why is this cut so valued over the saddle, which is more tender and less expensive? It probably comes down to aesthetics.

The arch of Frenched rib bones must just make people feel like they're dining at the Ritz, and they are, at Ritz prices. Another part of the rib loin is the least thought about of any cut on the lamb—the belly. If you can find it, it's great stuffed with sausage, rolled up, and roasted with fresh herbs.

SADDLE/LOIN

The saddle is the definition of luxury—it's the lamb version of the porterhouse and T-bone section of beef, which includes the loin and tenderloin. Whether the saddle is cut into chops or boned and tied into a roast, it's the best cut lamb has to offer. Ignore those people sneering at you over their plate of rib chops—you win.

LEG/SIRLOIN

Lamb leg is really versatile. You can steak it, cube it for kebabs and stews, chop it for tartare, grind it for chili, shred it for fajitas, or even pound it out for carpaccio. The list is endless. Because it is leaner than the rest of the lamb, you do need to treat it a bit more gently. If you're roasting, do it at a fairly low temperature (300° or 325°F), then give it a little blast of heat at the end to brown it. Lamb steaks can get by with just salt and pepper, but if you're planning on grilling them past medium-rare, you'd be well advised to marinate them first. The leg takes even very flavorful marinades well because the flavor in its hardworking muscles can stand up to almost anything.

Although the leg and sirloin are frequently sold together as leg of lamb, much of the forward section of the leg is actually sirloin.

Sirloin rules. It's tender, it has more flavor than loin chops but can be cooked just as hot and fast, and, best of all, it's usually a lot cheaper. I like it served as weird-looking chops or a boneless roast. Don't mess with it too much. All it needs is a little salt and pepper, maybe some olive oil, garlic, and herbs. What more can I say? Eat it.

SNEAKY BUTCHER SHOULDER RACK

Roasting a whole rack of lamb is really decadent. You'll get meat with a crusty, browned exterior and, once cut into chops, a bright red interior. The problem is that rack of lamb, because of all its desirable traits, is not cheap. However, if you can give up the elegance of those long, graceful rib bones, you can have nearly the same experience (I think it's even better, but hey, it's my recipe) by having your butcher cut the rib end of the shoulder into chops and then tie them back together. This may sound a little goofy, but if what you want is almost the same result without the pomp and expense, this will serve four people an unforgettable faux-fancy meal.

For this, you're going to need to go to a real live butcher and ask him to cut four 1-inch-thick chops from the rib end of one shoulder. Got that? They have to be cut from the same shoulder, or it won't look right when tied up. Since you're already at the butcher, have him tie the chops back together as a roast—or do it yourself at home, using butcher's twine and an overhand butcher's knot (see page 50) to form two snug loops around both the top and sides of the newly formed roast. **SERVES 4**

1 rosemary sprig, leaves only, finely chopped
2 garlic cloves, minced
3 tablespoons olive oil
1 tablespoon kosher salt
1 teaspoon freshly ground black pepper
Four 1-inch-thick lamb shoulder chops from the rib end, tied tightly together (see headnote)

SPECIAL EQUIPMENT
Instant-read thermometer

1. In a small bowl, combine the rosemary, garlic, olive oil, salt, and pepper and mix into a paste. Place the roast in a roasting pan. Put the rub all over the roast, taking care not to snag your hand on any sharp bones.

2. Preheat the oven to 375°F, letting the roast hang out in the roasting pan while the oven heats up.

3. Once the oven's at temp, throw that baby in there and rotate it every 15 minutes, until a thermometer inserted in the center of the roast registers 125°F or so. Budget 1 hour for cooking to be safe, but it could be less. Let the meat rest for 10 minutes, then cut the strings and serve.

LAMB BELLY PANCETTA

Making lamb belly pancetta is as quick and easy as home-cured projects come, and it will give you a fascinating flavor to work into dishes you might otherwise make using bacon, guanciale, or pork pancetta. Because lamb belly is fairly thin, it will cure in a week and be ready to use in about three weeks, which means a lot less time that your significant other or other housemate will have to deal with it hanging in the fridge. This is a stripped-down recipe that works well; feel free to add fresh thyme, coriander, garlic, or anything else that strikes your fancy.   **MAKES ONE 3-POUND PANCETTA**

1/4 cup kosher salt or coarse sea salt
2 rosemary sprigs, leaves only, roughly chopped
1 heaping tablespoon crushed red pepper flakes
A very small pinch of pink curing salt (see Resources, page 305)
1 lamb belly, about 3/4 inch thick, 12 inches long, and 12 inches wide and about 4 pounds

SPECIAL EQUIPMENT
Nonreactive food-safe container, roughly the size of the belly
Butcher's twine

1. Combine the salt, rosemary, red pepper flakes, and pink salt in a small bowl. Place the lamb belly in a large nonreactive food-safe container and rub the cure into the belly well on both sides, making sure to coat it evenly. Let it sit for 10 minutes, then coat it again with any remaining cure. Wrap in plastic and slide it onto the bottom shelf of your refrigerator.

2. Let the belly cure in your fridge for 5 to 7 days, turning it once or twice a day. At the end of curing, the belly should be firm and weigh about 25 percent less than when you started.

3. Rinse the cure off the belly and pat it dry. Roll up the belly tightly and tie it with butcher's twine. (You can add more fresh herbs before you roll it up if you want, just don't get radical.) Hang the pancetta in your fridge or in a cool, dry, dim, well-ventilated place. As with all curing things, keep it away from strong smells because the meat will soak them up.

4. You can use the pancetta after two weeks or you can let it hang out for months. If you find that the pancetta turns out too salty, unroll it and soak it for a few hours in cool water, and then let it dry before rerolling/tying/hanging.

CUMIN LAMB STIR-FRY

Lamb loves cumin, and one of the ways lamb can love cumin best is in a Chinese-style stir-fry like this one. I know, you're like, "Hey, dude, I don't have a wok; what good is this recipe going to do me?" Don't sweat it. If you have a good-sized cast-iron skillet or French steel pan, it'll work out fine. Just don't try this with a stainless steel pan or some such thing—it'll stick, and you'll get pissed off and never want to make it again. Also, you'll need a big metal spoon to move things around in the pan and remove them when need be. It's not traditional, but I like peanuts in my stir-fry. Feel free to skip them. Any ingredients you can't find at the store? Get on the Internet (see Resources, page 305, for my favorite sources).   **SERVES 2 TO 3**

1. Place the lamb on a cutting board and slice it into strips as thin as you can manage using a sharp 8- to 10-inch chef's knife. (Chilling the meat beforehand will make it easier to slice; place the package from your butcher in the freezer for 20 minutes.) If the strips are wider than 1/2 inch, stack them a few at a time and cut lengthwise in half.

2. Mix all the marinade ingredients well in a medium bowl and then toss the meat with it, coating thoroughly. It's best to allow this to sit overnight, covered, in your fridge, but if you don't have time, let it marinate, uncovered, at room temperature for 1 hour.

3. Heat a large wok or skillet over high heat until smoking hot. Add 1 tablespoon of the oil, then add the chiles and peanuts, if using, and let them sizzle until they start to blister and take on color. Add the meat and stir-fry until just cooked with some browning, about 2 minutes. If you need to add more oil to make the browning happen, then add a little more now and cook for 1 minute longer. Use a spoon to pull the meat and chiles out of the pan and onto a waiting plate.

4. Add more oil to your wok and get it very hot before adding the scallions. Stir-fry the scallions just until they turn bright green, about 2 minutes. Return the meat and chiles to the pan and toss for a few moments longer, just until everything is hot but not so long that the scallions get mushy, about a minute or less. Serve immediately, over rice.

1 pound boneless leg of lamb

FOR THE MARINADE
2 tablespoons ground cumin
2 tablespoons soy sauce
2 tablespoons Shaoxing rice wine
1 tablespoon toasted sesame oil
2 garlic cloves, finely minced
3 to 4 Sichuan peppercorns, crushed as best you can
1 teaspoon kosher salt
2 to 3 tablespoons peanut oil or toasted sesame oil
5 hot dried red Asian chiles (the little skinny ones)
1/2 cup raw peanuts (optional)
1 bunch scallions, cut into 3-inch lengths

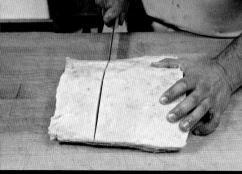

GRILLED MUTTON CHOP

Many cultures like the French really dig doing fancy stuff to the saddle of lamb: deboning, wrapping it in thin pork back fat, and rolling it up with beautiful whole sprigs of herbs and such. If that's the shape of your heart, please don't let me stop you, but I think the saddle is best represented by the simple and brutally awesome mutton chop presentation made famous by the legendary New York City steak house Keens. Almost cubic in form and confrontational in size, the mutton chop lets anyone who sits down in front of it know it means business. Ask your butcher for a mutton or lamb saddle chop as long as it is wide.

Extra points for cutting the chop off a whole saddle. Read the cleaver-buying advice on page 27 if you don't have a handsaw, and watch your fingers. **SERVES 2**

One 4-by-2-by-2-inch-thick mutton chop
Kosher salt and freshly ground
    black pepper

SPECIAL EQUIPMENT
Mallet
Large Weber charcoal barbecue grill,
    or the like
Medium-sized cast-iron skillet
Instant-read thermometer
Large cleaver or small handsaw
5-inch boning knife

1. If you choose to cut chops off a whole saddle of lamb/mutton yourself, instead of letting your butcher do it like a sane person, you'll need to get an inexpensive plastic cutting board. This is important, because it's likely you're going to do some damage to it. Also needed will be a boning knife and either a cleaver or a small handsaw. I prefer a saw to a cleaver here.

To use a saw: Start by figuring out how big you want the chop to be and then, using a 5-inch boning knife, cut through the meat, across the saddle, down to the bone. Do this on both sides of the saddle, then grab your saw. Make sure that you hold on to the saddle tightly with the other hand, or get some help and have the other person hold one end of the saddle while you hold the other. Gently saw through the bone, using fluid, medium-long strokes. Don't try to take too much at once, or the saw will bind and pop out, possibly damaging the meat—be patient! You may need to rotate the loin to cut completely through the bone without gouging the board. When you've finished cutting, use a spoon or the back of a knife to scrape off the bone dust before you season and grill the chop.

To use a cleaver: Using a boning knife, cut through the meat as above. Then, instead of sawing, place the cleaver inside the cut and on the bone where you want to cut. Grab a mallet and gently whack the back of the cleaver squarely and rhythmically until you have cut through to the board. Be careful not to get aggressive here, as it's pretty easy to hurt yourself when you're tangled up with a mallet and a cleaver. If you were hoping to hack away at the saddle with a cleaver like a cartoon character, sorry to disappoint you, but that sort of action takes years of practice. I'm trying to help you to succeed, thus the mallet. OK?

Recipe continues

2. To cook the chop, begin by seasoning it liberally with salt and pepper and then let it loaf around for an hour where you can gaze upon it but hungry pets cannot reach it.

3. Fire up your grill and preheat your oven to 325°F. Once your grill is hot as hell and your oven is ready, place the chop on the grill and give it a nice crusty sear on all sides, 2 to 3 minutes a side. Then place the chop in a medium cast-iron skillet and roast in the oven for 10 to 12 minutes, until it hits 120° to 125°F on an instant-read thermometer. Rest the meat for 10 minutes.

4. Debone the chop by following the X-shaped bone with a boning knife until all the meat is free, then slice the meat across the grain. Plate the chop by placing the sliced portions back on the bone roughly where they came from, in the most gruesome way you can figure out. Serve with a rustic red from the southern Rhône Valley.

The Maine Event

Trying to explain the Maine Event is like trying to describe your first kiss, or jumping out of a plane, or maybe your first acid trip. It's just too complicated. That said, I can describe it in terms of what it actually was: a weeklong summer camp for food-obsessed adult children at an achingly beautiful farm on Penobscot Bay, complete with chicken slaughtering, butchering demonstrations, and even a pizza night with a wood-fired pizza oven.

The Maine Event was a yearly tradition born during the crazy summer of 2009, a watershed moment for the Brooklyn food scene and a critical turning point in the lives of everyone involved.

I had just quit my job at the hottest butcher shop in the city, Marlow & Daughters, to open The Meat Hook with my partners in a space where we hadn't even begun construction, despite the fact that we were supposed to open in October. I was teaming up with my old chef, Caroline Fidanza (who was leaving her position as head chef of Diner and Marlow & Sons to open her own place as well); Millicent Souris, from the much-missed Queen's Hideaway (and a co-conspirator of mine from that summer's Queens County Farm Kegs-'n'-Cluckers event), who had just left the well-loved Williamsburg brunch spot Egg; my soon-to-be business partner Brent Young; and, of course, the event's boss lady and my wife-to-be, Annaliese Griffin. Did I forget to mention that I was getting married a few weeks later? And

Caroline, Millicent, Brent, and Annaliese were naturals to cook for the event. We had done dinners together in far more primitive environments before and managed to do better than just pull them off, but Spina? Spina was a self-taught cook whose previous job had been running a heavy metal record label. We'd had drinks. We'd talked food. I'd helped set up the Tea Room's meat program, but we'd never actually cooked together. Hell, I'd never even been to his house. (Come to think of it, I *still* haven't been to his house.)

Of course, the event was mostly Spina's idea: have a person who had never run a cooking school before (Annemarie Ahern, owner of Salt Water Farm) wrangle up a group of people who had never taught a weeklong event (us), charge what seemed like a lot of money for it, and raise expectations so high that they might be impossible to meet. Why not? What could possibly go wrong? The result would be a Rorschach blot of our collective interests and curiosity.

What do learning how to slaughter a chicken and an intoxicated BB-gun marksmanship contest lit by the headlights of a truck blaring classic rock on the radio have to do with each other? I'm not sure. I've never been on an all-inclusive vacation. I mean, my parents were too poor to send me to summer camp. Maybe it was a bad idea to have people whose idea of a good time is drinking Busch in the parking lot of a paintball field on Staten Island design a four-day food-dork dream vacation. Or perhaps it was the best thing ever.

It turned out to be a little bit of both.

Unlike typical culinary getaways where menus are set, food is ordered, and pantries are stocked, the Maine Event was an exercise in improvisation and panic management from the first day to the last. Since we all had real jobs with long hours and major responsibilities, we arrived only a day or two before the guests, initiating a madcap scramble to see what was available, in season, and awesome.

We swapped some pork for crabs and charmed our way into Zodiac boats to glean whelks and chanterelles from nearby islands. Some years there were blueberries or early peaches or sea urchins packed with uni; other years we lucked into just enough mackerel to garnish a salad course. One year we got calm, gentle Bresse chickens that practically leaped into the pot, others Freedom Rangers, known for, among other things, having a Terminator-like aversion to death. Life is like a box of chocolates, if the chocolate you get means the difference between success and your event turning decidedly crash-and-burn.

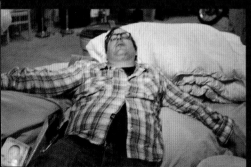

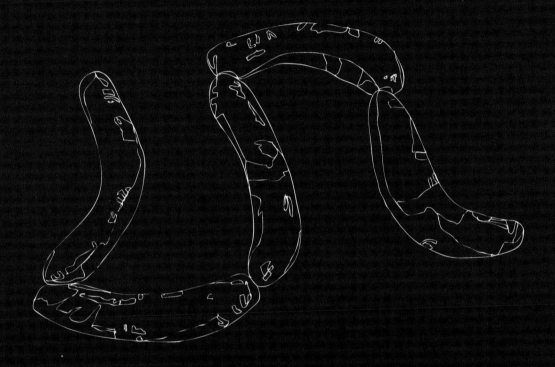

SAUSAGE

Making sausage is more like magic than anything else. With a little technique and a lot of delirious imagination, you can transform the odds and ends of a whole animal into sausages that taste like a slice of chicken Parm pizza, a bacon cheeseburger, or even a Spicy Bite from 7-Eleven. If that's not magic, I apparently wasted my early teenage years rolling ten-sided dice, reading Tolkien books, and listening to King Crimson. As with any kind of alchemy, you need to choose your tools carefully.

GRINDER

Please, please, please don't half-ass sausage making by buying one of those cheap plastic meat grinder attachments for a stand mixer. I'm not sure what they were thinking when they designed them—while they excel at doing things like grinding leftovers into baby food and the like, they aren't good at grinding raw meat. So when you are starting out, have your butcher grind the meat for you until you know for a fact you love making sausage so much that you'll spend your hard-earned cash to buy a real meat grinder. This will save you a lot of hassle and allow you to focus on actually making sausage, not on how much your grinder sucks. Failing to heed this advice will result in tears, domestic violence, and a complete lack of sympathy from me.

If you then decide that you are willing to invest $150 or so in your new hobby, choose either a high-quality manual grinder with a #22-sized plate or a good-quality #10 stand-alone electric grinder (see Resources, page 305). I realize that you may feel the urge to save a few bucks and buy a grinder on Amazon, but I recommend buying one from an online retailer that specializes in sausage making and meat processing, as they will stand behind their product and have a real-live person to call if you have any questions or issues. If you're on the fence about spending the money, keep in mind that grinders will do a lot more than just grind meat. They can rice potatoes for mashed potatoes, do a great job of crushing tomatoes for sauce, and quickly chop eggs for egg salad, to name just a few uses.

SAUSAGE STUFFER

There are a lot of different ways to stuff sausage, and you can get away with a lot if you're already familiar with the process. I've used the cut-off neck of a water bottle in a pinch, but I really recommend buying an actual stuffer for your first few attempts at sausage. The best style is the hand-crank piston type (see Resources, page 305), readily available online for around $100. These don't heat up or overwork the sausage meat, as the worm gear of a meat grinder with a stuffing attachment can. Overmixing your meat or getting the meat hot will cause your sausage to be crumbly and have a generally terrible texture. If you're unsure if you want to spring for a stuffer, ask around to see if anyone you know has grandparents or other folks with one kicking around in their basement that you can borrow. Barring that, check with local housewares shops or rod-and-gun clubs to see if they have one you can rent. If you are absolutely stuck using the stuffing attachment for a meat grinder, make sure to undermix the meat before you put it in the hopper, and take a Xanax.

SAUSAGE CASINGS

Most sausage casings are "natural" casings, which means that they are the scrubbed, scraped, and washed intestines of cattle, hogs, or sheep. They are bundled up and stored in salt or a strong brine to preserve them. There are different sizes for different types of sausages, but what we think of as normal grocery-store-sized sausage hog casings are what's called for here. To complicate matters, though, pork casings come in various sizes, measured in millimeters. Look for 29- to 32-mm casings. Although they can be purchased online in cheaper bulk packs called hanks, for a first attempt I would recommend presorted and individually tubed casings, as sorting casings is a nasty, smelly, and frustrating job. Some casings need to be soaked before they're used; others simply need to be flushed with cold water. Pay attention to the manufacturer's instructions on this, as soaking casings that shouldn't be soaked can make them soft and they can burst while you're stuffing them, which detracts significantly from the joys of making sausage.

SAUSAGE 101

To make sausages the right way, you're going to need a scale. All our sausage recipes are in grams, not because I'm a lazy asshole, but because grams are precise and yield predictable results, and I want to set you up for success.

A KILO IS A THOUSAND GRAMS

My first attempts at making sausage were real hit-or-miss propositions. I judged seasoning quantities by eye and feel and corrected the spices by trial and error. The worst part was that I could never seem to replicate a recipe that had turned out really awesome.

All that changed when Ben "Gram Master" Turley was talked into moving from Richmond, Virginia, to Brooklyn to work with Brent and me at Marlow & Daughters. Ben brought two things with him that would forever change us. One was an iPod full of Black Moth Super Rainbow, which would become the unofficial sound track to our lives, and the other was a stack of sausage recipes with the ingredients set out in grams.

If you weigh things in grams, you'll get good sausage every time. Volume measurements won't work. Recently, a bunch of good cookbook authors have tried to convince people to buy a scale and weigh their ingredients for baking or sausage making or what have you. Just do it. I'm pretty sure that you've spent way more money on something totally stupid or completely useless in the last six months. A decent kitchen scale costs as little as $25, so you have no excuse for not buying one.

FAT TO MEAT

The fat-to-meat ratio of a sausage is the most important element of any recipe. The baseline of 70 percent meat to 30 percent fat can't really be messed with, unless you want to set about reengineering the entirety of the recipe, ingredients, and techniques. The meat that we use for sausages is almost exclusively from pasture-raised heritage-breed pigs, which makes the job pretty easy when it comes to getting the perfect ratio of fat to meat.

Berkshire, Tamworth, and other "modern meat" heritage-breed pigs tend to have the perfect ratio of fat to meat built into them, provided they are allowed to grow to what we think is the optimal hot weight (weight after slaughter) of around 225 pounds.

In the event that you can only get meat from skinny pigs for your sausage, you can augment the missing fat with back fat, which you should be able to buy cheaply at a butcher shop. If you follow these recipes and your sausages end up too salty, you have too much fat; if they're bland and/or dry, you have too little fat. Mess around. Be OK with failure. You can always use your sausage mixture for a pasta sauce or chili, or stuff it into an old sock and throw it at the kids hanging out at the mini-mart, because those kids need to get fucking jobs.

SALT, PEPPER, AND GARLIC RATIOS

Three critical ingredients in a sausage recipe are salt, black pepper, and garlic. These give you the proper salinity, spice, and flavor that will allow you to build nearly any sausage recipe. If you're making breakfast sausage, you aren't going to want the garlic, and if you're making a recipe like bratwurst, which is more white-pepper-based, you'll need to substitute white pepper for black. Otherwise, our basic ratio is going to allow you to make sausage, throwing in whatever harebrained flavors you can think up, and if nothing else, your sausage is at least going to be properly seasoned. This is one of those "teach a man to fish" kind of formulas. Follow the ratio and use common sense.

THE BASIC SAUSAGE RATIO

1 pound pork to 9 grams kosher salt to 7 grams minced garlic to 1 gram freshly ground black pepper.

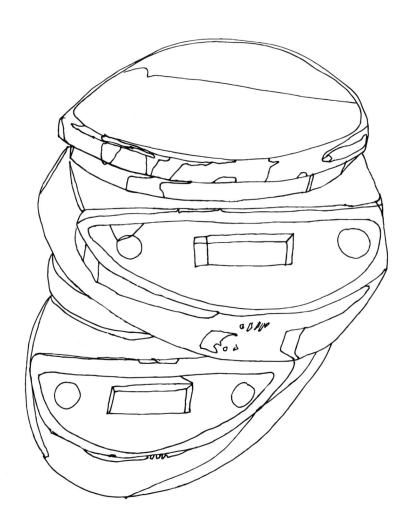

BEYOND HAMBURGER HELPER:
MEAT AS FLAVORING

Let's face it, good meat costs money. One of the most common criticisms of the local/sustainable meat/food movement is that local food in general, and meat from small family farms in particular, is too expensive for the average person, and certainly a person of low income, to afford. Without wading too deep into this controversy, I would like to offer my two cents about strategies for getting good food and meat into your diet without spending a lot of money.

I could have put this aside in nearly any section of the book, but I chose to include it in this chapter because sausage is such a flavorful and easy way to get good meat into your day-to-day meals for less. When you're having a big meat-centric backyard barbecue, there's no way around spending a fair amount of money if you're purchasing food you can feel good about serving. However, the same one or two sausages required to fill up one of your Fourth of July guests will feed up to six people if used as a flavor base for a pasta sauce, soup, or stew. When you buy good meat, it has more flavor and, with a little planning, that flavor can go a long way.

There is a popular refrain in the media that Americans eat too much meat. I have said it myself, and I stand by it. Rather than go the eco/small earth route here, I'd like to get to the spiritual heart of American meat culture, which developed in the post–World War II boom era. The nation had just emerged from a decade and a half of economic depression, unemployment, strict rationing, and global war. It makes perfect sense that our grandparents and great-grandparents wanted to kick out the jams and live a little once the economy started to expand rapidly in the late 1940s and early 1950s. After not being able to enjoy a good steak for fifteen years, who wouldn't want to?

The Eisenhower era saw an explosion in backyard barbecues and a culture that placed a lot of value on real knock-down, drag-out carnivore fests. If Herbert Hoover promised the meager chicken in every pot during the years that came before, Dwight, smiling in his khaki shorts with a porterhouse, seemed to promise two steaks on every grill. One of the interesting elements of this period of limited institutional farm subsidies is that if meat prices are corrected for inflation, they look an awful lot like the prices you would pay at a butcher shop like The Meat Hook today. Americans were, quite literally, putting their money where their mouths were and making a decision to spend a larger portion of their income on meat.

Fast-forward sixty years, and you find that, because of artificially low grain prices and a number of kinky bits in the Farm Bill, Americans have come to think of massive amounts of cheap meat as some sort of birthright. But while the Eisenhower years were chockablock with grilled steaks on the weekends, during the week the frugal housewife saved her pennies by preparing casseroles and pot roasts from inexpensive cuts. This, it seems, is a lesson that cheap Concentrated Animal Feed Operation (CAFO)—produced meat has allowed us to forget. If we're going to leave behind the bad agricultural ideas of the twentieth century and embrace good meat, we're going to need to reexamine our great-grandparents' ideas of thrift and learn to use meat primarily as an ingredient and flavoring, not as a main dish.

GARLIC SAUSAGE

I don't know what went into the first sausage ever made, but I suspect the recipe was something like this. The simple combination of salt, spice, and garlic is at the heart of nearly all sausages made anywhere on earth, whether the meat is pork, beef, lamb, or even more exotic "bush meats" like kangaroo or antelope. This basic recipe is also the starting point for most Western European fermented dried sausages, like the French *saucisson sec* and Italian *salame*. You can choose to think of this recipe as a starting point for your own recipes, or you can leave it alone and enjoy the pleasures of the pig.   **MAKES ABOUT 35 LINKS**

10 pounds boneless pork shoulder
   (70% lean meat/30% fat)
90 grams kosher salt
70 grams finely minced garlic
12 grams freshly ground black pepper
1/4 cup ice water
1 length 29- to 32-mm hog casing

SPECIAL EQUIPMENT
Meat grinder with medium plate
5-gallon food-safe plastic tub or
   extra-large mixing bowl
Disposable gloves
Piston sausage stuffer

1. Put the meat grinder and plate in the freezer for an hour or so. Cut the meat into chunks that will easily fit into the throat of the grinder, and put them in the freezer too.

2. Lubricate the ends of the shaft and screw the whole thing together according to the directions. Attach the plate and screw it down tight. Plate size? Larger, when just getting started, is better. Get fancy later. Grind the meat and transfer it to a food-safe plastic tub.

3. Now add your salt, garlic, and pepper to the bowl, sprinkling them evenly over the top of the pork. Put on your gloves and mix them in with a bread-kneading motion, making sure to rotate the bowl a quarter turn after each knead.

4. After about one complete revolution, pour in the water and knead it in with the same motion until you notice that, quite suddenly, the meat has gotten firm and bound together. Stop. Take a small ball of sausage, roll it between your palms, and see if it will stick together without falling off. Good. Now wrap the ball in foil, flatten it, remove the foil, and fry it gently in a small skillet over low heat for about 2 minutes a side, or until firm to the touch. This is your sausage test. Let it cool, then taste it. It should be pretty damned good and have a nice sausagey texture. If it's too salty, you can add bread crumbs soaked in cream, some sugar, or more meat to the mix. If it's not salty enough, take a big pinch or two of salt, mix it with some cold water, and mix gently into the meat. (Is the mix crumbly? Uh-oh, you overmixed. Better luck next time. Make a giant batch of chili or a pasta sauce with the sausage meat instead.) When you're happy with the taste of the sausage, put the bowl in the fridge to chill.

5. While your sausage meat rests, rinse the casings by running cold water through them a few times using water straight out of the faucet with the end of the casing resting in a bowl in the sink (so it doesn't escape down the drain).

Recipe continues

6. When the meat is well chilled, put one casing over the nozzle of your sausage stuffer. Fill the cylinder of the stuffer with your sausage meat, making sure to tamp it down well with your hands to eliminate air bubbles, until it is about 1½ inches from the top. Place the cylinder in the crank frame and lower the piston into the cylinder by turning the crank. Pull about 4 inches of casing past the tip of the stuffing horn and begin to slowly crank the piston until the sausage begins to fill the casing. No need to tie off the end at this point—it will allow any air to escape as the casing is filled. Continue to turn the crank with one hand while you guide the filling of the casing with your other hand. Make sure you fill the casing so that there are only a few air gaps, but not so tightly that the meat is packed into it. Less filled is better than filled too tight, as any slack in the casings can be fixed when linking them, but overfilled casings will burst and you will need to start over.

7. Twist the sausage into links by pinching off a 5- to 6-inch-long portion and spinning it once or twice, overhand for the first link, and then twist off the next link, underhand in the other direction; continue pinching and twisting off links, alternating the direction. I didn't talk about tying the ends off, did I? Well, you don't really have to if you leave 2 to 3 inches of casing empty at either end. You wanna tie them off? Go for it. I won't stop you. After your links are twisted off, stack them neatly end to end on a baking sheet and place them on the top shelf of your fridge, uncovered, to dry the casings overnight.

8. To cook, either place the baking sheet of clipped links in a preheated 325°F oven for 18 minutes or panfry or grill at a low heat, or they might split or blow up. Any sausages that you don't cook or give away to friends can be stored, covered, for up to 5 days in the refrigerator. Or pack them into Ziploc freezer bags, 4 to 6 links each, and freeze for up to 3 months. To defrost, place the bag in a large bowl of cool water for 2 to 3 hours at room temperature, or defrost overnight in the refrigerator.

ITALIAN SAUSAGE

Here's a variation on our basic garlic sausage recipe, with a few flourishes. One of our takes on the classic Italian-American sausage, it gets its signature flavor from the fennel seeds and, in this version, fresh rosemary that has been minced very fine to add more depth and rustic appeal to the flavor. Use the red wine to add even more bold Italian flavor. A good-quality Sangiovese or Primitivo works well. **MAKES ABOUT 35 LINKS**

1. Put the meat grinder and plate in the freezer for an hour or so. Cut the meat into chunks that will fit into the grinder and freeze them too.

2. Begin by placing the fennel seeds in a small dry skillet (no oil, please!) and putting it over the lowest heat you can muster to allow the seeds to toast gently until they are slightly browned and aromatic, about 5 minutes. Let cool.

3. Then get the salt, cayenne, black pepper, and paprika together and turn them and the fennel into powder in a spice grinder; doing this right before you make the sausage will make it extra flavorful.

4. Grind the meat as in the Garlic Sausage recipe (page 157), transfer to a food-safe plastic tub, and sprinkle the powdered spices, sugar, garlic, and rosemary over the meat. With gloved hands, mix the meat mixture, adding water, as in the Garlic Sausage recipe, then proceed as directed to stuff the sausages. Refrigerate overnight before cooking or storing.

5. *Buon appetito!*

5 pounds boneless pork shoulder
    (70% lean meat/30% fat)
8 grams fennel seeds
45 grams kosher salt
2 grams cayenne pepper
6.5 grams freshly ground black pepper
12.5 grams sweet paprika
20 grams sugar
35 grams finely minced garlic
5 grams finely chopped rosemary
1/4 cup ice water or dry red wine

SPECIAL EQUIPMENT
Meat grinder
Spice or coffee grinder
5-gallon food-safe plastic tub or
    large mixing bowl
Disposable gloves
5- or 10- pound piston sausage stuffer

CHICKEN BACON RANCH SAUSAGE

While the Chicken Bacon Ranch isn't perhaps the most outlandish sausage we've ever made, it isn't far off either. This is a great trashy grilling sausage for summer holiday weekend barbecues or an indulgent weeknight in front of the TV with a cold beer. A healthier alternative would be to grill up a few of these sausages, slice, and serve over romaine lettuce with buttermilk dressing and sliced red onion.   **MAKES ABOUT 35 LINKS**

1. Put the meat grinder and plate in the freezer for an hour or so. Cut the pork and chicken into chunks that will fit in the grinder and freeze them too.

2. Grind the meats as in the Garlic Sausage recipe (page 157), transfer to a large food-safe plastic tub, and sprinkle the dry ingredients, including the bacon and the seasoning packet, over the meat. Mix with gloved hands for 30 seconds, then add the buttermilk and proceed as directed in the Garlic Sausage recipe. Then stuff the sausages and refrigerate overnight before cooking or storing.

3³/4 pounds boneless pork shoulder (70% lean meat/30% fat)

3³/4 pounds skinless, boneless chicken thighs or breasts

60 grams kosher salt

12 grams freshly ground black pepper

5 grams garlic powder

5 grams onion powder

3 grams ground dill seed

Small pinch of celery seeds

1 pound bacon, cooked, cooled, and finely chopped

One-ounce packet ranch dressing seasoning

1/4 cup buttermilk

SPECIAL EQUIPMENT

Meat grinder

5-gallon food-safe plastic tub or extra-large mixing bowl

Disposable gloves

5- or 10- pound piston sausage stuffer

MEAT HOOK MEAT SAUCE

This meat sauce is what we make with the various Italian sausage blends that get left in the stuffer tube. Like so many things we make to use up the odds and ends from the week's animals and production, the sauce is never quite the same, changing from week to week depending on the stuff we have lying around. I guess that is just a drawn-out way of saying that what follows is more of a guideline than a recipe: feel free to improvise and change any elements of it, or not. Serve over your favorite pasta. **MAKES 2 QUARTS**

1 pound loose bulk Italian sausage
1 large onion, finely chopped
5 garlic cloves, finely minced
1 tablespoon all-purpose flour
1 cup pork or beef stock
One 28-ounce can whole tomatoes
1/4 cup unflavored vodka (optional)
Kosher salt and freshly ground black pepper
1/4 cup finely chopped parsley

1. In a large pot, cook your sausage over medium-high heat, smashing and cutting it up with your wooden grandma spoon. (No grandma spoon? You're screwed—get one!) The idea is to chunk up the sausage into bite-sized or smaller pieces.

2. After the meat has cooked for about 15 minutes, add the onions and garlic and cook until soft and translucent, 5 to 7 minutes. Add the flour and stir it in well until everything is sticky, 1 to 2 minutes. Add the stock and stir well, then add the tomatoes and vodka. (Feel free to omit the vodka, the not-so-secret ingredient in vodka sauce, if you like. I use it to help break down the tomatoes and make the texture smoother.) Reduce the heat to low and let the sauce simmer, stirring every 5 minutes or so, for about an hour, or longer if you have time.

3. Finish the sauce by seasoning with salt and pepper to taste, then add the chopped parsley. Leftover sauce can be refrigerated for up to 7 days or frozen for up to 3 months.

The Meat Hook
BRUNCH

Opening The Meat Hook, like any risky small business on a shoestring budget, was a real bitch. Lease negotiations and construction delays caused us to put off opening the doors for almost a month, and when we finally did open, it was because we had to: we were out of money.

Once we had made it through our first six months of working at the new shop, even though we were still putting in seventy-hour weeks, something strange happened: we started to get bored. One night, Brent and I closed together and walked over to the Roebling Tea Room to drink our after-work gallon of whiskey. Five or six whiskeys into the night, we decided that we needed to start serving brunch. Moreover, we wanted to make the Meat Hook brunch a sort of metaphor for all the ridiculousness of the New York City food scene in general and the popularity of chef-centric dining in particular. Exclusivity, excess, and the idea of the person footing the bill acting as a punching bag of sorts for the "chef" were the themes we decided to run with. What happened next, we couldn't have imagined.

The format would be one table of two every Saturday morning at 11:30 a.m., right in front of the butcher counter. Reservations could only be made by calling "Laurence" (Brent's cell phone) and leaving a message, along with sending him the most embarrassing picture on your cell phone. The cost was a prix fixe of $50 per couple, and it included all drinks and food. Seems like a dumb setup but kind of a good deal, right? Wrong. The catch was that you needed to finish every course before you were served another one, no matter what we served. Can't eat twenty marrowbones? Too bad, you failed. Your brunch is over.

Like most things truly stupid and exclusive that happen in New York City, the Meat Hook brunch became "a thing" within two weeks of the first service, and by month two, we were booked from March through October. We were blown away that something that started out as an elaborate joke—eating brunch at a table for two, surrounded by people waiting in line to buy sausages, and getting tortured with food—ended up becoming the kind of horrible thing that people sic their personal assistants on to try and coerce their way into getting a reservation for. I'd be lying if I said it didn't make me judge these people.

Needless to say, we no longer offer brunch. This is mostly because we're way too busy these days to cook food and sling sausages on a Saturday morning, but it's also because that brunch, the love child of boredom and alcohol, was getting boring itself. It did, however, lead to grander things, like our Midnight Mass Halloween–themed dinner with friends, St. John Bread with wine chef Lee Tiernan, and Rippers, our very own little restaurant in Rockaway Beach.

CHICKEN

Chicken suffers from a real image problem. In the popular consciousness, "chicken" is code for bland, conservative, and complacent food. Chefs look at chicken dishes on menus as the "safe" items for people on a diet or children who are picky eaters. All of this is complete bullshit. Well-raised chickens are among the most delicious meats you can cook, and they are by far the cheapest pasture-raised meat if you're trying to do well by your wallet while saving the planet.

Whether you cook it simply with salt and pepper or with fresh herbs, intense spices, or savory smoke, chicken is more versatile than any other meat when it comes to taking center stage as a meal. Rather than regarding it as the meat you choose when you've given up, I think of chicken as an opportunity to rediscover something that has been all but tossed into the culinary trash basket. And the fact is that it is the meat Americans eat more of than any other; if you want to change the way people eat meat, you should start by looking at what they eat most.

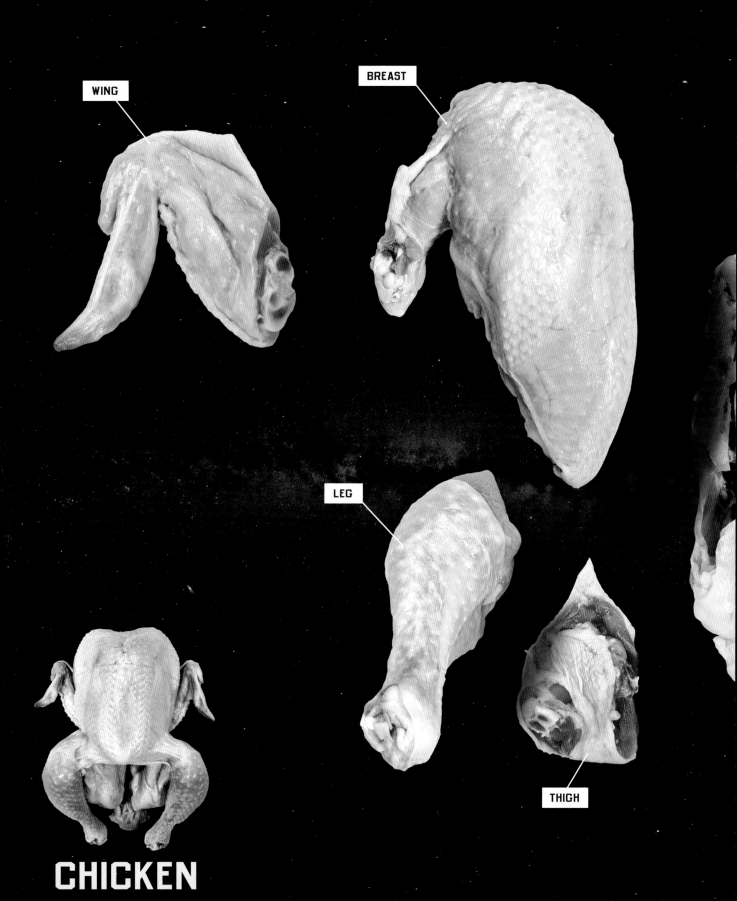

WING

BREAST

LEG

THIGH

CHICKEN

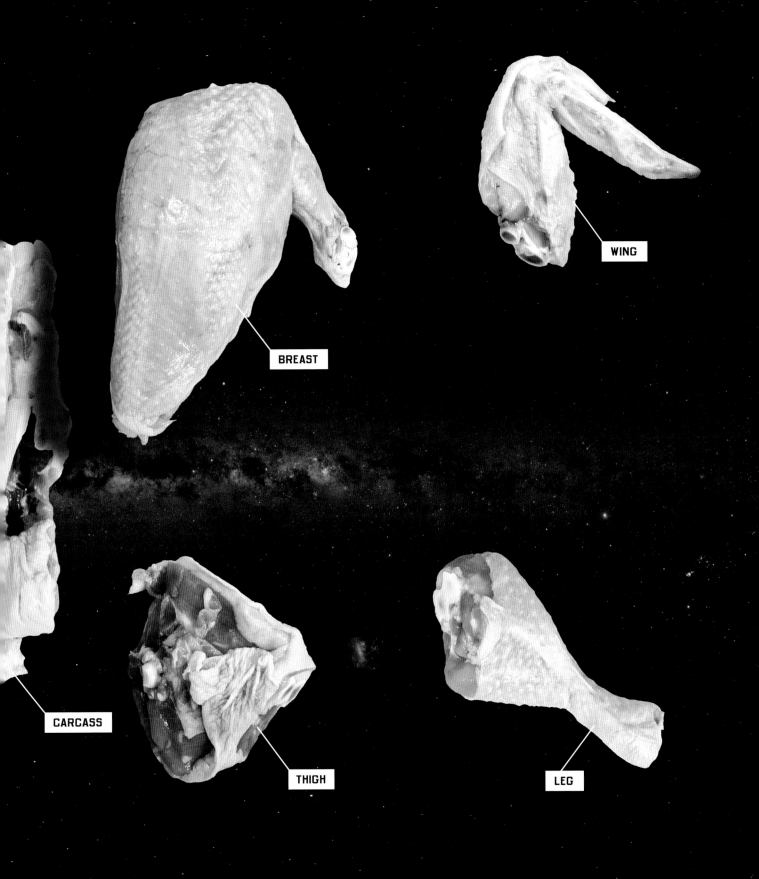

WING

BREAST

CARCASS

THIGH

LEG

CHICKEN CUTS

At The Meat Hook, we only buy whole chickens from our local producers, and then we break them down every morning. I won't lie to you, it's a huge pain in the ass. So why do we do it? Quality and peace of mind. The only thing standing between us and going out of business is our contract with our customers that we are selling them exactly what we say we are. If we bought pieces from some faraway chicken-cutting plant, we wouldn't know a damned thing about them—who cut them up, what the birds looked like whole, what farm they came from, or how they were raised. Here are the pieces you'll find on a whole bird.

BREAST

This is the most expensive and sought after of the cuts on chicken. It's also lean and it's unevenly shaped, making it difficult to cook the entire breast to the same temperature. It's great for stir-frying, kebabs, and other boneless applications. Butterflying and stuffing breasts is a great way to help them cook more evenly.

WING

Universally known for their flavor and juiciness, chicken wings have a high bone-to-meat ratio, which goes a long way toward making this the most succulent cut on the bird. That ratio also makes wings a great choice for broths and stocks, especially if you're looking for a stock with a lot of body to use as a sauce base. The downside is that the connective tissue, where the meat attaches to the bones, needs to be dealt with in some way. I recommend marinating wings in buttermilk, hot sauce, or some other acidic marinade before frying or cooking with high heat.

THIGH

Second only to the wing in juiciness and flavor, the thigh is great for making chicken salads, soups, and braised dishes, as well as frying and roasting. Boneless thigh meat is the absolute best cut for chicken sausage, forcemeat, and other more exotic applications, but is just as good roasted simply with salt, pepper, and sage.

LEG

This ugly duckling of the anatomy of the chicken suffers from the same problem as the breast—it is oddly shaped and difficult to cook evenly. The challenges of the drumstick are increased by the quantity of tendons and connective tissue in the meat, as well as the stringy texture of the long muscle fibers that make up this part of the leg. So this cut is usually best for braising and soups, though it can be transformed for deep-frying by "lollipopping," cutting around the small end of the drumstick and scraping the meat up to the top of the bone, thus eliminating the uneven shape.

BONES, FEET, AND NECK

These castoffs from the chicken carcass are a good base for stocks and broths. They are rich in collagen, which gives the stock body, and they can be either roasted to a deep golden brown to make a dark stock or blanched, washed, and simmered for a white stock. For more on stock making, see page 243.

HOW TO BUY A CHICKEN

Chicken labeling conventions are pretty confusing. What exactly are you getting when you buy a natural chicken versus a free-range, hormone-free, organic, air-chilled, or pastured bird? Certainly one can log on to the USDA website and see what the letter of the law is concerning these different types, but it only tells you part of the story—a lot of the terms are meaningless. Chickens, like life, are not a black-and-white proposition. One small natural-chicken producer's bird might be beautiful and, if you visited the farm, you might find that the chicken was raised in pretty pleasant conditions but was not certified organic. On the other hand, you could visit an organic farm and be horrified at the conditions the birds are raised in, and yet they are labeled with that buzzword you're seeking. An air-chilled bird from one producer may look gross—soft fleshed and swimming in weird muck—while another producer's air-chilled birds are firm, fresh smelling, and succulent.

Buying chicken is a lot like buying anything else: if you care about it, you have to figure out what you're looking for, ask questions, and, even if the answers you get conform to what you've read in a feel-good hippie magazine, let your senses be your guide. Many "conscious" consumers feel much more comfortable buying by the label in a supposedly healthy or organic supermarket chain, choosing to pay three times more for words like "free-range" and "sustainable," but in the end, what they get might not taste better or be any better for the animals or the environment than what they would get at a megamart on the other side of town.

A chef at a good restaurant wouldn't buy fish without peering at the gills or sniffing the belly, and you shouldn't buy chicken, or anything for that matter, without examining it closely. If a chicken looks misshapen, is missing skin on its back, smells off, feels sticky, or exhibits anything else that sets off your warning buzzer, don't buy it—or, if it's too late, don't buy from that store again and find your chicken somewhere else. That "somewhere else" is usually a farmers' market or, if you're lucky enough to live near one, a local butcher shop that specializes in high-quality local meat. Don't just assume that you're getting what you want even if you're at the counter of a fancy new shop that throws around all the right buzzwords. Channel your inner great-grandmother and look, smell, and touch before you sign on with anyone selling you a chicken.

HOW TO BUTCHER A CHICKEN

Chances are, if you have access to properly raised chickens at a farmers' market or farm stand, they're only going to be sold whole. Even if you're lucky enough to be able to get chicken parts from a supplier you feel good about, knowing how to butcher a chicken is a good skill to learn—you know, for when the zombiepocalypse comes.

I like to think of the way we cut up chickens at The Meat Hook as fairly unusual. Our method yields two elegant "airline breasts" (a boneless breast cut with the drumette still attached, made popular by hotels and airlines during the early postwar era) and two legs/thighs, as well as, of course, the chassis to make stock with. If you're looking for a more conventional way to cut up chicken, there are 1,500 YouTube videos out there waiting for you.

1. Start off by putting on your glove(s). Place the bird in the center of your cutting board. Remove the liver, heart, and any other offal in the cavity, wrap, and freeze for later use.

2. Using a 5-inch boning knife, cut the wing from the drumette by placing the blade exactly in the bottom of the V where the two joints come together. Repeat on the other side.

3. With your off hand, find the breastbone and cut two parallel lines on either side of it down to the bone with the boning knife or a sharp paring knife.

4. On the breast facing away from you, follow the rib cage around with the tip of the knife, freeing the breast down to the back.

5. Cut through each wing socket.

6. Cut down the middle of the V between the leg and the pelvic area of the chicken carcass. Repeat on the other side.

7. Cut between the bottom of each breast and the top of the leg and between the thigh and drumstick. You now have 2 wings, 2 airline breasts, 2 legs, 2 thighs, and the carcass. Wrap in Ziploc bags (be sure to press out all the air before sealing). Fresh chicken will keep in the fridge for about 2 days, and it freezes well for 2 to 3 months.

1 whole chicken

SPECIAL EQUIPMENT
Cut-proof glove (see Note, page 23) or disposable gloves
Cutting board
5-inch boning knife
Paring knife (optional)

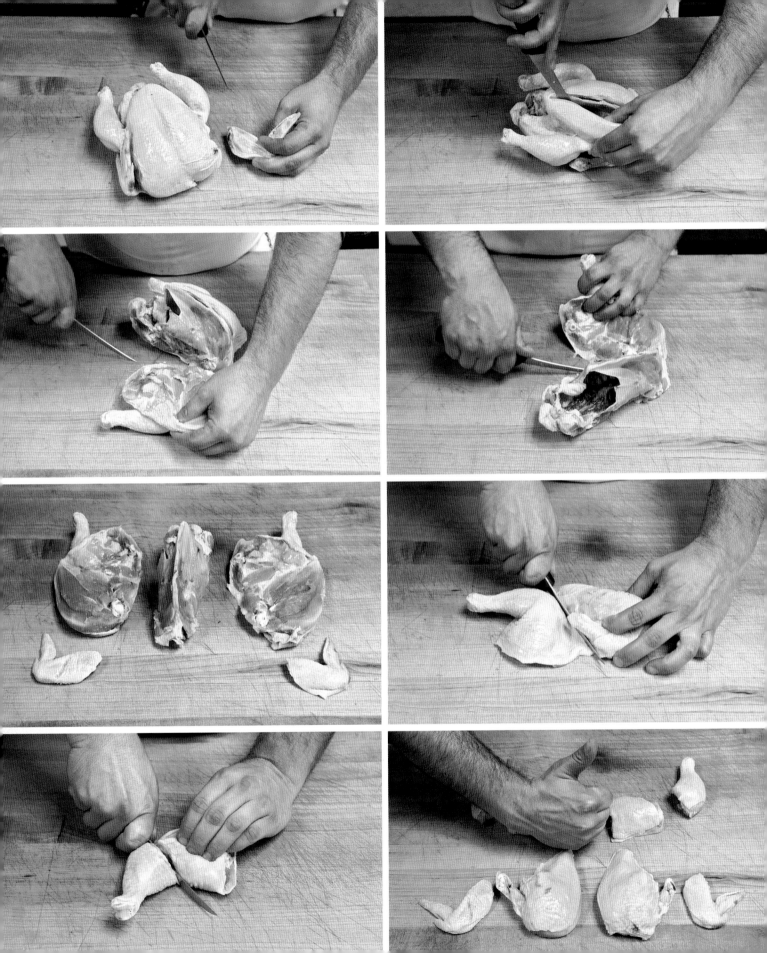

PIES-'N'-THIGHS LIL' SUPPER

Pies-'n'-Thighs, a Williamsburg fried chicken institution, **was the first successful restaurant business opened by someone I knew. It showed me that you** *could* **take a huge chance and actually succeed. Inspirational bullshit aside, Pies-'n'-Thighs makes damn good fried chicken. Carolyn Bane is the Pies-'n'-Thighs fried chicken czar, and this is the dream dinner.** **SERVES 4**

1. Combine all the ingredients for the brine in a large pot and bring to a boil over high heat, then turn off the heat and let cool to room temperature. Transfer the brine to a large bowl or nonreactive food-safe container, cover, and refrigerate until completely cold.

2. While you're waiting for the brine to chill, pull out a cutting board, 5-inch boning knife, and chicken, and put on your gloves. Cut off the leg/thigh by running the knife between the thigh and the pelvis on one side of the chicken. Repeat on the other side. Separate the thighs from the drumsticks by cutting through the knee joints.

3. Next, cut out the back of the chicken by following the natural line where the bottom and top ribs meet in the rib cage with your knife, cutting down on either side. Then split the whole breast in half by cutting through the breastbone. Be careful here, as you'll need to use some force to get through the bone. Finally, cut each breast crosswise in half. Freeze the carcass for stock.

4. Place the chicken pieces in the brine. Cover and let sit overnight in the fridge.

5. The next day, pour the peanut oil into a large, deep cast-iron skillet (it should be 1½ inches deep) and heat over medium heat to 325° to 350°F—no hotter.

6. Put the flour and salt in a large Ziploc bag and shake it for about 30 seconds to combine well. Throw the chicken straight from the brine into the bag—you want the chicken to be wet so that the flour really adheres. Seal the bag and give the chicken a 30-second shake. Transfer the pieces to a plate and discard the bag.

7. Fry the chicken in batches of 2 to 3 pieces, turning every minute or so, until golden and cooked through, about 12 minutes. Don't overcrowd the pan, and make sure your oil gets back up to temperature before putting in the next batch. Place the finished chicken pieces on several layers of paper towels and allow to drain while you finish the rest.

8. To serve, cut or pull the chicken off the bone and thickly slice it. Spread mayonnaise and barbecue sauce on both sides of each bun. Place slices of fried chicken on each bun, top with pickles, and serve.

FOR THE BRINE

1 cup kosher salt
½ cup plus 1 tablespoon sugar
2 tablespoons cayenne pepper
2 tablespoons paprika
1 tablespoon freshly ground black pepper
4 quarts water

1 chicken, 3½ to 4 pounds
2 cups peanut oil
2 cups all-purpose flour
2 tablespoons kosher salt
4 potato buns, split
Mayonnaise
4 tablespoons MH Barbecue Sauce
　(page 55)
Dill pickles, sliced into thin rounds

SPECIAL EQUIPMENT

Large bowl or nonreactive
　food-safe container
5-inch boning knife
Cut-proof gloves (see Note, page 23)
　or disposable gloves
Deep-fry thermometer

Chicken

HOW TO KILL A CHICKEN

The first time I ever really thought about killing a chicken was the night before I killed almost fifty of them. I'm pretty sure that sounds bad, so let me back up here. One Friday afternoon, I got a call from my friend—well, at that time my acquaintance—farmer MGR (Michael Grady Robertson). He was working to turn the Queens County Farm Museum in Glen Oaks, Queens (the oldest continuously worked piece of farmland in the five boroughs), from the petting zoo it had become back into a real working farm.

"Hey, man, my rooster population is out of control," MGR said to me. He had about fifty roosters on his hands, which was about forty-nine too many. "You want to come out and slaughter a bunch of chickens?" Of course I did. But everything I knew about processing fowl came from a chapter in *The Omnivore's Dilemma.* "Uh, sure," I told him. "I'd love to. Do you have any kill cones?" MGR had no kill cones. "No problem," I said. "We can use orange traffic cones." Were these words really coming out of my mouth? "Great," MGR said. "See you tomorrow."

What to do? I knew that almost everything was available on YouTube videos. And so, with a stiff drink in one hand and my computer mouse in the other, I set about exploring chicken snuff films.

Most of the videos I found were full of earnest farm types wearing full work gear. These people were well organized and well equipped, and the whole scene made me feel like my last-minute, low-budget endeavor was doomed to fail. I had no kill cones. No chicken pluckers. No gutting tables. No vats of ice water in which to chill the birds. I had no chance.

Then I found it. Well into my third tumbler of bourbon, I came across what I was looking for: a video of two guys in a backyard, slightly intoxicated, processing chickens with little more than a knife, a hose, and, yes, a bright orange traffic cone. The man gutting the chicken was making a heavy-metal face and spraying water into the air, singing, "We're going DOWN to the CHICKEN FA-A-ARM!!!" Suddenly I was home. They weren't well prepared or earnest or even sober, but they were having a great time killing and gutting chickens.

I watched the five-minute movie over and over. The methods they used were basically the same as those in the other videos, just with fewer fancy tools. The chickens died just as well and were as cleanly processed (the guts and windpipe removed, then the cavity hosed out), yet the whole thing seemed infinitely more possible because, honestly, if those guys could do it, anyone could.

The next morning I woke up before the alarm to shower and organize my knives. By the time I arrived at the farm, MGR was already out front. "Do we know what we're doing?" he asked. "Yeah, we're good," I replied. "I watched a bunch of YouTube videos about it last night." MGR started laughing hysterically. "Of course—perfect!"

Since those bad old days, I have gotten a chance to kill a lot more chickens and see people who actually know what they're doing kill chickens, and now I pretty much know what I'm doing. What follows is Chicken Slaughter 101, and what that means is that it is a pretty breezy overview. If you're serious about killing your own chickens, please research the subject a little more deeply. That said, if you're stuck with a bunch of chickens and just this book, you'll probably do all right, but you might want to check out some YouTube videos first.

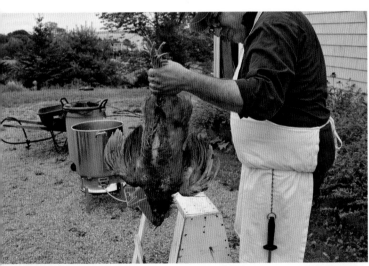

1. Start by setting up your killing station: Using a sharp knife, cut enough material off the top of the traffic cone to allow the neck of a bird through, but not its shoulders. Attach the cone to the sawhorse as securely as possible, using heavy-duty nails or screws. Next, fill a large pot with water and get the water heating to 140°F on an outdoor burner. Fill a bucket or basin with ice and water and position a trash can between the two.

2. When you're ready, grab your chicken by the feet and try to clutch it to your chest so that it can't flap its wings. This will keep you and the bird much calmer. Now, holding the chicken by the wings and feet, lower it into the cone, headfirst. Once it's in the cone, hold onto the feet with one hand and pull the neck through with the other. Be quiet and gentle when doing this, or you'll risk the bird getting pissed at you, and you do not want that.

3. With your off hand, cradle the chicken's head between your first and second fingers, with your thumb pulling the feathers of the neck toward you and exposing the skin where the arteries are. Let me be clear: you cannot cut cleanly through feathers. Please take your time and pull them back completely. Even one feather can screw up your cut.

4. Next, with your boning knife, make two cuts on either side of the neck that are roughly parallel to the angle of the beak. If you hit the arteries, there will be a fair amount of blood (2 to 3 cups). If not, try again until you get it. Stay calm—don't freak out!

5. Once the cuts are made, hand off your knife or set it in a safe place and use your knife hand to hold the legs of the bird as it bleeds out to make sure it doesn't thrash around and possibly get loose and fly around, spraying blood all over you—which will happen to you at some point if you kill enough chickens. The chicken will take 30 seconds to 1 minute to die. Keep holding it, even after you think it's dead, for an extra 30 seconds, just to be sure.

6. Once the chicken is dead, plunge it into the 140°F water, holding the legs and moving it up and down in the water with a sort of plunging motion for 20 to 30 seconds. Then pull it out and yank on some feathers. If they come out cleanly and with little effort, move the chicken over to the trash can and start plucking the feathers. If they don't come out, plunge the chicken into the water again for another 10 seconds and then see if the feathers come out. Whatever you do, don't use boiling water for this task; it'll parcook the bird and burn the hell out of you. You want to pluck off all the feathers using a motion perpendicular to the skin of the chicken. This may take a while if this is your first time, but stay with it and be very thorough—no one wants to eat a stray feather! If the feathers aren't pulling out easily, feel free to give the chicken another quick dunk in the scalding pot.

7. Once the bird is plucked, grab your knife and cut a small shallow slit just above the tail (also called the pope's nose) in the fat area below the narrow tips of the breasts. Work your hand inside the bird and along the top of the underside of

SPECIAL EQUIPMENT
5-inch boning knife
Medium orange traffic cone
(you may need a smaller or larger one, depending on the size of your chickens; you can find these at your local lumber and hardware depot)
Sawhorse or similar sturdy wooden shelf to attach the cone to
4 heavy-duty nails or screws
Hammer or screw gun
Large burner for heating water
Instant-read thermometer
5-gallon bucket or a laundry sink for ice water
Trash can to pluck chickens over and eviscerate them into
A hose attached to a water source
One person other than yourself who is OK getting blood all over him (optional)

the breastplate, then down in a scooping motion, grabbing all the guts and pulling them out toward you. Don't squeeze too hard, or chicken poop may shoot out the vent at your face or chest. Once the guts are out (look inside and make sure you got everything), hose the blood and guts off and out of the chicken and plunge the chicken into the chilled water bath for 10 minutes. Then remove the bird, shake off the extra water, and place in a large plastic bag. Refrigerate immediately.

8. Once the processing is done, you want to either cook the chicken right away or wait at least 24 hours for the rigor to come and go. Failing to do this will result in rubber-bullet-tough meat.

CHICKEN IS THE REAL GATEWAY MEAT

While grass-fed beef and pastured heritage-breed pigs get the lion's share of the foodie spotlight, the humble chicken is really where it's at if we're going to try to turn the industrial food system around and be able to feed the masses a healthy and relatively affordable meat that they can feel good about. Why? The short answer is time. While it can take up to two years for pigs and up to four years for grass-fed/grass-finished beef to go from conception to slaughter, the turnaround time with pasture-raised chickens can be just a few months. If this doesn't shed enough light on why chickens are so important to rescuing our food system from CAFOs, it might be helpful to think about it from the perspective of a farmer.

Say you're a farmer doing commercial dairy, commodity corn, or another relatively profitless, high-input method of farming and you hear from a guy in the next county that he's making pretty good money in pastured meat. If you're looking to get into that line of farming, would it make sense to start by forking out thousands and thousands of dollars to rent a thousand acres of pasture, install fencing, buy four hundred head of cattle, and then wait two to three years to start slaughtering and marketing your beef? Or would it make more sense to spend a few thousand dollars to build mobile chicken coops and buy some chicks to run on the few spare acres behind your house and see how it goes?

Farmers, by and large, are a fairly cautious lot. They have to be, as making one mistake or hitting a string of bad luck with weather, disease, or what have you could mean losing the farm that has been in the family for generations. Financially it makes much more sense for them to keep doing what they know farmingwise and maybe try out pastured chickens for a few summers before deciding to add some hogs, sheep, or cattle, rather than jump in with both feet and risk losing everything. Bacon may well be the gateway meat for wayward vegetarians, but chickens are the real gateway meat for changing the way the country farms and eats.

TWENTY-MINUTE CHICKEN LIVER MOUSSE

People make such a big deal **out of preparing charcuterie items—like they deserve a medal or something for pureeing some livers or baking a terrine. I don't get it. This recipe for chicken liver mousse is both fast and easy. It's delicious, too, so I suppose you can feel free to make a big deal out of it.**

Serve with crusty bread, cornichons or a similarly delicious pickle, and mustard. Or with Ritz crackers. Or on Wonder Bread with grape jelly. The mousse will keep, covered, in the refrigerator for 1 week. **SERVES 8 TO 12 AS AN APPETIZER OR SNACK**

1 large yellow onion, thinly sliced
2 tablespoons olive oil or chicken fat
Kosher salt and freshly ground
   black pepper
2 thyme sprigs
2 oregano sprigs
2 rosemary sprigs
1/3 cup port or brandy
6 whole chicken livers (or 12 split pieces),
   about 1 1/2 pounds, cleaned and rinsed
1/3 cup dry red wine
2/3 cup very cold heavy cream
8 tablespoons (4 ounces) cream cheese,
   sliced into tablespoon-sized chunks,
   chilled

SPECIAL EQUIPMENT
Mason jars, ramekins, or a terrine mold
   (you'll have 2 1/2 to 3 cups of mousse
   you'll need to pour into a good-looking
   vessel or vessels of some sort)

1. In a large sauté pan or cast-iron skillet, cook the onion slices in the olive oil (or chicken fat, if you have some lying around) over medium heat, stirring occasionally, until lightly golden, 5 to 7 minutes. Season with salt and pepper and cook until the onions are caramelized and brown, 3 to 5 minutes longer.

2. Add 1 sprig each of the thyme, oregano, and rosemary and smash them in with the onions. Deglaze your pan with the port, using a wooden spoon to scrape up the good bits from the bottom of the pan. Cook until all the liquid has evaporated, about 5 minutes. Transfer the onions to a bowl, pulling out the herbs and discarding them, and let cool.

3. Wipe out your pan with a paper towel and place over medium-high heat. Add your livers and sauté until browned on both sides but still medium-rare, about 2 minutes on each side. Add the remaining herb sprigs and deglaze the pan with the red wine, scraping up the bits on the bottom of the pan. Cook just until all the liquid has evaporated, about 5 minutes; don't let the livers start to stick to the bottom of the pan. Transfer the livers to a plate or bowl to cool, discarding the herbs.

4. Toss the cooled livers and onion into a blender (a food processor will also work, but a blender will yield a smoother texture) and turn it on. After the livers have been spinning for about a minute, slowly add the cream and cream cheese and blend to a puree. Taste for seasoning. The mousse should be slightly salty; if it's not, add more salt 1/2 teaspoon at a time. You can add more black pepper too, if you wish.

5. Pass the blended livers through a fine sieve and pour the mousse into the mold(s) of your choice and chill in the refrigerator for at least 30 minutes before serving. The mousse will keep, covered, in the refrigerator for 1 week.

CHICKEN NUGGETS

Let's face it: two immutable food truths are (1) chicken nuggets taste really good and (2) industrial chicken nuggets are, generally speaking, pretty creepy. What is a nugget-loving, conscientious carnivore to do when overcome by the desire to stuff his face full of fried chicken blobs slathered in barbecue sauce? Make them at home. It might seem impossible to replicate such a mass-produced mystery meat in your own kitchen, but I assure you it is not only possible, it's actually fun.   **MAKES ABOUT 20 NUGGETS**

1. Place the chicken, egg yolks, bread crumbs, and 2 teaspoons salt in a food processor and pulse a few times until the meat is well chopped but not a paste, about 1 minute. Spread the mixture, 1 inch thick, evenly onto a parchment-lined baking sheet or pan and allow to chill and set up for 30 minutes in the refrigerator.

2. Meanwhile, mix the potato starch together with the big pinch of salt and the pepper in a medium bowl.

3. Once the meat has set up, use a knife or cookie cutter to cut it into nugget-like shapes. Gently toss the nuggets in your seasoned flour.

4. Pour the peanut oil into a large pot, attach a deep-fry thermometer to the side of the pot, and heat the oil to 375°F over medium-high heat.

5. Add half the nuggets and fry for 5 minutes, or until golden brown. Transfer to a paper-towel-lined plate to drain. Cook the remaining nuggets, making sure to allow the oil to return to temperature before you add them to the pot.

6. Serve immediately, with the barbecue sauce (or honey-mustard dressing). We could both pretend that you're going to share these, but you're not.

Note: You can use either potato starch or flour for the coating, but potato starch yields a better, crispier texture. If you like thicker breading, dredge the nuggets first in potato starch or flour, then in beaten egg whites, and then again in the starch.

8 boneless chicken thighs, cut into small chunks, or 1 chicken, deboned (see page 183) and cubed

2 large egg yolks

1/2 cup fine dried bread crumbs or crushed soda crackers

2 teaspoons kosher salt, plus a big pinch

2 cups potato starch or all-purpose flour (see Note)

1 teaspoon freshly ground black pepper

4 cups peanut oil or other oil for deep-frying

MH Barbecue Sauce (page 55) or honey-mustard dressing

SPECIAL EQUIPMENT
Cookie cutters (optional)
Deep-fry thermometer

INSIDE-OUT CHICKEN POTPIE

This is a goofy play on the potpie that uses a whole boneless chicken as the crust and a pie tin for the fillings. It might just be the perfect way to maintain your low-carb lifestyle in the fall and winter months. In my early days as a protobutcher, I broke down a lot of chickens. They're small and you get to go through the same motions over and over, trying to eliminate any unnecessary movements and leaving no bit of usable flesh on the chassis. It was the first act of butchering I became good at and had pride in. Cutting up chickens became like a dog trick, like playing fetch—I just wanted to do it over and over again.

My chicken butchering zealotry led me to rent a technique DVD by legendary French chef, author, and teacher Jacques Pépin, and I was blown away by how fast he could completely debone a chicken from the inside out. My first attempts were, let's say, primitive, but I practiced often and eventually I became good at it—leaving me with a lot of boneless chickens to figure out what to do with. One of my favorites is the inside-out potpie that was born from leftover filling and one of those chickens.

This isn't a beginner butchering project. You might want to wait until your boning knife skills are a little bit more solid. And you might want to wear cut-proof gloves. **SERVES 3 OR 4**

FOR THE FILLING

1 cup whole milk or Basic Brown Stock (page 243)
3 tablespoons unsalted butter
3 large button mushrooms, finely chopped
1 celery rib, chopped into medium dice
1/2 yellow onion, chopped into medium dice
1/2 carrot, peeled and chopped into medium dice
3 tablespoons all-purpose flour
Kosher salt and freshly ground black pepper

One 3 1/2-pound chicken
Kosher salt and freshly ground black pepper

SPECIAL EQUIPMENT
Cut-proof gloves (see Note, page 23) or disposable gloves
5-inch boning knife
Chef's knife

1. Start by making the filling, so it has a chance to cool before you stuff it into the chicken. In a small saucepan, warm the milk over low heat. Keep warm.

2. Meanwhile, melt the butter in a large skillet over medium heat. Add the mushrooms, celery, onion, and carrot and sauté until bright and slightly softened, 5 to 7 minutes. Add the flour and cook, stirring for 1 minute, then add the warmed milk a little at a time, stirring constantly, until you have a nice thick filling. Season with salt and pepper to taste. Set aside to cool while you butcher the chicken.

3. Preheat the oven to 375°F.

4. Get out your cutting board and put on your gloves. Using a 5-inch boning knife, start to remove the backbone of your chicken by flipping it breast side down and cutting along each side of the backbone. Then work down the back on both sides to the pelvis, hip sockets, and wing sockets, freeing them up as you go. Scoop out the oyster (the small piece of dark meat on the back near the thighs). Continue cutting around the rib cage until you get to the breast.

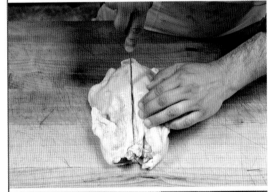

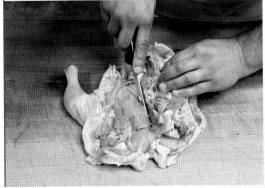

Recipe continues

5. Next, cut around the wishbone from the front, then pull it toward the back and out. Then force two fingers on each side of the breastbone under the breast. If you can get under the tenders, do that; if not, don't sweat it and just gently pry the breasts off the breastbone and back toward the tail, freeing up the flesh as you go with the knife, until the partially boned chicken is sort of coming off the carcass like a tube sock. Continue gently and patiently pulling and freeing up the chicken until it comes off completely. Wrap the carcass and freeze it to make stock (see page 243).

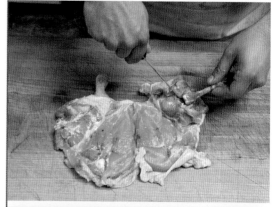

6. On to more chicken-removal-type stuff: Scrape around the base of each thigh bone until the meat starts pulling away from the bone, and force it off down to the knee. Gently cut around the knee and scrape/press the flesh off the bone down to the end of the drumstick, then push the bone back into the meat sock. (That's the best way I can describe the process.) Once the bone is back in, take the spine of your chef's knife and whack the base of the drumstick to break the bone, so you can remove it in its entirety.

7. Now for the fun part! Take a small roasting pan, your boneless chicken, disposable gloves, and the now-cool potpie filling, and let's begin.

8. Generously sprinkle salt and pepper all over the floppy bird and then plop it, skin side down, into your roasting pan in a splayed-out manner. If you couldn't get the tenders off with the breasts, place them in the meatless gaps between the breasts and thighs. Now start to dollop the filling onto the center of the breast area and the legs. Not too much at once! Using your gloved hands, gently stuff the filling into the legs and drumette areas. Add more filling to the center and then eyeball your chicken-to-filling ratio. You'll need to be able to wrap the chicken around the filling; if you put in too much, pull some out and heat it up in a baking dish later to serve with the bird.

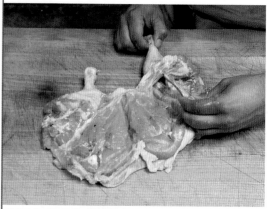

9. Begin to fold the two sides of the chicken toward each other, tucking in the neck skin and generally trying to make yourself a nice-looking chicken package. Gently flip it over in your roasting pan, doing more tucking as you go. Don't stress—you are likely going to screw the pooch the first few times, so just go slow and maintain your sense of humor. Use your gloved hands to stuff any escaped filling back into the bird and do your best to cover it with chicken skin.

10. Roast for about 1½ hours, until an instant-read thermometer registers 165°F. Remove and let rest for 10 minutes, then slice and serve.

Roberta's

Roberta's is a pizza place. At least that's how their chef, Carlo Mirarchi, described it to me over the phone a couple of months before they opened. If I remember correctly, he wanted to buy meat or learn to butcher or something. I was crazed at the time, butchering for four restaurants in a tiny metal shack behind Diner and listening to the same Black Sabbath tape over and over all day long every day, so I couldn't help him. What Roberta's has become since that conversation in 2008 is remarkable. Somehow, a restaurant opened from scratch for what most fancy restaurants pay to stock their wine list (and located in what was once a very sketchy part of Brooklyn) has become an internationally known destination restaurant. This by itself might not sound as extraordinary as it is. But how many internationally renowned restaurants have you heard of that have a built-in radio station fashioned out of shipping containers, or a tiki bar, or a yearly block party that is headlined by Andrew W.K.? None. That's how many. It's one thing to make it to the top, and it's another thing altogether to make it to the top in a marginal neighborhood of Brooklyn—but what's really the thing is that they've made it to the top on their own terms. We got into bed with the gentlemen of Roberta's long before we opened our Rockaway Beach shack, Rippers (see page 94), with them and way before we opened The Meat Hook. I can't actually remember not knowing them.

If I had to pick one place and time to mark the transition from our "fooling around" period to our "going steady" future with Roberta's, it would have to be the night in early summer 2009 that the future Meat Hook team headed out the door of Marlow & Daughters to the Lower East Side for an art opening. I'm fairly sure it was an art opening, anyway. The event took place inside a boutique of some sort owned by friends of friends and it was very crowded and hot, with cheap red wine everyone was guzzling out of plastic cups. Having spent the last eleven hours serving the crush of customers at

Marlow & Daughters on a busy Saturday, I took a break from the impromptu gallery sweat lodge and headed for the nearest liquor store to secure my alcohol independence. I can't piece together what led to my returning with a bottle of absinthe, a huge jug of terrible sake, and a pocket full of airplane liquor bottles, but I do know that when I returned, a strong contingent of Roberta's men was standing front and center, and they wanted us to help them buy a boat.

The boat in question was a twenty-six-foot S-2 sailboat manufactured in the 1980s, a model that had developed something of a cult following in the years after the company ceased production. Roberta's, knowing something about cult followings, had decided to buy the boat as a sort of company "yacht," and they wanted us to go in on it. Once the edge of the horrific collection of spirits I had amassed had kicked in, we came to understand just exactly what they meant by "buy" a boat. We, the future partners in The Meat Hook, would be purchasing exactly one-third each of one-fifth of the boat. Despite the fact that none of us had any money, we agreed that buying one-fifth of a small sailboat was a really good idea. I'd like to think that we sealed the deal by toasting with airplane bottles of Jim Beam in the street, but since I had not eaten a proper meal in days and was running on very little sleep and lots of alcohol, I can't recall if this actually happened or not. However, like many of my memories in and around Roberta's, I choose not to remember it any other way.

Well, the boat is long gone, but Rippers and our relationship with the ladies and gentlemen of Roberta's has survived, among other things, a devastating hurricane, personnel changes, shouting matches, and early morning surf lessons. Whether or not we do anything else together in the future, Roberta's will always be a part of our family.

TURKEY

A somewhat little known fact about the bird that Benjamin Franklin nominated as our national emblem during the formation of the Republic is that turkeys are, in their present state of breeding, pretty stupid as domesticated animals go. Many years ago, when I was trying my hand at being a self-supporting food writer, I spent the better part of an hour talking with a turkey farmer in Upstate New York about exactly how stupid the noble icon of all things wholesome and family-oriented really is. She recounted tales of turkeys smothering each other in a poultry pile when confronted by foxes and weasels (to be fair, this is a fairly common thing among domesticated birds), drowning in six-inch-deep water troughs, and even sometimes meeting their end while staring up at falling rain with their mouths open in a kind of neural glitch, not unlike a seizure, during which their lungs fill up with rainwater and they suffocate.

Lest you assume that *all* turkeys are prone to such fates, anyone who has spent time around wild turkeys will agree that they are a pretty street-smart animal when compared to their domesticated brethren, if quirky and prone to their own strange behavior.

The saving grace of domesticated turkeys is that they will, when raised on pasture, consume up to 25 percent of their total daily intake of food in grass and bugs, unlike chickens, which only get about 10 percent of their daily feed in free grass. That 25 percent represents a significant savings in the cost of raising these birds, especially as grain prices continue to rise despite governmental subsidies, and it starts to make turkey look like something we shouldn't sideline until the holidays roll around every year.

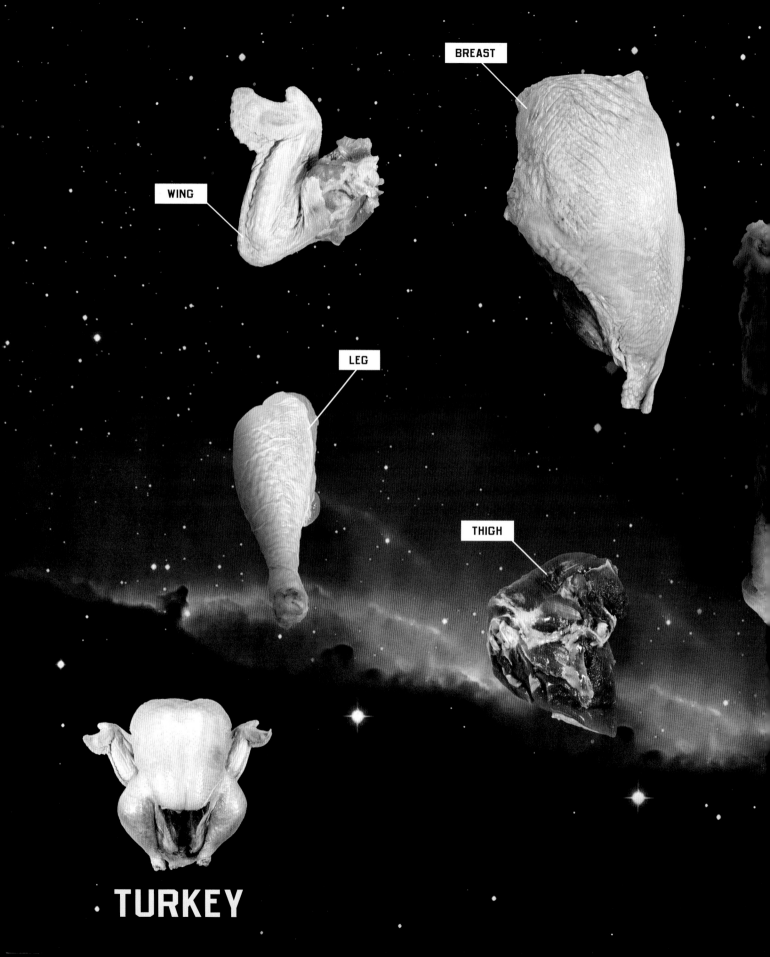

BREAST

WING

LEG

THIGH

TURKEY

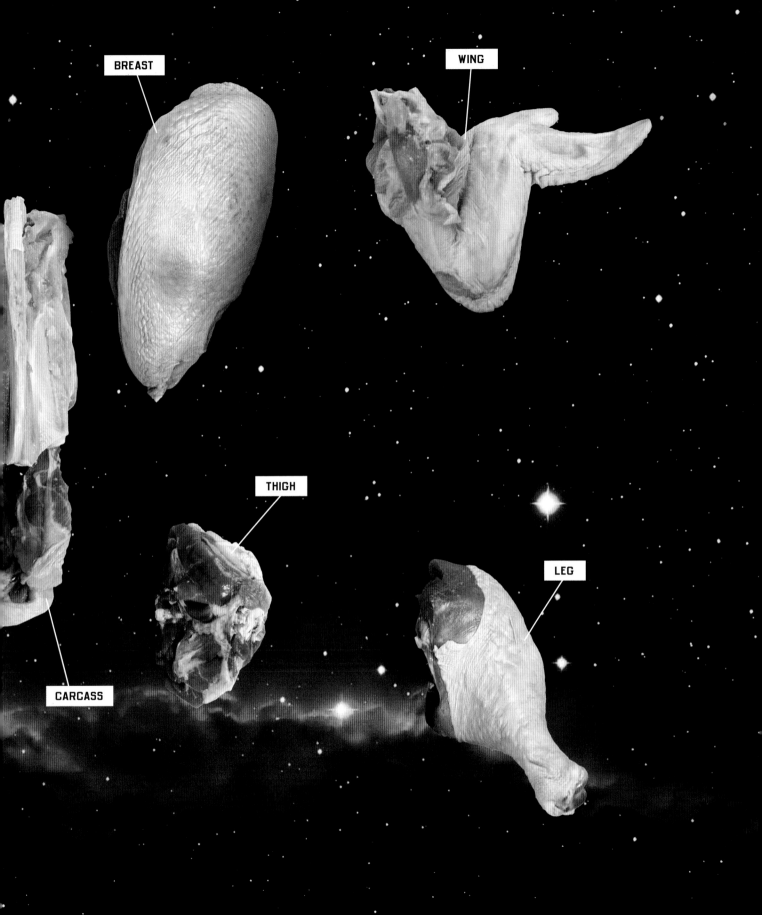

BREAST

WING

THIGH

LEG

CARCASS

TURKEY CUTS

Turkeys are real beasts, and their cuts are macro as well. One breast half is enough to feed a small family with leftovers, and one thigh is enough to satisfy a couple's intense craving for Thanksgiving in the middle of July. Because these cuts are so large and are usually sold whole, you should be prepared to deal with leftovers, just as you would at the holidays with a whole bird.

BREAST

Like the breast of any domesticated bird, the breast of the turkey is tricky to cook perfectly and easy to over-cook and dry out. So brining the beast before cooking is highly recommended. Adding butter or chicken fat under the skin is better still. If you're roasting a breast by itself, you should cook it at under 300°F until it is within 15 degrees of your target temperature of 170°F, then crank up the heat to brown the skin.

WING

Turkey wings, unlike those of chickens, are a little on the tough side, with a lot of chewy tendons and such. I like to steam them for 1½ hours to help dissolve the connective tissue before roasting them in the oven with high heat to crisp and brown the skin. Roasted wings are also a great choice for making extra-flavorful turkey stock because of their greater surface area of brown skin and all the collagen in the tendons.

THIGH

Turkey thighs are not something you usually see kicking around in the grocery-store meat case, probably because they end up getting made into turkey bacon or something strange like that, and that's unfortunate. Turkey thighs, like chicken thighs, are fantastic when roasted, with plenty of intramuscular fat to keep them juicy. And boneless ground thighs are a great meat to use in Turkey Tamale Pie (page 205) too.

LEG

Nothing says Renaissance faire like gnawing on a turkey drumstick! The drumsticks, like the wings, are a little on the tough side if not cooked slowly, and they benefit from being brined for at least 24 hours before cooking to keep them moist. My favorite way to prepare turkey drumsticks is to brine them and then smoke them for 8 hours at 200°F. Bodices, jerkins, and chain mail are optional.

BONES, NECK, AND THE REST

Using the leftover carcass or bones from your feast is a classic frugal move, and while turkey stock isn't as versatile as chicken stock, it's certainly handy to have around if you're stuck with more leftover turkey meat than you planned for. Because turkeys are bigger birds, with harder cartilage and tougher tendons, you should plan to simmer turkey bones for at least 8 hours, if not 10, to extract the maximum amount of flavor from them.

HERITAGE VERSUS BROAD-BREASTED WHITE

There seems to be a recently accepted orthodoxy that the best turkeys for any and all are the old American heirloom or heritage breeds like Bourbon Red, Narragansett, Standard Bronze, and so on. Food-lover types look down their nose at the lowly and common Broad-Breasted White, which has been the standard grocery-store turkey for something like seventy-five years. Very little seems to be said about turkey-raising techniques, cooking complications, or the texture of the meat—everyone just goes around hollering about flavor and biodiversity (like a turkey with its head chopped off, if a headless turkey could be smug).

In the spirit of full disclosure, I was one of the first people to pile onto that bandwagon. One holiday I hauled home a ridiculously overpriced Bourbon Red that, if I could, I would have dressed up in a onesie and strapped to my chest like a proud papa. Turkey perfection was mine. The angels of Slow Food smiled down on me. I was winning at life! Well, until I pulled the turkey out of the oven on the big day. After all my brining, trussing, and fussing over temperature and time, my guests and I ate a turkey that was tough, dry, and chewy. Thank God for good wine.

It was in light of this huge disappointment that I started to delve below the surface of all the hullabaloo, and I discovered the many pleasures of the very same breed carelessly tossed aside by the fooderati in their dash to find the newest, coolest thing: the Broad-Breasted White. I came to understand that this bastion of blandness was really a damned good bird when raised on pasture, all the while remaining fairly idiotproof in the oven as well as tender and juicy on the plate.

I don't want to come across as some sort of heritage hater who cares nothing for biodiversity, small farms, children, and puppies. Heritage birds do have their place, but unless your holiday kitchen is a French Laundry—esque palace of Zen, you're much better off with a properly raised Broad-Breasted White.

HOW TO BUTCHER A TURKEY
(AND MAKE TURKEY STOCK)

We cut up turkeys the same way we butcher chickens (see page 170), except it's easier. Where a wrong turn of your boning knife can completely screw up a chicken cut, turkey bones are so hard and substantial they almost scream out the instructions. The directions here cover both how to butcher a turkey and how to make a turkey stock.

1. Before you get started, preheat your oven to 425°F so you can begin roasting the bones as soon as you've finished the butchering.

2. Put the turkey on a cutting board. Put on your gloves and remove anything you find in the cavity. Place the giblets in a Ziploc bag and refrigerate or freeze for later use, and throw the neck into a large roasting pan.

3. Use a 5-inch boning knife to cut the wings from their sockets at the base of the breast. Set these in the roasting pan with the neck.

4. Now make two cuts on either side of the breastbone from the front to the back all the way down to the hard bony plate of the breast. At this point, the wishbone will have been partially uncovered from the breast; take the tip of your knife and run it down the breastbone on each side, keeping the blade parallel to the breastplate as you do. Then follow the ribs around to the bottom of the bird and cut the breasts free on each side. Set the breasts aside.

5. Now, using both hands, grasp the "knees" of the legs and press them down toward the cutting board to pop the legs out of their sockets. Grasp one leg and use the tip of your knife to free the base of the thigh from the pelvis/back of the bird. Do this on the other side, then toss the carcass into the roasting pan and place the pan in the oven to brown, about 1 hour.

6. Separate the drumsticks from the thighs by cutting through the knee of each. Wrap all the pieces in Ziploc bags (press all the air out before sealing). Fresh turkey will keep in the fridge for about 2 days and freezes well for 2 to 3 months.

7. When the bones are ready, throw them into a large pot filled with cold water and bring to a boil over high heat. Turn down the heat to low and simmer the bones for 8 hours.

8. Remove the bones, then strain the stock and let cool. Refrigerate for 1 week or freeze for up to 4 months.

1 whole turkey

SPECIAL EQUIPMENT
Cutting board
Cut-proof gloves, (see Note, page 23) or disposable gloves
5-inch boning knife

HOW TO HAVE A STRESS-FREE THANKSGIVING

Perhaps no holiday issue is more fraught than the freaked-out-over Thanksgiving turkey. That one meal holds all our emotional baggage concerning family, friends, and the stress of the season. And so, in the name of creating the perfect bird, we obsess over heritage breeds, brines, under-skin butters, times, temperatures, and much more. I even know some bastards who flip the turkey mid-roast and apply bags of ice to the breasts. Please. Stop. Take a deep breath and decide to relax and maybe even have a little fun cooking for your holidays this year.

First of all, excuse me for saying this, but turkey, even when done the best it can be, is *just not that good*. I'm not saying you should replace your holiday turkey with lobes of foie gras or porterhouse steaks, but I'd just like everyone to be honest and lower the bar a little. Admitting that what you're really attempting is to channel all the glory of American history by elevating a humble, relatively bland beast to the heights of culinary excellence is the first step toward sanity. Second, remember that this is not any of your guests' first rodeo. Chances are that no matter how badly you may botch the job of cooking your bird, the people sitting around your dining table have eaten *much* worse. Guaranteed, someone in the room has attended a Thanksgiving dinner so heinous that they ended up ordering takeout at a Chinese restaurant. Are you feeling a little less anxious? Great! Now you can begin to plan a stress-free day of thanks.

But let's talk first about what is really important: booze and snacks. A hungry guest who cannot find a drink is an angry guest. A hungry guest who drinks but has nothing to soak it up is a guest who's at risk of feeling up someone's roommate. Protect yourself and your holiday: have booze and snacks at the ready. Start a party with the nice stuff, to reward the guests who show up on time, then break out the box wine later, during the loud, close-talker portion of the evening's program.

About the bird: What kind of turkey you purchase is bound up in personal convictions and identity politics. Whether you get a supermarket turkey or a pedigreed pastured bird that had its feet rubbed down with artisan cider every evening, just know what you're buying and plan accordingly. If you have an industrial Butterball-type of bird, you can get away with roasting it hard and fast at 425°F. If you choose a pastured, heritage, or wild turkey, you'll have to brine it for at least a day and roast it at or below 325°F for much longer to allow its firmer flesh to become tender. Figure out how early in the morning to get up to start cooking your precious showpiece, and maybe add on an extra hour for the sake of sanity.

Stuffing naturally follows the turkey, and all I can say is: please, please, please do not put your stuffing in the turkey. I know all the flavor and tradition arguments are pro–turkey stuffing, and I don't care. Find your flavor somewhere else and keep it out of the cavity of your bird. Why am I so staunchly antistuffing? Time, pure and simple. All stuffing is different, and any of it will screw with your planned roasting time and thus add an element of the unknown to the equation. Stuffing causes randomness, and randomness causes stress. Keep stress out of your turkey.

As for what side dishes to serve, I suggest you stay focused on the classics. I have seen the most creative and forward-minded line cook nearly reduced to tears upon learning that there were no sweet potatoes with marshmallows at the table. Don't be the person who makes somebody cry because you couldn't resist putting bottarga in the stuffing or decided to replace mashed potatoes with a roasted root vegetable puree. Give the people what they want. Try to keep the bold-flavor-foodie thing in your pants, stock up on Bell's poultry seasoning, and embrace all that is mediocre and amazing about your mother's back-of-the-box stuffing recipe.

Finally, whatever you do, remember that Thanksgiving really isn't about you, it's about *them*. Keep your guests boozed up and free from hunger, and don't screw up their beloved holiday dishes, and you're 80 percent of the way to loosening the icy grip of fear that torments all cooks as they lie in bed the night before Thanksgiving. Keep it simple. Keep it safe. Maybe even take a Xanax and truly enjoy the warm glow of having a house full of crazy people.

ROASTING THE BIRD

Roasting a turkey can get complicated. *Very complicated.* But I figure if you're reading this book and not some treatise on culinary foams, you'd like the process to get simpler. We can do that.

First, it's a good idea to brine your bird. You don't have to. Your mom probably got along pretty well without doing it, but brining does make roasting a bird a little more forgiving—and it's especially recommended if you're using a heritage or wild turkey. Things you should know if you choose to brine your turkey: (1) your bird will take a little longer to cook, so plan on an extra hour or so if you brine; (2) your pan drippings will be saltier than normal, so make sure you have extra turkey stock on hand to dilute it with if you're using it to make your gravy; and (3) you will need to bump your heat up earlier to get crispy skin, because after soaking in brine for 12 hours, the skin will be much wetter than it would otherwise be.

To make a brine, fill a pot with hot water from the tap and vigorously stir in enough salt and sugar to make it slightly saltier than you'd like: ⅓ cup sugar and 1 cup kosher salt for every 10 cups of water. Then add 6 cups of ice cubes to cool it down. Feel free to omit the sugar (though it helps with browning and meat texture), and add whatever herbs you like before adding the ice. About 2 gallons of brine should be more than enough for most birds.

Rather than take all the precious room in the refrigerator, I suggest you brine the bird over ice. The night before the holiday, place the bird in a brining bag with the brine, place it in a 5- to

7-gallon bucket or other appropriately sized leakproof container, and cover the whole thing with ice. No matter what anyone tells you, don't brine a bird for more than 24 hours. After the one-day mark, you're rapidly giving your turkey a weird cured-ham sort of texture that is yucky.

On the big day, set your alarm for about four hours before you're going to start cooking. Pull the turkey out of the brine, and let it sit out at room temperature somewhere safe from your cat or dog, to warm up and dry off. Does this make you feel uncomfortable? You should have bought a nice, clean pastured bird instead of that antibiotic bomb, shouldn't you? Don't worry; the turkey will be fine. Letting it come to room temperature will make it cook more evenly (less thermal inertia and stuff) as well as crisp up better (the skin won't be waterlogged).

After you've had your first cup of coffee, pull out some butter to soften up (I like to make a fresh herb butter the night before: 1 cup chopped fresh herbs, such as sage, thyme, savory, or marjoram, mashed into 1/2 pound softened unsalted butter). Use paper towels to blot off any remaining moisture on the bird.

Once the time to roast your turkey has come, preheat the oven to 325°F and give the turkey a butter/herb/salt/pepper/poultry seasoning/whatever rubdown, loosening the breast skin and getting some butter under it as well. Plop the turkey into a roasting pan and throw it in the oven.

How about some cooking times, you say? Unless you're cooking up a baby-dinosaur-sized bird, four hours is a good standard cooking time. I like to add about an hour safety gap just in case any number of other potential mishaps throw off your dinner plan. If you get ahead of schedule, you can pull your bird out of the oven and let it rest covered on the kitchen counter.

Right about the time that the bird is getting close to done (you're aiming for 165° to 175°F in the thigh), crank the oven up to 425°F to crisp up the skin. If the turkey is sharing the oven with pies and whatnot, this might not be an option, but at least try to turn up the heat. Be warned! It's usually about this time that everyone has had a decent amount of wine and is getting rowdy, so make sure you set a timer for 40 minutes to remind yourself to take the bird out of the now-blazing oven.

When is the turkey done? I pull my turkey out of the oven when the leg/thigh gets really wiggly to the point that I feel like I could almost pull it off the turkey. Most food professionals will consider this overcooked, but it's the way I like my turkey. Again, for me, simpler is always better.

Last, let your turkey have a rest with a foil tent over it. About 20 minutes should be fine, but go longer if it's huge. Keep in mind that the turkey will carryover cook by 5 to 10 degrees, so plan accordingly if you're a temperature queen.

Once the turkey has rested, carve away! Unless you've carved many a holiday turkey, I find it's best to do this task in the relative safety of the kitchen. I like to take off the breasts using a 5-inch boning knife (it's *much* easier) and then slice them with a very sharp chef's knife. If you aren't sure your boning knife is up to the task, use a serrated bread knife to get through the tough skin cleanly and then finish with a chef's knife. The thigh bones can be pulled out by hand and then the meat sliced like the breast, across the grain. In the event that you completely blow the carving part or you've overcooked your turkey, just pour gravy over the meat on a platter and sprinkle a bunch of fresh herbs over the top. No one will know but you.

GARLIC MASHED RED-SKINNED POTATOES

I think anyone who loves food and cooking has had a moment that changed him from a person who likes to eat into a person who is really interested in food. For me, it was the first time I ever ate New American food, or at least what stood in for New American food in my hometown of Orange, California.

The restaurant was called the Citrus City Grill, and it opened in the old town circle. I had just gotten my financial aid check, allowing me to take my girlfriend there for her birthday despite the bill's being what we would normally spend on two weeks of groceries. I had the salmon and she had the roast chicken, and while my meal was completely serviceable, what ended up turning my head around was not the herb roast chicken (*fresh* herbs?) but the garlic mashed red-skinned potatoes. My mind was blown that something so good could be assembled out of the workaday boiling potatoes I had eaten for dinner nearly every night of my pre-pubescent life. Deeply moved and inspired, I set to figuring out how to make those potatoes at home.

However, in my early twenties, I had absolutely no idea how to cook, let alone develop a recipe. My movements in the kitchen were gross pantomimes of things I'd seen on cooking shows, and the long and short of what I knew about "gourmet" food was that it involved butter, wine, garlic, and a large pepper mill. Not being able to afford a pepper mill, I set to work with my meager quiver of culinary arrows. After stealing a Styrofoam soda cup of white wine and several heads of garlic from my pizza delivery job, I dutifully chopped potatoes with my Ginsu, minced garlic, and used the only fancy cooking technique I knew, marinating the potatoes in white wine, garlic, and salt for an hour before boiling the whole mess and then mashing in butter and sautéed garlic. To my surprise, the results were fucking delicious!

Fast-forward ten years to a time when I actually knew how to cook, and I still marveled at just exactly how such an ill-conceived dish continued to work despite all of the nonsensical bullcrap it had going on. As much as I can figure, this recipe works because

5 pounds red-skinned potatoes, scrubbed and quartered
1 head garlic, separated into cloves and peeled
1 bottle (750 ml) dry white wine, such as Pinot Grigio
Kosher salt
1/2 pound (2 sticks) unsalted butter, softened
One 8-ounce container sour cream
1 bunch scallions or chives, or 1/2 bunch of each, finely chopped
Freshly ground black pepper

SPECIAL EQUIPMENT
Immersion blender, potato ricer, or potato masher

the acidity of the wine lightens, brightens, and generally makes the garlic and potato flavors pop and keeps the butter from making the whole thing greasy. What follows is a more refined version of the original. Make it for Thanksgiving or on any old Thursday night. Either way, I think you'll agree that it's delicious, even if the recipe doesn't make much sense.   **SERVES 8 TO 10**

1. Start by throwing the potatoes, half the garlic, half the white wine, and a handful of salt into a large pot filled with cold water. Bring to a boil over high heat, then turn the heat down to a simmer and cook for about 1 hour, adding a few glugs of wine to the pot every 15 minutes or so.

2. While the potatoes cook, roughly chop the remaining garlic. Add the garlic to a medium saucepan along with the butter, and melt the butter over low heat for 10 minutes or so. Remove from the heat and keep warm.

3. Once the potatoes are easily pierced with a fork or knife, drain, place them back in the pot, and mash in the sour cream, scallions, and butter/garlic mixture. I use an immersion blender for this task, but you can stay classy and use a potato ricer to rice the potatoes into the pot, or an old-fashioned potato masher, if you want. Stir in pepper to taste, and add some more salt if needed. Serve hot.

FOIE GRAS GREASE GRAVY
(and Seared Foie Gras)

My friend Millicent and I were cooking Thanksgiving dinner for three other people at a friend's house a few years back, and someone brought a lobe of foie gras to cook as an appetizer. After we had seared off slices of the fatty duck liver, we were left with half a cup of foie gras fat in the pan. Millicent, being the thrifty line cook that she is, decided to make that fat the base for the gravy roux. It was delicious, and it used up something decadent that would have normally gone in the trash.

The best part of this recipe is that the gravy can be made before the bird is finished cooking, as you don't have to wait for the drippings. It's a big help not to have to make your gravy at the last minute, when you're trying to get everything else ready to serve. Plus, you and your guests get to eat foie gras, which ain't bad.   **SERVES 8 TO 10**

1 lobe duck foie gras, about 1 pound
Kosher salt
$1/2$ cup all-purpose flour
4 cups turkey stock (see page 192),
    at room temperature
One 16-ounce can cheap pilsner beer
1 teaspoon poultry seasoning,
    preferably Bell's
1 teaspoon freshly ground black pepper

SPECIAL EQUIPMENT
Chef's knife

1. Place the lobe of foie gras on a cutting board. You're going to be slicing the lobe into $1^{1}/4$-inch-thick slices, but in between each slice you're going to need to run your chef's knife under hot water for 20 seconds to heat it up and allow it to make clean slices.

2. Once you've sliced the foie gras, put a large sauté pan over high heat and season the slices liberally with salt while the pan gets hot. When your pan is so hot that a drop of water dances across the surface (about 3 minutes over high heat), sear the slices in batches, cooking 2 slices at a time and searing them for 45 seconds per side. Transfer the cooked slices to a plate to serve to your guests as an appetizer. You should have about $1/2$ cup of grease left in the pan.

3. Reduce the heat to low and whisk in the flour a little at a time. Keep whisking the roux for 3 to 4 minutes, until it darkens slightly. At this point, you want to slowly whisk in your turkey stock and cheap beer a bit at a time, whisking until all the liquid is incorporated. Add the poultry seasoning and pepper and whisk for another 15 or 20 seconds. Taste the gravy and add salt if necessary. Remove from the heat and set aside, covered, until needed.

4. Rewarm the gravy for 5 minutes over low heat and transfer to a gravy boat to serve.

STUFFING

In keeping with the relaxed, foolproof theme of my holiday bird primer, this stuffing recipe is basic, traditional, and easy. If you are at all worried about ruining your stuffing, then stash some Stove-Top instant stuffing somewhere in the kitchen in case of emergency. I am not kidding. **SERVES 8 TO 10**

1 large or 2 smaller loaves of really good bread, cut into stuffing-sized (1-inch) pieces
1 tablespoon kosher salt, or to taste
1 teaspoon freshly ground black pepper, or to taste
1/2 cup oil (peanut, olive, or vegetable)
2 tablespoons poultry seasoning, preferably Bell's, or to taste
4 celery ribs, chopped
1 large onion, minced
2 tablespoons peanut oil
2 quarts turkey stock (see page 192) or dark chicken stock

1. The day before the meal (or even several days before), preheat the oven to 375°F.

2. Put the cubed bread into an extra-large mixing bowl. Sprinkle on the salt, pepper, 1/2 cup oil, and poultry seasoning and toss the bread thoroughly until fully coated. Spread the bread evenly on two baking sheets and bake until crispy, about 40 minutes. Don't overdo it; it's better to have light brown bread cubes than ones with black bitter edges. Set aside to cool completely. Don't be alarmed if the bread is still a little soft—it will firm up as it cools. Once the bread cubes are cool, you can store them in a Ziploc bag at room temperature until needed; they keep for about 1 week.

3. The morning of your meal, in a large skillet, sauté the celery and onion in the 2 tablespoons peanut oil over medium heat until the onions are halfway translucent, about 7 minutes. Toss the onions and celery into that same extra-large mixing bowl, add the bread, and toss again. Set aside.

4. When you're 1 1/2 to 2 hours out from turkey time, heat the stock in a large saucepan over high heat until warm, about 5 minutes. Then start lightly pouring it over your bread and vegetable mixture, tossing well. Taste for seasoning; now would be a good time to add some salt/extra poultry seasoning/pepper if needed. Pour some more stock in and then mix thoroughly. Pour and mix until just before you think you have enough liquid, then stop. The stuffing should be moist but not soggy, and each piece of bread should still be separate and distinct. Remember, you can always add more stock later, but you can't remove it. Allow the stuffing to sit for 15 minutes, then add some more stock and/or salt if needed.

5. Load the stuffing into a buttered baking dish or a slow cooker. If you're baking it in the oven, you only need to make the top of your stuffing crispy by giving it a good blast at 425°F for 20 to 30 minutes, right after the bird comes out of the oven to rest. If you're using a slow cooker, just set the cooker to low and let it cook for 20 or 30 minutes. If you're running late, turn off the cooker, and the stuffing will be nice and warm for at least an hour.

6. Stuffing, like most things, will look fancy if you sprinkle some fresh herbs on top right before the big reveal.

Turkey

TURKEY TAMALE PIE

Invariably, after the holiday crush, we're left with a good number of unclaimed turkeys that find their way into the freezers of The Meat Hook. So we're left to thaw, debone, and grind up these stragglers for packages of ground turkey.

When I was growing up, my stepmother didn't do much cooking, preferring to let my dad clatter around in the kitchen making a mess and pumping out Quixote-worthy dishes of his own conception. Occasionally, though, she would disappear into the kitchen and emerge an hour later with this dish, which I'm assuming was a synthesis of her casserole-loving Wisconsin upbringing and the decade or so she'd spent living in Las Cruces, New Mexico. This is a great low-maintenance dish, using ground turkey (or ground pork, veal, beef, or chicken, for that matter).   **SERVES 4 TO 6**

1. To make the crust, place the cornmeal, cold water, chili powder, and salt in a medium saucepan and cook over medium heat, stirring, until thick, about 10 minutes. Add the butter and cheese and give it a quick stir to melt the butter, then remove from the heat and set aside.

2. To make the filling, place a large skillet over medium heat and add the oil. Allow the oil to heat for 30 seconds, then add the onions and garlic and sauté until fragrant and soft but not brown, 5 to 7 minutes. Add the turkey and cumin and cook, stirring often and breaking up any clumps of meat, until the turkey is lightly browned and cooked through, about 10 minutes.

3. Preheat the oven to 375°F.

4. Add the flour to the turkey and stir until everything gets gluey, 1 to 2 minutes, then add the corn, chiles, tomato sauce, and water. The mixture should have the texture of chili; if it is a little thin, simmer over low heat for another 20 minutes to thicken it. Taste and season with salt and pepper. Remove from the heat.

5. Dump the meat mixture into a medium casserole dish (there's no need to grease the dish) and level it out using a spoon. Top the filling with an even layer of the crust mixture, and more cheese if you like. Bake for 40 minutes, or until the crust is golden brown on top and a knife inserted into the crust comes out clean.

6. To serve, spoon into bowls and top individual servings with the sour cream, black olives, more green chiles, and perhaps salsa. Serve with ice-cold Tecate and limes.

FOR THE CRUST
1 cup yellow cornmeal
2 cups cold water
1 teaspoon chili powder
$1/2$ teaspoon kosher salt
1 tablespoon unsalted butter
$1/2$ cup shredded pepper Jack cheese, plus (optional) more for topping the casserole

FOR THE FILLING
2 tablespoons oil (olive, peanut, whatever)
1 medium onion, chopped into small dice
2 garlic cloves, minced
1 pound ground turkey
1 tablespoon cumin seeds, toasted and finely ground
2 tablespoons all-purpose flour
1 cup fresh or frozen corn kernels
One 4-ounce can chopped roasted green Hatch chiles or the like
$1/2$ cup tomato sauce or salsa
$1/2$ cup water
Kosher salt and freshly ground black pepper

TOPPINGS
About $1/2$ cup sour cream
About $1/4$ cup sliced black olives
Salsa (optional)

THE ROEBLING TEA ROOM

The Roebling Tea Room had a strange genesis as a restaurant project. It was started by Syd "Squid" Silver, who had decided to give up her life on the road as the bassist for the popular 1990s female assault band the Lunachicks, and it was originally cheffed by Stephen Tanner, bassist for the art metal band Harvey Milk. Stephen, who would later open Pies-'n'-Thighs and the Commodore nearby, chose for his sous-chef of sorts his friend photographer Dennis Spina. Tanner left after not too long to follow his culinary fiddle foot and tour with Harvey Milk, leaving Dennis, who had no formal training as a cook, in charge of the food for the eighty-seat restaurant.

After a few years, the Tea Room had been transformed from a third-run brunch place to one of the most interesting restaurants in Brooklyn, if not all of New York City. Spina read cookbooks obsessively, experimented extensively, and continued the Tanner legacy by never hiring anyone who had actually been trained to cook. The result is a strange mixture of Jersey-Shore-meets-Thomas-Keller, with macrobiotic vegetable-juiced ceviches topped with deep-fried leeks and mountainous burgers served "all-the-way" with whopper sauce and a fried egg.

My relationship with Dennis began after he was left in charge of the Tea Room. He would come by around the time I got off work at Marlow & Sons to ask me where to get the more exotic stuff he wanted to mess around with. Our relationship evolved as we jerked and stumbled through implementing "the Program" at the Tea Room. The Program was a harebrained scheme whereby I would take the bus to Fleisher's butcher shop in Kingston, New York (which I was selling meat for on the side), to cut a side of local beef on my only day off from butchering at Diner to sell to Dennis, in an effort to raise money for my wedding. The most memorable moments of that period, a weird summer where it seemed to rain every Friday at around 6 p.m., were the weekly sprints from my job at Diner to the Tea Room's back patio, where I would frantically cut up and portion an 85-pound lamb using only basic hand tools in a desperate race against the inevitable early evening rain showers.

We've both come a long way since those good old days. We're now both business owners, Dennis having opened the River Styx, his new wood-oven mother ship, which we supply with Meat Hook meat. Despite the years that have passed, the Tea Room remains at the center of many of the nights and days of my life; it's where I get out of the cab from the airport, luggage in hand, to have a drink. It's a true home away from home.

BASTILLE DAY

Somewhere, hiding in plain sight, at the bottom of each daily menu at the Tea Room is the countdown to the next Bastille Day. Dennis, an Italian from New Jersey, just loves the shit out of all things French, and Bastille Day is what he loves the most. Normally he's a pretty disciplined chef, making sure that creativity does not come at the detriment of food costs, but on that one special night a year, a big middle finger is raised to frugality and profits. He serves dishes ranging from a simple plate of sliced ripe tomatoes drizzled with Armagnac to much more bizarre and sometimes punishing dishes like "Corn Washington" that can only be described as conceptual, but, you know, in the best possible sense.

ZERO

RUM OMELET 8	HEAD SAUCE GRIBICHE / SURROUNDED BY PARSLEY / $10.	TOMATOES IN ARMAGNAC / 10.
SALT COD BLACK BUTTER / 10.	OVERCOOKED BEANS / CREME FLEURETTE / $12.	OYSTERS WITH CHAMPAGNE POURED ON THEM / $3.
FRICADELLES BROTH / TOMATO / ROBERT SAUCE / $12.	CORN WASHINGTON EGG MEURETTE / $10.	RATATOUILLE $ 7.
ITALIAN BLOOD PASTES 1 2 .	CONSOMME CLAM AND PORK / WHITE MEAT FORCE MEAT / $8.	SHRIMP MERMAIDS COLD SALMON DRESSED / $12.

REGRETS

E $15.	CHEESE $16.	STEAK TARTAR ENTREE EDITION $22.
SWEETBREADS BUTTERPOACHED MUSHROOMS / SAUCE MAGNIFICENCE / MUSSELS $24	ZOO MEAT CAFÉ DE PARIS SAUCE / $40.	CHICKEN VERJUS AND MEDIEVAL SPICES / $23.
SOUSED TUNA PROVENCALE / $23.	BALTIMORE "TOURNEDOS" $ 2 3 .	BLOOD SAUSAGE SAUCE NANTUA / $23.
WHOLE ROAST DUCK WITH IT'S JUICES / DUCKFAT POTATOES / GIZZARDS / LIVERS / GARNISHES / CASSIS / $70.	STRIKER $ 1 6 .	GARBURE CHABROT / $23.

2013

Menu, For Now.

July 16th 2011 A.D.

Liberté

Ratatouille 6.
Egg Meurette / 4.
Heirloom Tomatoes in Armagnac / 10.
Devilled Cockscombs / 6.
Tongue With Sauce Romaine / 6.
White Anchovies That have been Sitting By a Fire 7.
Beef Cretons / 7.
Eagle Rock Oyster / 3.

Égalité

Snails in Soubise / 10.
Preserved Pigeon / 12.
Larded Meatballs in Broth / 9.
Estofinado / Salt Cod / Eggs / Walnut Oil / 10.
Bone Marrow / Croissant / Gribiche / 10.
Chicken Liver Pate / Sweet Chili Aspic / Garnishes / 9.
Mussels Cooked Over Pine Needles / Mayonnaise / 12.

Fraternité

Ask Us About The Sun King / 27.
Lamb Neck / Anchovy / Mustard / Red Wine Vinegar / 15.
Blood Sausage / Duck Fat Potatoes / Over Dressed Salad / 17.
Soused Swordfish / Eggplant / Tabil / Harissa / 10.
Rump Steak / Cooked on One Side / Bearnaise / Fries / 17.
Meat Ravioli / Cooked in Meat Juices / 15.
Wanderer's Chicken / Preserved Lemon / Olives / Rice / 17.
Duck Breast / Roasted Over Grape Vines / 15.
Le Cheese / Fries / 15.
Wild Striped Bass / Cucumber Hollandaise / 16.

Our meat is on a program.

CHRISTMAS PARTY

The year we opened The Meat Hook, Dennis thought it was a good idea to give us (broke, tired, and desperate) $750 to cater the Tea Room's Christmas party for the staff. What resulted from that single irresponsible decision can be seen in many of the more ridiculous recipes in this book, and, I'm just now realizing as I write this, went a long way toward shaping us as a shop.

DUCK

Ducks are a strange bird. They are pretty much the only bird with red meat (naturally red-colored flesh in its raw state) that we eat on a regular basis. With the exception of squab, geese, and the occasional ostrich burger, duck is pretty much *the* red-meat bird. How much does duck taste like beef or other more common red meats? Well, you can split a duck down the back, flatten it out, dry-age it suspended from a wire hanger, and cook it to medium-rare, and it'll become tender and flavorful just like a side of beef. You can't do that with a chicken.

Ducks are also much heartier than many of the other feathered friends we eat for dinner. Insulated by a layer of thick fat and equipped with waterproof feathers, they are extremely buoyant and are natural swimmers. While ducks have been bred to fit our purposes over the course of the past thousand or so years, we haven't changed them in any essential way from what they were ten thousand years ago. Although it's common to see ducks much like the ones we raise for the table softly quacking around a park pond or waddling comically across a roadway, we don't often see undomesticated birds that resemble chickens pecking around the edge of a public playground. Ducks are survivors, and I like that.

The relatively enormous amount of fat that a duck has allows it to float and keep warm, but it may also allow us to put on a few pounds. While chicken and turkeys might be the poster children for a low-fat-diet lifestyle, ducks are more like pigs, tempting us to indulge in all things rich, luscious, and fatty. Duck has a homey flavor that invites us to a land where it's always sweater weather and beach-body season is far, far away.

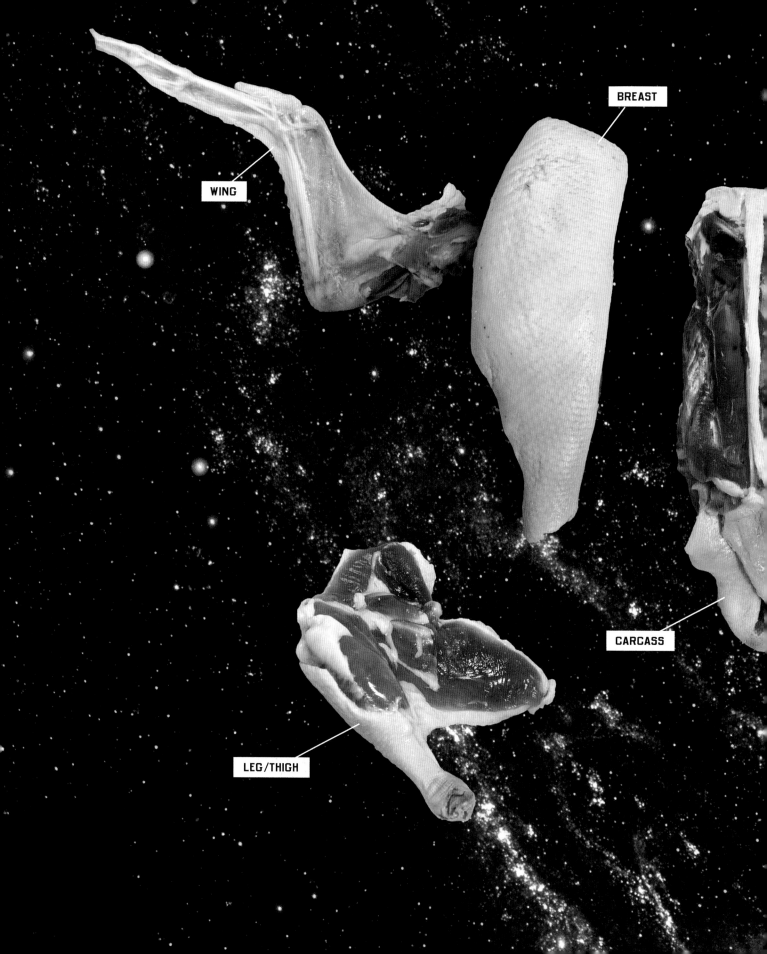

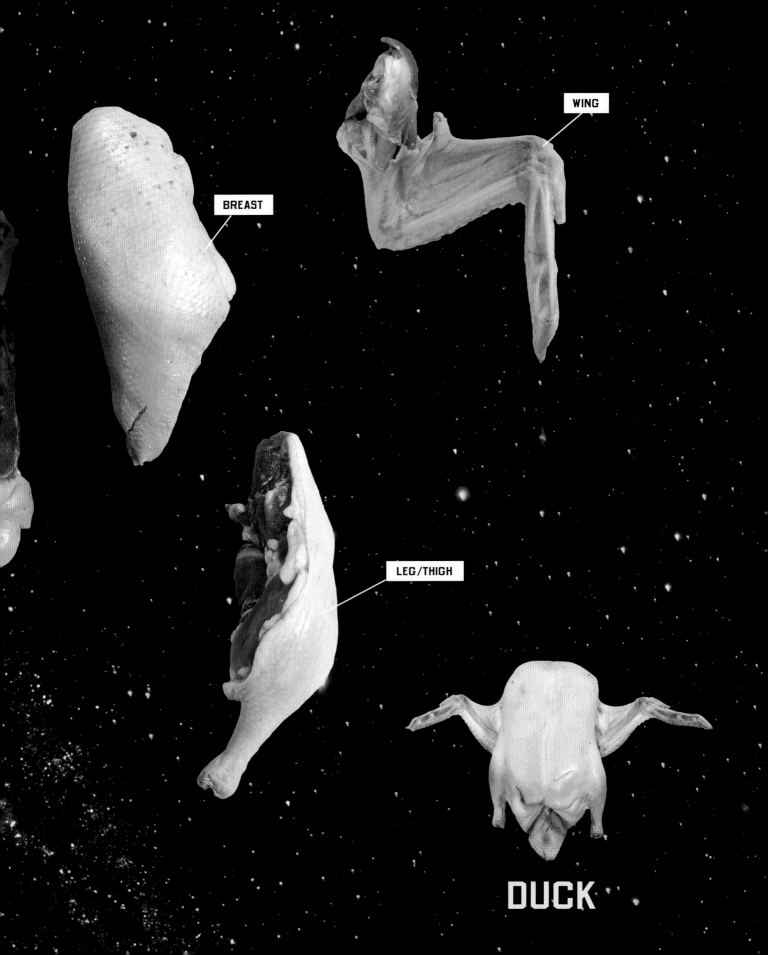

BREAST

WING

LEG/THIGH

DUCK

DUCK CUTS

Unlike chicken or turkey, ducks really only have two cuts, as the thigh and drumstick are pretty much never separated. Why this is, I can't really say, but I suspect that it has something to do with the small size of the drumstick.

BREAST

The duck breast is the main event: tender, fatty, expensive, and notoriously difficult to cook well. Few meats rival the New York strip cut of beef for dining luxury, but duck breast does. Besides being elegant, the breast is extremely versatile. It can easily be made into duck bacon by curing and smoking it, or even made into duck prosciutto by salting and air-drying. Try doing that with a New York strip!

LEG

Duck legs are rich, sticky, and lip smacking whether slow-roasted, confited in their own fat, or braised with herbs in wine. Because of a fair amount of connective tissue, they aren't well suited to being cooked hot and fast, but they can be cooked low and slow and then seared off in a hot pan to crisp the skin. Did I mention that they're cheap? If you have the palate of Brillat-Savarin but the pocketbook of a college student, the duck leg is your economy-class ticket to duck city.

HUDSON VALLEY FOIE GRAS

Hudson Valley Foie Gras is probably the most famous duck farm outside of France. It has been written up in *The New York Times* and seen on TV shows with the likes of Anthony Bourdain. They make some of the finest foie gras in all the land (don't let someone from Quebec hear you say that), and their products sell for a lot of money to the best restaurants on the East Coast and beyond. We, however, not being particularly fancy, buy the parts of their ducks that don't end up on TV— namely, the hearts, tongues, gizzards, fat, and legs.

Foie gras can be controversial, because to get ducks or geese with nice fat livers, the birds need to be force-fed twice a day, using a tube and a funnel filled with grain. It sounds pretty bad, but in reality, force-feeding is only as gruesome as the individual farmer makes it. I don't have a problem with foie gras, or at least not with the way Izzy Yanay and his lovely staff at Hudson Valley Foie Gras do it. We just don't sell very much of it except around the holidays.

Foie gras has become a sort of animal-rights whipping boy in the last few years, with bans or rumors of potential bans on its production becoming an easy way for politicians and animal rights people to act like they're doing something important. In fact, they're just targeting a tiny cottage industry made up largely of small family farms that don't have money for the high-priced lawyers that industrial meat producers have waiting in the wings.

Having visited Hudson Valley Foie Gras, I can attest that the animal welfare at these places is about 1,000 percent better than at any commercial laying hen or meat chicken operation I've seen. Izzy and other small foie gras farmers may have hundreds of birds in their spacious, well-lit, and well-ventilated barns at any given time. When you compare this to the thousands upon thousands of birds that may be jammed into a typical grocery-store meat-production facility, it seems pretty straightforward as to who should be getting banned and who should be left alone to muscle out an honest day's work doing something special.

HOW TO BUTCHER A DUCK
(AND RENDER THE FAT AND MAKE DUCK STOCK)

Breaking down a duck isn't much different from breaking down a chicken, but ducks are bigger, longer, and oddly shaped. When you butcher a duck, you want to be ready to render the fat too (you'll thank me later) and get some duck stock going as well.

1. Preheat the oven to 425°F, ready for roasting the bones for stock.

2. Put on your gloves and place the duck on a cutting board. Start by removing the duck's innards, if there are any. Put them in a Ziploc bag and throw it in the fridge to deal with later.

3. Use your boning knife to cut off the neck flap and the fat around the cavity to make it easier to remove the breasts and legs. Toss this fat into a small pot and set it over low heat to begin rendering the fat (for more on rendering fat, see page 260).

4. Next, run your fingers along one of the legs near where the legs meet the breast to make a clear determination of what is breast and what is leg—this is to make sure that when you cut the leg off, you're not removing the fat from the tip of the end of the breast, which would mess up its good looks. Then slice along the edge of the leg.

5. Once the fat has been freed from the leg, grab the bird by the leg so you can use its weight to help you remove it from the carcass and run your knife up the side of the back while applying tension to the leg, pulling it away from the body. This will ensure that you take all the good meat with you.

6. Once you've carved out the oyster, you'll run into a snag: the hip socket. Put the bird breast side down and wrench the leg free of the socket, pulling it up and toward you, finishing the move by nicking any tendons that are keeping it attached with your knife.

7. Pulling the leg toward you, use your knife to free up the last bit of leg meat. Do the same thing on the other side, and then move on to the breasts.

8. Just as when butchering a chicken, find the breastbone with your fingers and cut a slit on either side of it, keeping the cuts as close to the breastbone as possible.

9. Now, using long, shallow cuts, follow the breastbone and free up the breast on both sides. Be aware that unlike a chicken's, a duck's rib cage dips away suddenly to the interior just after the breastplate stops. Don't screw that up, or you'll be busting out the meat glue.

1 whole duck

SPECIAL EQUIPMENT
Cut-proof gloves (see Note, page 23)
   or disposable gloves
5-inch boning knife

10. Once you've freed the rear of the breast, you can carefully cut down the wishbone to the wing socket and nick around it until the breast is free. Don't worry, chances are you're going to fuck this up the first few times you do it. Don't take it personally—everyone sucks at breaking down ducks the first ten to twenty times! Repeat on the other side.

11. Put all the pieces in Ziploc bags (be sure to press all the air out before sealing). Fresh duck will keep in the fridge for about 2 days, and it freezes well for 2 to 3 months.

12. After you finish taking the meat off the carcass, trim the raggedy-looking pieces of fat off everything, cut all the fat off the carcass, toss it all into your rendering pot, and cook until the fat has shrunk by at least half and is light golden brown.

13. Place the carcass in a roasting pan and brown the bones, 30 to 40 minutes. Then throw the roasted bones into a large pot, cover with cold water, bring to a simmer, and simmer gently for 6 to 8 hours. Remove the bones, then strain the stock and let cool. Refrigerate for 1 week or freeze for up to 4 months.

14. Meanwhile, allow the rendered duck fat to cool for 20 to 30 minutes, then strain it through a fine-mesh sieve into a storage container. Cool completely before refrigerating or freezing it. The duck fat is good for 2 to 3 weeks refrigerated and indefinitely frozen.

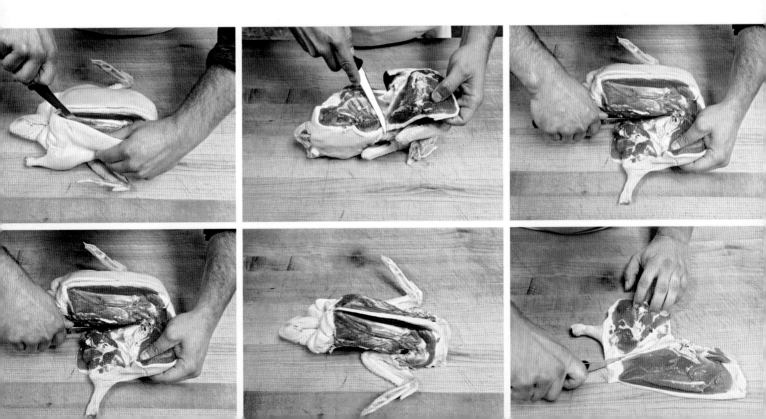

GRILLED DUCK HEARTS

This is a good recipe to make if you want to be the "cool offal-eatin' dude" in your group of friends, without having to pretend that eating beef liver doesn't make you want to run off to find a nice private spot to retch. Duck hearts, when properly handled, taste better than duck breasts and are infinitely cheaper and easier to cook to boot. They do require that you plot and scheme several days in advance to marinate them (the more time, the better). You simply cannot rush this step. Try to get away with just an hour or two of marinating, and it's a one-way trip to rubber-bullet city for you and your duck hearts. **SERVES 6 AS AN APPETIZER**

1. Rinse off the hearts, making sure to get out any blood that might be hiding inside, and pat dry.

2. Mix all the other ingredients in a large bowl, then toss the hearts and the marinade into a Ziploc freezer bag. Marinate in the refrigerator for 2 to 4 days. If you like playing with your food, you can flip the bag every day, but it doesn't really matter.

3. When you're ready to eat, get your grill going very hot.

4. Drain the duck hearts. If you're grilling small duck hearts (we use jumbo ones from Hudson Valley Foie Gras ducks [see Resources, page 305] that are 5 to 6 hearts to the pound), put them on skewers before grilling to prevent them from falling through the grate, and for easy flipping.

5. Use tongs to place the hearts on the grill, and turn them every minute or so—like most red-blooded things, duck hearts are perfect when cooked to medium-rare, with some red juices seeping out, so cook for 2 to 3 minutes per side.

6. Serve immediately.

Note: If you want to make more work for yourself, try stuffing the hearts with chorizo or another rustic sausage and then par-roasting them for 12 minutes at 350°F before grilling.

1¹/₂ pounds duck hearts

FOR THE MARINADE
¹/₄ cup grapeseed oil
¹/₄ cup olive oil
¹/₂ cup red wine vinegar
2 garlic cloves, minced
1 big rosemary sprig, leaves removed and roughly chopped
1 teaspoon crushed red pepper flakes
1 teaspoon kosher salt
1 teaspoon freshly ground black pepper

DUCK RILLETTES

There are some fancy people in the world who would like to make you feel like the average person is neither capable nor worthy of making this recipe. Screw them. I'll also assume that someone will say this recipe isn't totally authentic. My answer to that is I don't live in France and this is how I make it. Duck rillettes are a great thing to make when you buy a whole duck, cut off the breasts for one meal, and are stuck with the legs. **SERVES 6 TO 8 AS AN APPETIZER**

1. The night before you plan to serve the rillettes, place your duck legs in a non-reactive food-safe container. Put on your disposable gloves and rub the legs all over with the salt and quatre épices. Cover and refrigerate overnight.

2. The next day, preheat the oven to 275°F.

3. Place the duck legs, duck fat, garlic, and whole thyme sprigs in a baking dish that will just hold them all comfortably. Cover with two layers of foil and throw in the oven for about 3 hours. When the meat slips easily off the bone, you know it's ready (be careful of the hot steam when you check on the legs). Once you take the duck out of the oven, gingerly remove the foil, and cool for 45 minutes to an hour, until you can handle the legs comfortably with gloves.

4. Pour the duck fat into a medium bowl and throw in the thyme leaves to flavor the fat. Carefully pull the meat off the bones, keeping an eye out for small bones and such, then shred it into the bowl. Do the same with the skin if it's not too floppy. Squeeze out the garlic cloves from their skins and add to the bowl.

5. Mix with your hands (if you have a stand mixer, you can do this in there, using the paddle attachment on the lowest setting), making sure to squish everything together by squeezing the mixture. Once you have a cohesive blob of sorts, give the mixture a taste and add a few splashes of vinegar (sometimes I throw a little Texas Pete in too), salt, if needed, and pepper. You're looking for balance: the acid in the vinegar should make the fatty paste not seem greasy and also make the flavors pop. When you add salt, keep in mind that you're not going to be eating this hot, so you should make it a bit saltier than you would otherwise. If you're happy with the seasoning, proceed to mix the hell out of the mixture until it becomes almost a paste, then pack it tightly into jars or ramekins and refrigerate.

6. Take the ramekins out of the refrigerator 2 to 3 hours before you want to eat. This is a good snack for a hot summer night when you don't want to cook. Serve with Dijon mustard, cornichons, and saltines.

2 duck legs

2 tablespoons kosher salt, plus more to taste

1 tablespoon quatre épices (French 4-spice powder; see Note and Resources, page 305)

1 cup duck fat (see Resources)

2 to 4 garlic cloves, unpeeled

8 thyme sprigs, 3 left whole, leaves from remaining 5 removed and reserved

1 tablespoon sherry vinegar or red wine vinegar, or to taste

1 tablespoon hot sauce, such as Texas Pete, or to taste (optional)

Freshly ground black pepper

SPECIAL EQUIPMENT
Disposable gloves
Stand mixer with paddle attachment (optional)
2 pint-sized ramekins or glass jars

Note: Quatre épices, or French 4-spice powder, is equal parts ground ginger, pepper, and mace, with a couple of big pinches of ground cloves.

SMOKED DUCK HOWSEWICHES
with Longan Honey

This is a lot of work for a sandwich. **The first time we made these, they somehow got the name crackwich. You know, like crack cocaine, only a sandwich. However, once I sat down to write this recipe, I realized that (a) David Chang had trademarked any food with the word** *crack* **in it and (b) no food, no matter how addictive it is, is like crack. At all. Crack smells like burning socks that have been dipped in burning rubber. These sandwiches don't smell anything like crack, I assure you.** SERVES 4

1. Fire up your smoker so that it is cruising at around 275°F and add a handful of wood chips or a chunk of wood.

2. Using a boning knife, cut off all the fat flaps from the cavity end of your duck. Put the fat in a Ziploc bag and stick it in the freezer so you can render the fat later. Score the skin 1/8 to 1/16 inch deep with a sharp paring knife all over the breasts and legs and place the duck in the smoker, with the baffle open, so it will only be drying out and cooking, not smoking.

3. While your duck is in the smoker, make your mop and the sauce. For the mop, just whisk together all the ingredients in a small bowl and set aside.

4. For the sauce, combine all the ingredients in a small saucepan and bring to a simmer over low heat, stirring to dissolve the sugar. Reduce the heat and simmer slowly for 20 minutes. Let cool.

5. At this point, your duck should have started to render fat and be getting slightly golden on the edges. Using a natural bristle paintbrush, coat the duck with a layer of the mop, then flip the duck over. Add some wood to the smoker, close it up, dial in the baffle, and go away for 40 minutes. Repeat the mopping and flipping procedure every 40 minutes for about 4 hours.

Now bump up the heat of your smoker to 375°F. Or pull the duck out, place it in a medium roasting pan, and finish it in a preheated 375°F oven for 25 to 30 minutes. The duck should be starting to fall apart.

6. Let the duck rest while you get your sauce hot again. Carve the duck, making sure to get meat and skin in each slice, coat the slices in sauce, and serve in the hamburger buns, topped with the scallions and cilantro.

1 duck, about 5 pounds

FOR THE MOP
2 cups cider vinegar
1/2 cup longan honey (see Resources, page 305, or look for it at a Chinese grocery; or use regular honey)
1/4 cup light soy sauce
2 tablespoons Chinese 5-spice blend

FOR THE SAUCE
1 cup hoisin sauce
2 tablespoons cider vinegar
2 tablespoons Sriracha sauce
1 tablespoon brown sugar
An 8-pack of supermarket hamburger buns
1 bunch scallions, thinly sliced
1 bunch cilantro, leaves removed and very roughly chopped

SPECIAL EQUIPMENT
Smoker (see "Smokers," page 284)
Charcoal (not self-lighting)
3 pounds wood chips or chunks, preferably cherrywood
5-inch boning knife
Natural-bristle paintbrush

GRANDMA DESJARDINE'S ROAST MUSCOVY DUCK

If you asked my grandmother, there was really only one breed of duck that mattered and only one way to cook it. Whenever she was coming to visit during the holidays, I would dream about her roasted duck for weeks beforehand, fantasizing about stealing bits of crispy skin while the duck rested in the kitchen before she carved it. Don't walk away from this recipe because it's not fancy enough—it doesn't have to be fancy; it's really good. **SERVES 4 TO 6**

1 Muscovy duck, about 5 pounds
3 tablespoons kosher salt

SPECIAL EQUIPMENT
Cut-proof gloves (see Note page 23) or disposable gloves
5-inch boning knife
Kitchen twine

1. Preheat the oven to 325°F.

2. Put on your gloves. If your duck has a bunch of innards inside it, fish those out and set them aside to make gravy or something else, then rinse out the cavity with cold water and pat the whole bird dry with paper towels.

3. Put your duck on a cutting board and use your boning knife to cut off the huge neck skin flap and the glob of fatty skin near the cavity opening. (Just kind of make the duck look like a prepared chicken.) Score the skin ⅛ to ¹/₁₆ inch deep with a sharp paring knife all over the breasts and legs. I like to make a nice tight diamond pattern, but if the best you can muster is a bunch of uneven squares, that's fine.

4. Tie the ends of the drumsticks together snugly with kitchen twine. Holding the duck by the legs, like a handle, rub the salt liberally all over it.

5. Now throw it onto a roasting rack set in a roasting pan and stick it in the oven for about 1 hour.

6. After the hour is up, pull the duck out and, using your sharp knife, prick the skin all over to release the fat that has rendered but is still trapped in the skin. Make sure you get the back too! Put the duck back in the pan, back side up for even rendering/browning, and roast for another hour.

7. Repeat the same pricking and flipping procedure, and throw the duck back in to cook for another hour.

8. Pull the duck out of the oven and pour off the fat (save it in an old jelly jar or something equally grandma-like and store, covered, in the refrigerator). Crank up your oven to 425°F and put your bird back in for 25 to 30 minutes, to make it brown and crispy. Let rest for 5 minutes, while you herd everyone to the table, then carve and serve.

Duck

Brent loves to throw a barbecue. Really. He loves a barbecue like Andrew W.K. loves a party. His views here may not represent those of The Meat Hook. Especially the push-up contest part.

HOW TO THROW A BBQ

By Brent Young

I'd say 90 percent of butchering is really a dick-measuring contest. Everyone in the shop is constantly trying to one-up one another, and all butcher shops, in turn, are trying to one-up one another, which leads to a lot of ridiculous challenges. The same goes for barbecues. We're not talking "authentic" Texas, North Carolina, or Tex-Mex barbecue here, we're talking a party with Ice-Cold Dunks (page 238), Long Dong Buds (see page 15), and dosing your friend's hard lemonade with LSD. This is where we, The Meat Hook, flop our dong on the table and present to you the Man Steak (page 65). It's the steak to serve for the end-all, be-all of barbecue one-upmanship. If you bring a Man Steak to the table, you'll shut up your brother-in-law for the next six summers. Here's how to throw a party Meat Hook–style.

STEP ONE

The first key to a good barbecue is music. It's often neglected at a casual gathering, where the host thinks he can just throw on some tunes and everyone will be happy. This approach is negligent and stupid. Every party builds, and your music should reflect this. Your playlist should have waves and levels. Keep things chill at first, with some Doobie Brothers, Steely Dan, Mike Jones, and Todd Rundgren. Build with Soulja Boy, 36 Mafia, and Katy Perry. Yes, Katy Perry. This isn't the time to enlighten your friends about your obscure jazz flute collections. When everyone is really drunk, it's time to bring out the Wacka Flacka Flame and LMFAO. Fuckin' party, dude.

STEP TWO

Next is the food. Keep things simple. Buy one huge piece of meat (see Man Steak, above), and throw it on the grill. You only have one cooking surface, so you want to make your life as simple as possible. Half chickens, thick-cut pork shoulder chops (see The Inevitable Pork Chop, page 113), and Dinosaur Ribs (page 55) also fit the bill. Think simple. Think BIG.

STEP THREE

Make sure you have a cooler full of ice-cold cheap beer. Cheap beer is the secret to 98 percent of all good times. Don't get fancy, and don't waste your money on nicer beer. It's hot outside, so let your friends guzzle the cheap stuff.

STEP FOUR

Last but not least is competition. This is where fraternities actually get things right. You should always have a cornhole game or maybe some light archery or other competition going on during your barbecue. When I was in college, my roommate and I were too cheap to buy a set of horseshoes one Fourth of July, so we invented a very similar game we called Proximity Brick, using an old piece of rebar and a pile of bricks in our backyard. Get creative. Arm wrestling or push-ups will do just fine if you're in a pinch. Just keep the party going by whatever means necessary.

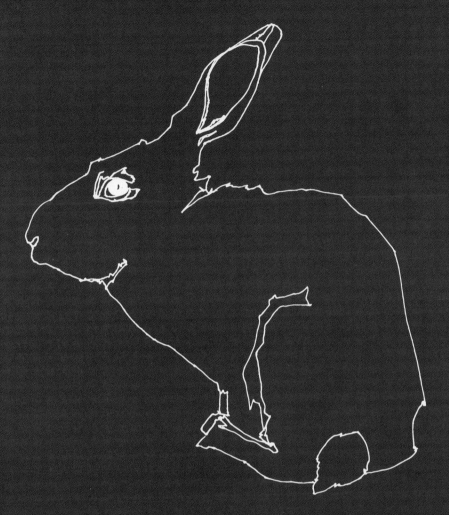

RABBIT

Rabbit has a way of making itself more intimately known to me than, say, chicken. We sell a lot of chickens, but no one gives them more than a passing thought. With rabbit, though, everyone from our farmer, a great character named John Fazio, to our barber, Gaspare, who will trade a haircut for a rabbit, really has a taste for these damned things.

If you've never eaten rabbit, you should. And if you've never tried cooking it, you must. Just remember rabbit is very lean and thus does not suffer being overcooked or in any way mishandled in the kitchen. But don't let that scare you away. Giving it a soak in buttermilk beforehand and keeping a little closer eye on it while it's cooking will go a long way toward making rabbit get into your blood too.

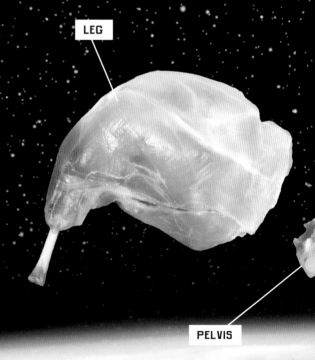

SHOULDER

LEG

PELVIS

RABBIT

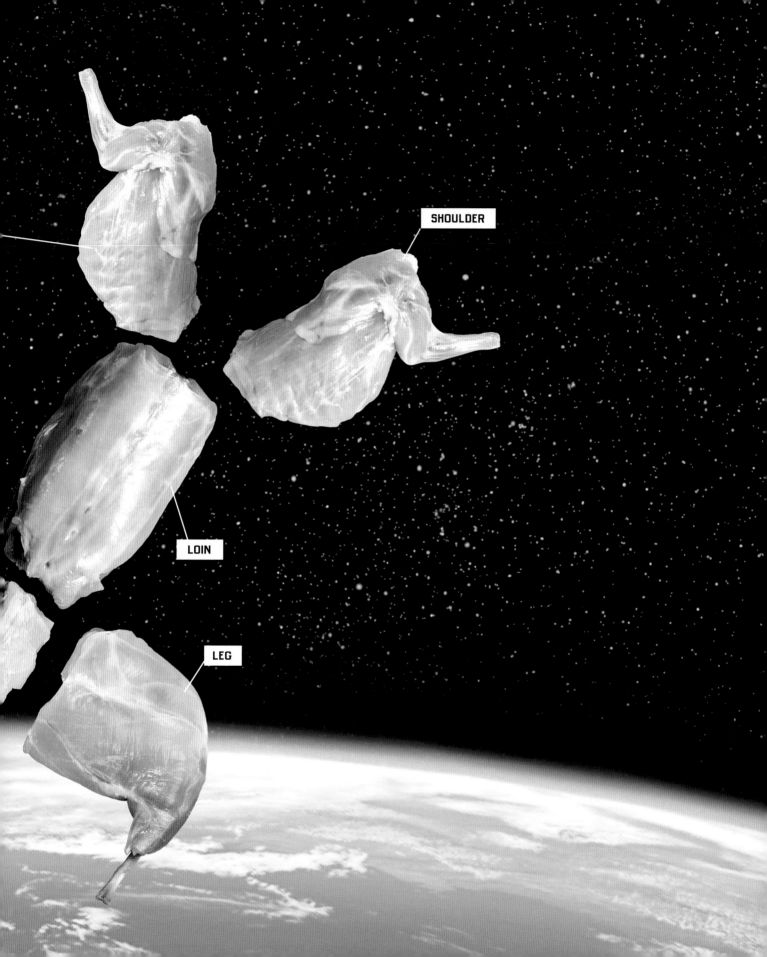

RABBIT CUTS

Rabbit is a really little critter compared to beef, lamb, and other four-legged animals, but it still has very distinctive cuts that reflect its larger relations' complexity. While it's expensive compared to, say, a chicken, a rabbit is really three different meals in one package. You can marinate and fry the legs, sauté the loin, and braise the shoulder—or just roast it whole. Add to that the long and varied history of rabbit preparation that includes nearly every country, region, and ethnic group around the globe, and you have more than just an animal on a cutting board, you have a passport to the past, present, and future of meat cookery.

LEG

Rabbit legs are the meatiest and most substantial cut and thus are the focus of most rabbit recipes. Many of these recipes recommend soaking the legs in buttermilk or yogurt or some other acidic liquid for hours before cooking. The practice harkens back to rabbit's roots as wild game, when soaking game was de rigueur, but soaking or marinating the leg is still a good idea, helping to break down the muscle and make it tender. It's especially important because the leg contains very little fat to make it juicy, so perfectly cooked legs are the only way to ensure juicy meat.

LOIN

When cooking rabbit loin I treat it like expensive diver scallops or medallions of beef tenderloin. It should be cooked quickly, with plenty of fat (like butter), over fairly high heat until it is just barely done. When in doubt, cook it less than you think—keep in mind that it will carryover cook for a few minutes after you remove it from the pan. The loin can be soaked or marinated, especially if you fear it may be tough, but make sure to rinse it off and pat it dry before it hits the pan.

SHOULDER

The shoulder is a solid braising cut because of its many muscles, connective tissue, and bones. It's important to use moist, moderate heat applied over a long period to make the meat tender and succulent instead of dry and stringy. One of my favorite methods is to gently poach the shoulder in duck fat until the meat starts to pull away from the bone, then brown it quickly in a hot pan using a bit of the poaching fat to get the meat to take on a bit of tasty color.

CHOOSING A RABBIT

We don't sell a lot of rabbit. I wish we did. I wish we could get wild hares with their fur still on. I also wish *The West Wing* were still on TV and that I could shoot lasers out of my eyeballs, but them's the breaks. When it comes to choosing a rabbit, I have only one absolute hard-and-fast rule for you: it must be fresh. While I suppose it's possible to produce rabbits in some sort of awful industrial nightmare concentration camp, most farmers who raise them do it more as a hobby than anything else and aren't willing to invest the money in a huge operation—mostly because Americans just don't eat much rabbit. We request that the rabbits we buy are killed the morning we get them, and if you've found a guy at your farmers' market to get rabbit from, you should do the same. If you're stuck somewhere where you can't get fresh rabbit, you can order it frozen online (see Resources, page 305). That is less desirable than fresh, but it's better than nothing. Whatever you do, do not buy frozen rabbit from a grocery store. You can be sure that it has been sitting in that freezer for a very long time (*see* "Americans just don't eat much rabbit," above).

Beyond being fresh, your rabbit should be plump and meaty looking. If the rabbit you're being offered is spindly and bony, move along, as it is likely to be tough and stringy. Rabbit doesn't have much fat, but a good rabbit should have one-eighth-inch-wide streaks of fat where the hind legs and the body meet.

HOW TO BUTCHER A RABBIT

Butchering a rabbit is pretty satisfying: all you need is a rabbit, a cutting board, a knife, and ten minutes of your time to turn a carcass into three distinct cuts. Here are the basics, but keep in mind that this is a starting point. There are innumerable butchering techniques from other chapters that you can apply to these basic cuts. Let your imagination run wild, and when you're comfortable, try your hand at deboning, stuffing, and rolling. Great things come in small packages.

1. Put on your gloves, set up your cutting board, and grab your rabbit. Look inside the cavity for the liver and kidneys. Pull these out and discard them (or feed them to your cat). Could you do something useful with them? Well, yes, but really, what are you going to do with one tiny liver and two minuscule kidneys?

2. Use your chef's knife to cut through the body of the rabbit where the legs and the loin meet. Next, splay out the rear legs and split them right down the middle.

3. Place your knife directly behind the rib cage, where it meets the loin, and cut through the body again. Last, split the rib cage and shoulder down the middle, like you did with the rear legs.

4. Place all the pieces in a nonreactive food-safe container, cover, and refrigerate until you need them. Or wrap in Ziploc bags (be sure to press all the air out). Rabbit will keep for 2 to 3 days in the refrigerator, and freezes well for 2 to 3 months.

1 rabbit, 3 to 4 pounds

SPECIAL EQUIPMENT
Cut-proof gloves (see Note page 23)
    or disposable gloves
8- to 10-inch chef's knife
Medium nonreactive food-safe container

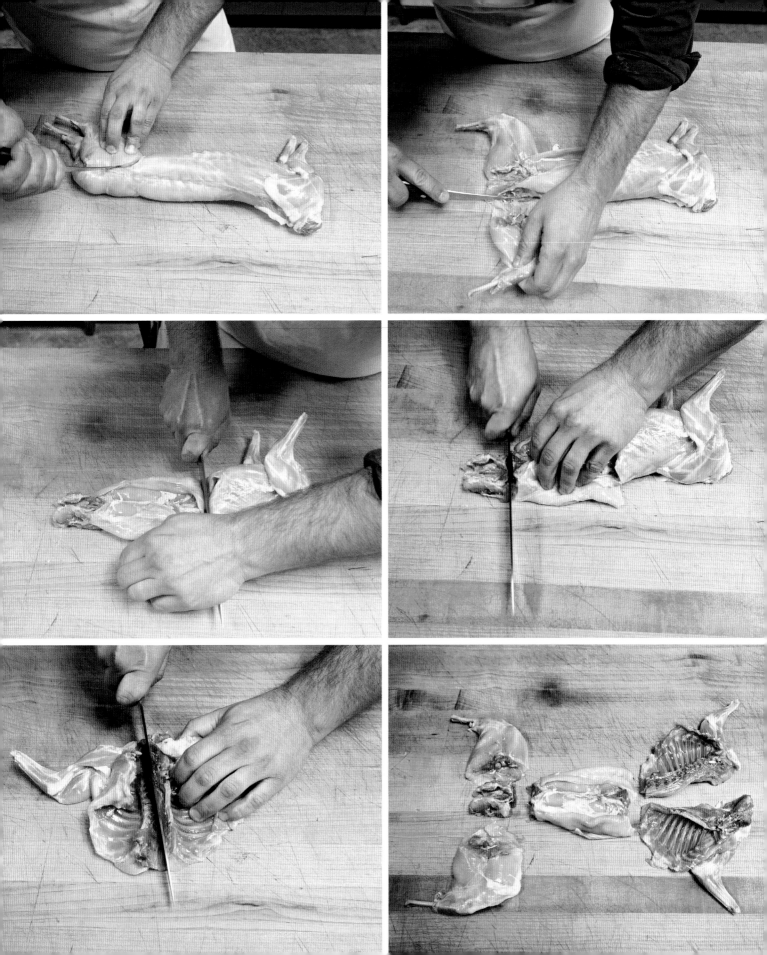

RABBIT RAGOUT

I hate little pieces of bone in my food. I know, butchers are supposed to be savages, eating raw beef, sucking out marrow, and drinking pigs' blood, but, seriously, tiny bones just really gross me out. With that in mind, this recipe is not a completely traditional ragout, with the bones left in. You braise the rabbit in the sauce most of the way there, then pull it out, cool it off, and take the meat off the bones before you finish it.   SERVES 4 TO 6

1 cup all-purpose flour
2 tablespoons kosher salt, or to taste
1 teaspoon freshly ground black pepper,
    or to taste
3 tablespoons olive oil
1 rabbit, 3 to 4 pounds, cut into 6 pieces
    (see "How to Butcher a Rabbit,"
    page 230)
1 onion, finely chopped
2 celery ribs, finely chopped
1 carrot, peeled and finely chopped
4 garlic cloves, minced
3 to 4 thyme sprigs
4 sage leaves
One 28-ounce can crushed tomatoes
2 cups Basic Brown Stock (page 243)

1. Combine the flour, salt, and pepper in a medium bowl and mix well.

2. Put a medium Dutch oven over medium-high heat and add the olive oil. While the oil heats, dredge the rabbit pieces in the seasoned flour. Place 3 pieces at a time in the hot oil and brown well, 3 to 4 minutes a side. Transfer to a plate.

3. Add the onion, celery, carrot, garlic, thyme, and sage to the pot, drop the heat down to medium-low, and cook, stirring every few minutes, for about 45 minutes, until the vegetables are soft and caramelized.

4. Add the tomatoes, stock, and browned rabbit and bring to a bare simmer over low heat. Cover and cook for 1½ hours, or until the meat is just beginning to fall off the bones.

5. Pull the rabbit pieces out using a slotted spoon and set aside on a plate to cool for 10 to 15 minutes. Cover the pot again and allow the sauce to continue cooking.

6. Once the rabbit is cool enough to touch, pull all of the meat off the bones; discard the bones. Return the meat to the pot and simmer for another 30 minutes or so to allow the meat and sauce to marry. Taste and adjust the seasoning. Serve the rabbit over Drop Dumplings (recipe follows) or pasta (ideally homemade), with a good bottle of Beaujolais.

DROP DUMPLINGS
MAKES 4 CUPS
3 cups all-purpose flour
4 large eggs
2 teaspoons kosher salt

Fill a 12-quart pot with 8 quarts of water and bring to a boil over high heat. Meanwhile, combine the flour, eggs, and salt in a large bowl and mix thoroughly with a dinner fork for 1 to 2 minutes, or until the batter is very difficult to stir.

When your water is at a boil, using two large soupspoons or the like, scoop up a spoonful of batter and use the second spoon to push the batter off and into the boiling water. (This should sort of feel like you're making the batter walk the plank.) Continue doing this with the rest of the batter, then boil the dumplings until they have all floated to the surface, indicating that they're done. Turn off the heat and let the dumplings sit in the water until you're ready to plate the ragout (they can sit for several hours). Use a slotted spoon to transfer the dumplings to your serving platter—draining them in a colander and then transferring them to the platter will make them both cold and ugly.

HASENPFEFFER

The first real farm-to-table restaurant I ever ate in was a strange little place in Greenpoint, Brooklyn, called The Queen's Hideaway, owned by Liza Queen. The entire kitchen ran out of a used home refrigerator, with extra cold storage in Liza's own refrigerator in her apartment next door. Every morning, Liza and her sous-chef, my friend Millicent Souris, would go to the farmers' market to buy meat and vegetables, spend all day prepping, and cook all night.

The food was good, but the neighborhood wasn't ready for the spot, and fatigue and money issues forced The Hideaway to close. Liza moved to Vietnam to cook, and Millicent and I became drinking buddies. Years passed before Liza returned to open Potlikker, in Williamsburg. The following recipe is a classic from the old Hideaway days. It involves marinating a cut-up rabbit in a ridiculous number of ingredients to make it tender and flavorful.

SERVES 3 TO 4

1. Put the rabbit in a medium food-safe container, preferably one with a lid.

2. To make the marinade, mix all the ingredients together in a bowl. Pour the marinade over the rabbit, cover with the lid or plastic wrap, and refrigerate, ideally for at least 24 hours, turning the pieces after 12 hours.

3. Pull the rabbit from the marinade and wipe it dry with paper towels. Strain the marinade and set aside.

4. Dump the cup of flour into a medium bowl. Dredge each piece of rabbit in flour, shake to remove the excess, and set aside on a plate.

5. Heat 2 tablespoons of the lard in a Dutch oven over high heat. When the fat is hot, brown the rabbit in batches of 3 pieces each, sprinkling with salt and pepper as you go, about 3 minutes a side. Transfer to a plate.

6. Drain the fat from the pot, add the strained marinade, and deglaze the pot over high heat, scraping up the bits with a wooden spoon, about 2 minutes. Add the remaining 2 tablespoons lard, the stock, and the brown sugar. Add the rabbit to the pot and bring the liquid to a simmer. Cover, reduce the heat to low, and simmer for 45 minutes to 1 hour, or until the meat is tender and just starting to fall off the bones.

7. Divide the stew among four plates and serve.

1 rabbit, 3 to 4 pounds, cut into 6 pieces (see "How to Butcher a Rabbit," page 230)

FOR THE MARINADE
2 cups cider vinegar
1 cup chicken stock
1 cup sturdy, fruity red wine
1/2 cup extra virgin olive oil
4 large yellow onions, sliced
10 garlic cloves, sliced
A few thyme sprigs
2 tablespoons mustard powder, preferably Colman's
1 tablespoon crushed toasted juniper berries
7 whole cloves
10 bay leaves, preferably fresh
1 teaspoon crushed red pepper flakes
1 tablespoon kosher salt
1 teaspoon freshly ground black pepper

1 cup all-purpose flour
1/4 cup lard or chicken fat
Kosher salt and freshly ground black pepper
1 cup Basic Brown Stock (page 243)
1/2 teaspoon light brown sugar

SPECIAL EQUIPMENT
Medium nonreactive food-safe container

DRINKING WITH THE MEAT HOOK

Whether it's shots, mixed drinks, or beer, for as long as there has been a Meat Hook, drinking all kinds of awful concoctions has been an integral part of making our shop what it is. Cavalier intoxication and senseless celebratory energy are part and parcel of the high-highs and low-lows of working in food in general and working at The Meat Hook in particular.

Cocktail culture may have taken over the hearts and minds of a significant swath of Brooklyn, but, aside from the occasional gin martini, we tend to stay away from anything that requires careful measuring, exotic bitters, or an ingredients list as long as your arm.

To say that we "like" beer is like saying that we "like" oxygen or water and sunlight. What those elementals of homeostasis are to living organisms, beer is to the members of The Meat Hook. I occasionally swear off beer, specifically cheap beer, when I take a gander at my growing midsection and resolve to sip fine wine in moderate quantities, but it never sticks. Try as I may, there is just no escaping the siren song of cheap canned beer and its longtime partner, whiskey.

We tend to prefer beer in cans, not for any sort of ironic or nostalgic reasons, but because these tend to be inexpensive, light tasting, and especially efficient to store, which is always a consideration when allocating space in a cooler full of bulky carcasses. More than that, a can of beer just feels good in the hand, and it offers the added bonus that, when the mood strikes, it can be shotgunned, crushed, or flattened against our foreheads. I hope you have as much fun drinking the Meat Hook way as we do.

Note: I would like to emphasize that the recipes and drinking activities that follow are not solely of my own imagining—they are iterations of activities passed on to me through the natural order of drinking games. Rules and styles may vary, as well as names, contents, and quantities. Please (do not) try this at home.

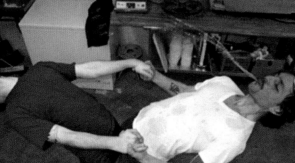

SNOWSHOES

In our lovely neck of the woods of Brooklyn, there is a local tradition at the few remaining old-school Italian butcher shops and pork stores that between Thanksgiving and New Year's every year, the counters start sporting liquor bottles and plastic shot glasses to help everyone get through the season with a minimal amount of stress. Wanting to fit in to the neighborhood and never having met a drinking tradition we didn't like, we gladly offer up our own minibar to help our patrons through the happiest time of the year.

Snowshoes are a holiday tradition at The Meat Hook that was imported to Brooklyn by way of Pittsburgh, straight from the holiday tradition of Brent's father, Bud Young. I'll admit that the combination of peppermint schnapps and whiskey sounds disgusting, but it's actually surprisingly delicious and refreshing. Try one or, really, try four, and you'll see what I mean.

SERVES 1

³/₄ ounce mediocre whiskey
³/₄ ounce peppermint schnapps
Combine in a 2-ounce shot glass and shoot immediately. Follow with another Snowshoe, or two.

SCOPE SHOT

Blame this shot on Carlo Mirarchi. The half-Panamanian chef of Roberta's and Blanca's came back from a trip to Panama with a giant bottle of seco, the country's national drink, as a thank-you for letting him work at Marlow & Daughters in 2008. Brent and I were very happy to have someone to talk to besides each other at the time, so the seco wasn't really necessary. The second event that led directly to this truly awful shot was that the manager at Diner, aware that we had been stealing whiskey from them, gave us a mostly full bottle of crème de menthe as a hint that we should stop pilfering his booze. The truly remarkable thing about this shot is that it tastes exactly like Scope.

SERVES 1

1¹/₂ ounces seco or any white rum or cane liquor
Crème de menthe
Pour the seco into a shot glass and add crème de menthe until it's the color of mouthwash. Drink.

COFFEE BOMB

The Coffee Bomb is a hybrid of two of my obsessions: sake and coffee. It was born during the dawn of the ill-fated, ill-advised Meat Hook brunch (see page 164), when we were functioning more or less on very little besides coffee and alcohol. While sake and coffee may sound pretty disjointed and even gross, I assure you it's quite good, as long as you use a mild, slightly fruity sake and a robust but not acidic bean.

SERVES 1

8 ounces medium- or dark-roast drip coffee, hot or cold
2 ounces light ginjo (premium) sake
Sugar (optional)

Pour the sake and coffee into a vessel that will handle the volume of the two, mix, and enjoy. No cream, but add sugar if desired.

BEAR FIGHT

Bear Fights are a really stupid idea. Don't drink them. But if you feel somehow compelled to give them a try, please make sure you do the following things first:

- Hide any and all dangerous, sharp, or heavy objects.
- Know where the nearest bathroom is.
- Have someone you trust stow your phone, wallet, house keys, and all hard alcohol, and make them vow to keep you away from anyone's significant other, sister, brother, or pet that you might become amorous toward.

Now you're as ready as you'll ever be.

This recipe is straight from the mouth of the bear: James Lum III, aka the Jizzler. The Bear Fight is an advanced move with its origins in two lesser power-drinking activities, the Jäger Bomb and the offensively dubbed Irish Car Bomb—but, you know, combined into one drink.

SERVES 1

FOR THE JÄGER BOMB

1 shot Jägermeister
6 ounces Red Bull

FOR THE IRISH CAR BOMB

1/2 ounce Irish cream
1/2 ounce Irish whiskey
8 ounces Guinness

Drop the shot of Jägermeister into a pint glass filled with the Red Bull. Chug the contents. With all due haste, drop the liqueur/whiskey combination into a pint glass filled with Guinness. Chug the contents. Here you will discover why this drink has been aptly named. It will feel as though two bears are battling in your abdomen.

THE ICE-COLD DUNK (OR ICD)

The ICD is a reimagining, if you will, of the classic shotgun. A three-man operation, it should probably be performed outside in warmer weather.

1 can cheap beer (such as Busch or Natural Light), prepped to be shotgunned (if you do not know what this means, you should probably not be attempting this advanced form of the activity)
1 midsize cooler, filled halfway with ice and then the remaining way with water

Have Friend #1 stand with the beer at shotgun-ready position. Place your hands on either side of the cooler's edge and submerge your head. Friend #2 should, at this time, lift up your body by the ankles to make things more dramatic. Once you are no longer willing or able to remain submerged, kick your feet erratically to signify to Friend #2 that you would like to be let down. Immediately, without hesitation, take said beer from Friend #1 and perform shotgun.

Due to the lack of oxygen in your cranium, the severe shock of the icy water, and the rapid ingestion of alcohol, you should feel a sense of euphoric light-headedness.

BONES

Most people don't give bones more than a fleeting thought, perhaps right before they fling them carelessly into the middle of the tray at a barbecue joint, and that is really too bad. Bones, cartilage, and connective tissue can make up 50 percent or more of an animal by weight. Throwing them away is like throwing away half the animal!

   At The Meat Hook, we're always trying to figure out different things to do with all the bones left over from butchering our amazing animals. Anytime we have to throw away bones because we couldn't do something with them before they got funky, I feel like the terrorists have won. This chapter includes just a few of the many things we do with this less glamorous half of the animal. If you want to try your hand at using bones for more than treats for your dog, here are a few pointers.

BUYING BONES

Bones from your local butcher should be very cheap, and some shops may even give them away (we do). Develop a relationship with your butcher, and ask him what days of the week are best for getting bones from them. No matter what kind of bones you get, make sure that they are fresh and meaty. By fresh, I mean either butchered-that-day fresh or frozen when they were fresh. Freezing doesn't affect bones one bit, so long as they don't get freezer burn. Still, it's best to get your bones the day you're going to use them so they don't take up space in your freezer or fridge for very long. And bones must be meaty, or there is no point in making stock with them—the meaty parts are where all the flavor is. Of bones from four-legged animals, the neck bones are best, as they have the most surface area and meat, as well as connective tissue that will give your stock body and viscosity.

BASIC BROWN STOCK

This recipe for brown stock can be made with pretty much any type of bones from almost any kind of animal. A brown stock is a stock made from browned-off bones, water, and various aromatic vegetables. Keep in mind that not all bones are the same flavorwise, and that you should use the stock accordingly. While chicken and pork stock have a sort of neutral savoriness that makes them suitable in any recipe that calls for stock, lamb, duck, and game stocks have very distinctive flavors that may only jibe with other complementary big flavors, so plan accordingly!

A few other notes on making basic stock: Use only fresh bones. If they smell fishy, sweet, or any other unmeat-like way, don't use them, or your stock and the many hours it took you to make it will be wasted.

Since all bones have different densities, weight is not really important when making stock, volume is. So don't roll into your local butcher and ask for 3¾ pounds of veal bones. Tell him you need enough bones to fill up your X-sized stockpot. Feel free to halve this recipe if you don't have a huge stockpot on hand. **MAKES 8 QUARTS**

7 pounds fresh, meaty bones
2 to 4 carrots, chopped into
   2- to 3-inch pieces
1 to 2 onions, quartered
3 to 4 celery ribs, chopped into
   2- to 3-inch pieces
About 8 quarts cold water

SPECIAL EQUIPMENT
Large roasting pan
16-quart stockpot
Large strainer
Cheesecloth
Plastic freezer-safe containers

1. Preheat the oven to 425° or 450°F (depending on at what temperature your oven starts to set off the smoke alarm—go a little lower than that).

2. Place the bones in a large roasting pan, without crowding. Crowded bones won't brown right. If you will be using this stock to make a heavy-duty meal like beef stew, you might consider roasting the vegetables along with your bones to give the stock a deeper flavor.

3. Roast the bones (and perhaps the vegetables) for about 45 minutes before you start checking on them. Chances are you'll know they're getting close to done because they'll start to smell amazing. You're looking for a nice rich brown (not light brown or burnt black).

4. Put the roasted bones and vegetables (roasted or not) in a 16-quart stockpot. Don't forget to scrape up the nice brown stuff in the roasting pan and put that in there as well. Add 8 quarts cold water, or enough to cover, and bring to a simmer over medium heat. Notice that I said simmer, not boil. Simmering makes nice clear stock. Boiling makes stock that is cloudy and can sometimes be a bit muddy tasting. Reduce the heat to low and simmer, uncovered, skimming off any yucky stuff that floats to the top, until the cartilage on the bones starts falling apart. Chicken stock will be done in about 4 hours; beef will take more like 6 to 8 hours.

5. Strain the stock through a large strainer lined with cheesecloth into a large container or pot and refrigerate overnight.

6. In the morning, carefully skim the solidified fat from the top of the stock with a spoon. If the stock is gelatinized and you want to pour it into containers for storing, heat it just a little to make it fluid again. Then pour into freezer-safe containers, seal tightly, and refrigerate for up to 5 days, or freeze for up to 4 months.

Note: If you want to make a white stock, instead of roasting the bones, blanch them in a large pot of boiling water for 5 to 10 minutes, drain, rinse under cold water, and proceed with the recipe.

SMOKED STOCK

Making smoked stock is foolishly easy, and it's great to have on hand if you're making beans, gumbo, split pea soup, and the like.   MAKES 8 QUARTS

1. Combine the pork, onions, peppercorns, and cold water in a 12-quart stockpot and bring to a simmer over low heat. Simmer, uncovered, for 6 to 8 hours.

2. Pour the stock through a large strainer lined with cheesecloth into a large container or pot. Use the broth immediately, or chill overnight.

3. In the morning, carefully skim the fat from the top of the stock with a spoon. If the stock is gelatinized and you want to pour it into containers for storing, heat it just a little to make it fluid again. Then pour into freezer-safe containers, seal tightly, and refrigerate for up to 5 days, or freeze for up to 4 months.

3 to 5 pounds smoked pork of some sort (bacon ends, ham hocks, pig's feet, ham, etc.)
2 to 3 onions, halved
1 teaspoon black peppercorns
8 quarts cold water

SPECIAL EQUIPMENT
12-quart stockpot
Large strainer
Cheesecloth
Plastic freezer-safe containers

CHINESE CHICKEN BROTH

I hate to begin this recipe with a cliché like "I learned how to make this from an old Chinese man," but I did actually learn how to make this light, delicious broth from an old Chinese man. I started making it regularly because it has become hard to get good Chinese soup, which is one of the few things I crave from my childhood and one that I cannot give up. This broth is just the thing to throw noodles, dumplings, or wontons into (you can use frozen; I won't snitch) on a chilly evening in late fall.   **MAKES 8 QUARTS**

A 2-inch knob of ginger (unpeeled)
3 bunches of scallions
3 to 4 very fresh chicken carcasses
    or 6 chicken backs
3 garlic cloves, unpeeled
1 cup Shaoxing rice wine
10 quarts cold water
Sea salt

SPECIAL EQUIPMENT
12-quart stockpot
Chef's knife or cleaver
Large strainer
Cheesecloth
Plastic freezer-safe containers

1. In a large stockpot, bring 8 quarts of water to a boil.

2. While the water is coming to a boil, beat the shit out of the piece of ginger with the side of a chef's knife or a cleaver. Cut 2 of the bunches of scallions into 3- to 4-inch pieces.

3. Once the water comes to a boil, add the chicken carcasses and blanch for about 5 minutes. Drain and rinse the carcasses under cold water to get the blood and such off.

4. Wash out the pot and add the blanched carcasses, along with the ginger, sliced scallions, garlic, and wine. Add the 10 quarts cold water and bring to a gentle simmer over low heat. Skim the floaty gross stuff off the top and let simmer, uncovered, for 4 hours.

5. Add the remaining bunch of scallions and simmer for 30 minutes more.

6. Strain the stock through a large strainer lined with cheesecloth into a large container or pot. Add salt to taste. You can use the broth immediately, or chill overnight.

7. In the morning, carefully skim the fat (save that shit for noodles—it's delicious!) from the top of the stock with a spoon. If the stock is gelatinized and you want to pour it into containers for storing, heat it just a little to make it fluid again. Then pour into freezer-safe containers, seal tightly, and refrigerate for up to 5 days, or freeze for up to 4 months.

RAMEN BROTH

Ramen people generally fall into two categories: college student-types who rely on the packaged dry noodles for most of their caloric intake and people who have turned meticulously assembled broth and handmade noodles into a vision quest. My personal journey to the ramen holy land started with salty packaged ramen and ended with me nearly throwing up outside the cultiest cult ramen joint in the world: Ramen Jiro in Mita, Tokyo.

Most ramen nerds are a pretty uptight bunch who insist that the broth must be made exactly one way or the other using this type of bones or that kind of kombu (the dried seaweed used to make the stock base, dashi) and only this type of sea salt. While it's cool that such a simple food has captured the imaginations of thousands, if not millions, of obsessive food lovers, it might do everyone good to take a deep breath and realize that ramen is, at its core, an attempt to make world-class food out of what amounts to the junk parts of a food system. Ramen is cheap because it uses stuff that would otherwise be garbage: bones, pig's feet, and bacon ends, as well as inexpensive ingredients like leeks, onions, apples, whatever, and water. What makes a ramen broth delicious resides with the person who makes it, not the laundry list of ingredients someone tells you has to be in the pot.

This ramen broth is different almost every time I make it because it serves, first and foremost, to use whatever leftovers I have on hand. Some weeks I throw in the smoked pig's feet that didn't move because the weather was too warm; other times I'll make it with the mountain of chicken carcasses left over from some special order. Almost anything can end up in the pot, so use the recipe here as a guideline and then go your own way. **SERVES 6**

1. First, set aside 2 hours to watch the classic 1980s Japanese ramen movie *Tampopo*. It'll put you in the right mood to make ramen broth. This is a great time to roast your bones (see page 243).

2. Next, combine all the broth ingredients except the salt in a 16-quart stockpot and bring to a gentle simmer over low heat, skimming off the foam. Continue to simmer, skimming often, for 3 hours.

Recipe continues

FOR THE BROTH
7 pounds bones (any kind except lamb or other gamy stuff), roasted
1 to 2 pounds bacon ends, smoked ham hocks, or pig's feet
A hand of fresh ginger, unpeeled, bruised with the side of a chef's knife
1 to 2 cups sake or other rice wine
2 to 3 onions, halved, or 3 to 4 leeks, white and pale green parts, roughly chopped
1 head garlic, halved horizontally
8 quarts cold water
Sea salt

OPTIONAL BROTH INGREDIENTS
Soy sauce
Miso paste
White or rice wine vinegar

FOR THE NOODLES
One package (6 nests) thin Chinese dried egg noodles (see Resources, page 305)
Skimmed fat from ramen broth
6 scallions, thinly sliced
Chinese BBQ Pork (page 117)
Toasted sesame seeds

SPECIAL EQUIPMENT
16-quart stockpot
Large strainer
Cheesecloth
8- to 10-quart pot

3. Taste the broth: it should be round and savory. If it lacks umami because you used chicken bones, add some soy sauce or miso. If it's flat tasting, add up to 2 tablespoons vinegar to make it pop. If it needs salt, add up to 2 tablespoons sea salt. Stir, and retaste.

4. Let the broth simmer for about 5 hours longer, or until the hocks, bacon, or pig's feet fall apart. Taste it again. When it's perfectly balanced, strain the stock through a large strainer lined with cheesecloth into an 8- to 10-quart pot and keep warm over low heat.

5. Bring 6 quarts of cold water to a boil in a medium pot. Meanwhile, in a large bowl, soak the noodles in enough cold water to cover for 2 minutes before adding the noodles (still in the baskets) to the boiling water. Cook for 5 minutes.

6. To serve, place each serving of noodles in a bowl. Ladle enough broth on top to cover two-thirds of the noodles. Add a splash of white or rice wine vinegar and top with the reserved skimmed fat, scallions, Chinese BBQ Pork, and toasted sesame seeds.

When I moved to Brooklyn ten years ago, there really wasn't much of anything to do on a Friday night except head in to the city to spend $10 a drink at a bar packed full of jackasses (way too rich for my wallet) or go to the Brooklyn Brewery for their open house. It didn't cost anything to get in, and $20 would buy you a fistful of wooden nickels to trade for beers at the bar. The open house was a true island of misfit toys, collecting all of the broke, newly arrived yokels like myself, along with neighborhood regulars and a random smattering of tourists and kids from Long Island. It was a great place to meet people, to find a roommate, a significant other, a band member, or just someone to talk to. Did I mention that you could get pizza delivered there?

After a few months, I stopped going as frequently, but the brewery always occupied a very warm and grateful place in my heart. So when Ben and company at Brooklyn Brewery started dropping off cases of beer for us at the shop and asked us to provide the food at the brewery events not long after we opened The Meat Hook, I felt like somehow I had come full circle, helping to provide a bit of the same experience for other people that the brewery had provided for me. It's my sincere hope that we can do half as good a job of becoming an iconic Brooklyn institution as they have and, maybe, become a warm memory for our customers as well.

TRASHY AND CLASSY

By Ben Hudson, Brooklyn Brewery

The Brooklyn Brewery began holding quarterly parties to introduce our newest beers right around the time The Meat Hook opened for business. From the get-go, Tom, Brent, Ben, and Sara Bigelow (their general manager) enthusiastically agreed to throw their business model to the wind and provide free food for our friends four times a year. While coordinating these parties, we can always count on the team at The Meat Hook to never, ever return an e-mail, or give us even a one-word confirmation that they'll be there, or answer a single message to let us know that, yes, they understand when the party is and how much food to bring.

But we can always count on them to turn up with some incredible concoction in tow. Every time. Like Batman at the scene of a crime, the Meat Hook team shows up at our parties with hunger-saving gadgets: table-length banh mi sandwiches, country pâté for three hundred, smoked Austrian street sausages, hand-torched Reubens—the list goes on. Of course, other friends bring food to the parties, really good stuff too, but it's the Meat Hook table that always has the line. Who can resist their combination of the trashy and the classy? The generous and the caustic? The love of Busch Light and the respect for Brooklyn Lager? The appreciation for tradition and the irreverence toward the norm? No one.

HERE'S A BRIEF LIST OF THINGS I'VE WITNESSED THE GUYS OF THE MEAT HOOK EXCEL AT:

• Holding their own grand opening party weeks before the store opened or was even partly through construction. There's nothing quite like munching on high-quality cheese wheels amid airborne drywall particles.

Roasting a pig on a farm in the middle of Queens and drinking well whiskey till the break of dawn.

- Bringing together Brooklyn's skeptical old-school Italian food community and the borough's upstart, cocky, tattooed food community for the purpose of worshipping meatballs.

- Joining forces with the Brooklyn Brewery to throw a kickass Rockaways party named Boardrockin', featuring a 1980s cover band called White Wedding, with half the attendees getting citations for drinking on the beach.

- Wiping any number of animals' blood from their hands upon seeing me and my family in the shop to give me a firm handshake. Every time. Sure, it's a time-honored greeting, but it's also a confirmation of pride in their craft. It's bloody and gross and real and right.

- Flying their freak flag high during the chaos of Brooklyn's inaugural Great GoogaMooga food festival. As lines became endless, food ran out, and tempers flared, the Meat Hook crew did what they do best: downed tequila, sputtered nonsense, taught meat truths, and introduced an eight-year-old boy to the art of butchering before a delighted crowd.

HERE'S A BRIEFER LIST OF STUFF I'VE WITNESSED THE MEAT HOOK BEING BAD AT:

- Returning e-mails.

FAT

What do Americans have against fat? Fat is a key ingredient in making pretty much anything taste good, and a life spent freaking out about eating fat (or not eating it) is no life at all to me. And if we're actually trying as a culture to eat less but better-quality meat, we need to stop avoiding good fats from properly raised animals and start avoiding the bad fats in processed foods that can make us obese or sick. Cooking with animal fat is not only thrifty (and can help save the world), but it also adds subtle flavor to the foods cooked in it. If you ever wondered why those stir-fried string beans you ate at the China Palace with your folks when you were an annoying fourteen-year-old vegetarian tasted so good, it was probably because they were coated in duck or pork fat. It's not that anyone was trying to put something over on you—people who traditionally cook with animal fat don't really understand why you wouldn't want to eat anything, especially a vegetable, cooked in it. Sure, Bacon Butter (page 257) will make you fat if you eat it by the quart, but if you're eating anything by the quart, you have much larger problems than I can address here. Following are a few of my favorite fats to use in the kitchen.

BACON FAT

You'd think that no one would need the virtues of bacon fat explained to them, yet I know
lots of people who pour the fat from their skillets right down the drain but don't hesitate to shell
out $25 for a bottle of olive oil from somewhere I can't pronounce to cook with. I understand
that most Depression-era thrift stuff seems annoying and more than a little crazy in this day and
age, but your grandparents weren't wrong saving bacon fat in a jelly jar. You can use bacon fat
to sauté vegetables, cook burgers, and fry steaks. And not only is the fat essentially free, it's also
full of magic flavor crystals that alone can rescue all but the most poorly thought-out dishes from
mediocrity simply by letting them bask in their goodness.

Bacon fat is best used for shallow-frying (and it's tough to save up enough bacon fat to deep-fry
in unless you have a real five-pound-a-week bacon habit, in which case you should maybe skip fried
food and go spend a couple of hours at the gym). Be careful not to burn bacon fat over too high
heat—it contains some of the sugar from the bacon you fried as well as lots of tiny bits of pork and
whatnot that can give your food a burnt flavor right quick if it's not tended to properly.

SCHMALTZ

What bacon fat is to pork, schmaltz is to chicken. With its ability to make any poultry cooked in it seem as if it were rubbed down with MSG, schmaltz is the best cooking fat that no one except for Jewish grandmas has ever used. Not only is it an amazing-tasting fat, it's also the most thrown away, since we consume more chicken per person in this country than anything else (except for, perhaps, reality TV).

So stop throwing away chicken fat and start using it for cooking chicken breasts and making roux for gravy. I will give you $5 if your life isn't changed in at least a semiprofound way by using this secret fat.

DUCK FAT

What we usually call duck in the United States is actually duckling, which is smaller and less fatty than its more mature brethren. Whether duck or duckling, there is a lot of fat on these animals and so something needs to be done with it. After we've broken down our ducks for the week (see "How to Butcher a Duck," page 214), we meticulously pare off every single bit of fatty skin, then render it over low heat and strain it off to use for any number of recipes that don't necessarily call for duck fat but don't explicitly say not to use it either. You should do this too. For the basics of how to render duck fat, see Making Schmaltz (page 260) and follow it exactly the same way, using duck skin instead of chicken.

Duck fat is not neutral, and it tastes awful if it gets burnt, but it's great for frying potatoes. Sara Bigelow, The Meat Hook's general manager, would like you to know, however, that duck fat should never, under any circumstances, be used to make refried beans.

LARD

Neutral, lard ain't. It is pork fat and therefore will make everything you fry in it taste vaguely porkalicious. It also has a somewhat low smoke point and burns easily, giving it and your food a truly disgusting bitter animal flavor. So use it carefully. It's excellent for certain savory baked goods and making slow-cooked beans. The best lard is leaf lard, which is rendered from the fat around the kidneys.

SUET

What the hell is suet anyway? It's the fat from around the kidneys of beef and veal. It's like the beef equivalent of leaf lard. Unrendered and crumbled up, it is the fat of choice for all manner of British savory meat pies and for Yorkshire pudding, and it's famous for creating the best-tasting French fries the world has ever eaten. Sadly, today no one much knows, or cares anything about suet, tallow, or any sort of beef-fat product in most of the United States, beyond those who make fancy soap and the remaining few who have clung to the old ways when it comes to delicious fries.

If there is something better (OK, besides duck fat) to cook French fries in than suet, I don't know what it is. It is also great for frying beef steaks and searing off stew beef. However, it's a little too strong for most other uses that aren't beef-centric.

GOOSE FAT MEMORIES

Much of what can be said about cooking with duck fat can also be said of goose fat—though a goose has much more of it. My grandfather Lester grew up in the northern woods of Minnesota during the dawn of the twentieth century, and his family's annual wild goose hunts kept them in that multipurpose fat for the rest of the year. He was pretty old when I was in elementary school in the mid-eighties, and one day his heart stopped working right. But a day or so after he underwent open heart surgery, I was ushered into his hospital room, and then everyone else mysteriously disappeared. Lester was a man of few words, but for some reason, he had decided that, having just faced his own mortality, he needed to tell me what the world was like when he was my age. He told me stories about trapping, hunting, and ice fishing in the brutal Minnesota winters with his brothers, long before anyone in that part of the world had ever seen an automobile. What stuck with me, however, was the detail he devoted to the ritual of putting on layers of wool socks smeared with goose grease before jamming his feet into oversize galoshes, to help keep his feet warm on their excursions. He'd never said many words to me at one sitting before that, but what really sticks in my mind from his long story that day is the goose fat part.

MAKING LARD

Rendered pork fat is found in abundance among nearly all pig-loving cuisines of the world and is used in countless ways. Especially in Europe, it is sometimes flavored with herbs or garlic and smeared on bread as a snack. When my thoughts turn to lard, I can't help thinking of the hog-killing chapter in the Laura Ingalls Wilder book *Little House in the Big Woods*—it is fixed in my mind as being as American as apple pie, if that apple pie has a pork-fat crust. **MAKES ABOUT 2 CUPS**

1. Chill your fat in the freezer for 30 minutes in the package you bought it in, then remove it and roughly chop it using a chef's knife or grind it through the medium die of a good grinder.

2. Add the pork fat and ¼ cup water to a medium pot and set it over low heat for 2 hours, stirring every 10 to 15 minutes. After 2 hours, the fat should be rendered and all of the water evaporated, leaving you with a pool of clearish oil. Allow to cool for 20 minutes, then strain into a pint-sized Mason jar or the like. It will keep for up to 2 weeks refrigerated, or up to a year frozen.

2 pounds pork fat

SPECIAL EQUIPMENT
Chef's knife or meat grinder
Strainer

BACON BUTTER

Bacon butter was a product born of desperation in the early days of the shop. Because we sliced all of our bacon from slabs, we were very soon faced with an alarming amount of bacon ends, the part that's left over after you slice slab bacon. The stockpile was growing each day despite our best efforts to use the ends in sausages, chilis, soups, and the like. Finally, I snapped. At the time, we couldn't make enough Marrow Butter (page 67) to keep on the shelves, so I decided to grind the bacon ends, cook them off, and use them to make the marrow butter recipe, only, you know, more baconish.

What can you use bacon butter for? Frying eggs, finishing steaks and burgers, smearing on hot bread, or coating a chicken before roasting. Honestly, I shouldn't have to talk you into making a recipe called bacon butter, should I? **MAKES ABOUT 3 CUPS**

1. Preheat the oven to 325°F.

2. Scatter the chopped bacon evenly into a large cast-iron skillet or small rimmed baking sheet and toss in the oven for 15 to 20 minutes to cook the bacon and render the fat. Remove from the oven and allow to cool for 15 minutes. Pour the bacon fat through a strainer into a medium bowl or the bowl of a stand mixer. Put the bacon bits in an airtight container and refrigerate for topping salads—or ice cream.

3. Add the butter, chives, hot sauce, and a good pinch each of salt and pepper to the bowl with the bacon fat and mix thoroughly with a sturdy whisk. If you're using a mixer, using the paddle attachment, mix at the lowest speed for 1 minute, then up the speed to the third setting for another 4 minutes. Taste for seasoning and adjust.

4. Packed into airtight containers, the butter keeps for 2 to 3 weeks in the fridge and for about 1,000 years in the freezer.

1 cup uncooked bacon ends, finely chopped (available for cheap at any shop that sells slab bacon)
1/2 pound (2 sticks) salted butter, cut into cubes and softened
1 bunch chives or scallions, finely chopped
3 to 4 good splashes hot sauce, such as Texas Pete
Kosher salt and freshly ground black pepper

SPECIAL EQUIPMENT
Strainer
A sturdy whisk or a stand mixer (optional)

CORN PONE

The first cookbook I ever bought was called *Hillbilly Cookin'*, picked up in the very early 1980s for $2.95 at what I can only describe as a prospector store. You know, the kind of place that sells gold-panning stuff, metal detectors, and books about lost treasure. I'm not really sure why I bought the book, but I'm sure glad I did, if just for this recipe alone. Think of corn pone as white trash polenta, but without all the fussing—plus it uses almost a cup of bacon fat. I like to eat it with chili or for breakfast with sausage, gravy, and eggs.   **SERVES 4 TO 6**

1. Preheat the oven to 350°F. Grease a medium cast-iron skillet or a round cake pan with a tablespoon of the bacon fat.

2. Sift together the flour, baking powder, salt, and baking soda into a medium bowl. Set aside.

3. Put the cornmeal in a large bowl and pour the boiling water over it. Add the remaining bacon fat, mix well, and let cool.

4. Using a wooden spoon, stir the buttermilk and cold water into the cornmeal mixture, then add the eggs as well as the sifted dry ingredients and mix together until no longer lumpy.

5. Scrape the mixture into the prepared pan. Bake for 25 to 30 minutes, or until golden brown. Serve immediately, or allow to cool and then reheat by frying portions in a skillet with some bacon fat.

$3/4$ cup bacon fat, at room temperature
1 cup all-purpose flour
2 teaspoons baking powder
$1^1/2$ teaspoons kosher salt
$1/2$ teaspoon baking soda
$2^1/2$ cups cornmeal
$1^1/2$ cups boiling water
1 cup buttermilk
$1/2$ cup cold water
2 large eggs, beaten

SPECIAL EQUIPMENT
Medium cast-iron skillet or 9-inch round cake pan

CHOPPED LIVER *with Schmaltz*

This is our general manager Sara Bigelow's recipe for the Jewish appetizing classic. I, like her, am from Southern California, and while one of my best friends growing up, Kevin Baron, was technically a chosen person, his family was about as Jewish as a pork chop with melted cheese on top. Thus, I never knew the pleasures of chopped liver until I moved to New York City and attended my first of many nights at the singular New York City Hebrew party dump that is Sammy's Roumanian Steak House. I'm not sure if their chopped liver made such an impression on me because it was so good or, more likely, because it was the only dish I was sober enough to remember, as it came out early, long before the Ketel One frozen in blocks of ice took hold and I found myself singing "Hava Nagila" like I was born with the Torah in my hand. I hope you love it as much as I do, frozen vodka or not.   **SERVES 3 OR 4**

3 tablespoons unsalted butter
1 large onion, minced
1 bunch thyme
1 pound chicken livers, cleaned
   and rinsed
Kosher salt and freshly ground
   black pepper
6 tablespoons schmaltz (recipe follows)
A splash of sherry or brandy
2 or 3 hard-boiled eggs, chopped

1. Melt the butter in a large skillet over medium heat. Add the onion and thyme and cook, stirring often, until the onions are golden brown and lightly caramelized. Remove from the heat and let cool.

2. Meanwhile, pat the livers dry and season lightly with salt and pepper. Melt a dollop of schmaltz (just enough to coat the bottom of the pan) in a medium skillet, over medium-high heat. Add the livers and cook until browned on one side, about 4 minutes. When the livers can be flipped, turn them over and cook for 4 more minutes, or until medium pink inside. Remove the livers to a plate to cool.

3. Take your chicken liver pan and get it hot over medium-high heat for about a minute. Deglaze it with the sherry, scraping up all the brown bits on the bottom of the pan, another minute or so, then pour the liquid into a small bowl to cool.

4. Remove the thyme from the onions.

5. Reserve one-third of the onions and livers. Transfer the remaining onions and livers to a food processor, add the rest of your schmaltz and deglazing liquid, and pulse to create a rough puree—this is chopped liver, after all. Transfer to a bowl.

6. Roughly chop the reserved livers. Add the hand-chopped liver and eggs to the chopped liver in the bowl, along with the reserved onions, and mash them together with a fork for 2 to 3 minutes. You're looking for a texture that is spreadable but not smooth. Add salt and pepper to taste.

7. Spread on rye toast and pretend you're living in a Woody Allen movie.

MAKING SCHMALTZ

Schmaltz, like bacon fat, isn't really *made* outright; it's collected from roasting pans and plates of chilled leftovers a spoonful at a time. However, should you want to make a large batch of schmaltz and can't wait to save it up from four months of roast chickens, here's how to do it.

MAKES 1 CUP
1 pound fresh chicken skin

Get a saucepan, add the chicken skin and 2 tablespoons cold water, and set it over medium-low heat. Once the water is mostly evaporated and the skin has started to render its fat, about 10 minutes, reduce the heat to low and allow to bubble, stirring well every 10 minutes, for about an hour.

At this point, your chicken fat should be rendered and the chicken skin should be golden brown. Turn up the heat to medium-high and fry the skins, stirring once a minute, until crispy and darker brown, about 5 minutes; be careful not to overheat the fat, or it will become bitter. When in doubt, err on the side of less brown. Turn off the heat and allow to cool for 15 minutes.

Pour off the fat into a glass jelly jar, transfer the skin to an airtight container, and refrigerate both. Schmaltz is good refrigerated for about 2 weeks and can be kept frozen indefinitely.

DUCK-FAT POTATO POUTINE

Duck-fat potatoes have come to be something of a casual fine-dining cliché over the past fifteen years. They can evoke visions of ill-advised remakes of classic dishes, unprofessional waiters, and overpriced wine lists. But duck-fat potatoes don't deserve that. They do deserve to be tossed with cheese curds and drenched in gravy. **SERVES 4**

1. Bring a large pot of salted water (add salt to the water until it is pleasantly salty, about 1 cup salt per gallon) to a boil, add the potatoes, and simmer over medium-low heat for 15 to 20 minutes, until they're just starting to get soft.

2. Meanwhile, warm the gravy in a large saucepan; keep warm.

3. When the potatoes are done, drain and transfer to a large bowl of ice water (50/50 ice to water) to cool.

4. Once the potatoes are cool, drain them and transfer to a large bowl. Dry the potatoes thoroughly with paper towels, transferring them to another large bowl as you get them dry. If you'd like more texture on your fried potatoes to hold on to that gravy goodness, smash the potatoes slightly as you dry them. Don't go crazy here—a little smash only, please!

5. Now, heat the duck fat to 375°F (use a deep-fry thermometer to make it easy) in a medium pot or deep saucepan. When the oil is hot, start adding your potatoes in serving-sized batches (that's one-quarter of your potatoes) to the hot oil and cook to a nice golden brown, 5 to 7 minutes. Use a spider or a slotted spoon to transfer the potatoes to a serving bowl and toss them with 1 cup of the gravy and 1 cup of the cheese curds. Serve right away.

6. Repeat these steps for the other 3 servings, making sure that your oil gets back to 375°F before adding the next batch, or you'll have soggy, greasy little buddies.

Kosher salt

3 pounds Peewee or other baby potatoes (no larger than 1 1/2 inches in diameter)

4 cups Foie Gras Grease Gravy (page 201)

3 quarts rendered duck fat (see Resources, page 305)

4 cups fresh cheese curds, at room temperature (see Resources, page 305)

SPECIAL EQUIPMENT
Deep-fry thermometer
Spider or large slotted spoon

FRENCHIES: LE COUTEAU D'ARGENT

Butcher-owner of the historic shop Le Couteau d'Argent, Yves-Marie le Bourdonnec came into the world of The Meat Hook suddenly, like a thunderstorm on a hot August evening, under the auspices of shooting a segment for a documentary for "the French HBO" (whatever that meant). He was loud, spastic, and hilarious in the way that only a cartoonishly stereotypical yet deeply knowledgeable French butcher can be, and his arrival at the shop in early 2010 ushered in a new era of internationalism for The Meat Hook.

After the initial shoot, Yves-Marie proceeded to charm and wow us by putting down his on-camera persona and picking up a boning knife to show us what is what in the key of French *boucherie*. However annoyed we might have been at first to find our busy little shop taken over by cameramen and lights, our hearts melted as Yves-Marie deftly parsed familiar primals into myriad French specialty cuts we had never dreamed of.

Months later, Yves-Marie and his entire crew of butchers from Asnières, a small suburb of Paris, descended on our shop for a demonstration of skill, talent, and dedication to craft that left us in awe of a culture that has never abandoned its allegiance to local family-owned shops or the craft of butchering. In our humble way, we attempted to show the band of Gallic misfits a good time during their visit to New York City. We couldn't have imagined then how overwhelmed and utterly destroyed by their generosity and ability to party we would be when we finally chiseled out a few days to visit them on their home turf in Paris, in the spring of 2011.

Yves-Marie is now all too busy to visit us under the weight of newfound popularity for his teacup-sized shop and the impossible task of cutting no less than four beef a week in its limited space for his eager fans. So we hope to someday visit him again and learn from him and his unlikely gang of misfit toys.

COOKING MEAT

Cooking meat can be intimidating. Being responsible for a big, beautiful hunk of expensive beef can send shivers down the spine of even the most experienced chefs or home cooks, causing them to doubt or second-guess themselves right into totally screwing up whatever they're trying to cook. With that in mind, a little pep talk is in order: Accept that every once in a while, you *will* completely blow it. An overcooked steak or a blackened chicken breast is not the end of the world—that's what take-out menus and a sense of humor are for. That said, I hope you approach this chapter understanding that my success is the result of many mistakes, but if you follow my cooking guidelines, you'll mess up a lot less meat than I did.

MEAT SCIENCE

The basis of any cooking method is science, pure and simple. But when I talk about "meat science," I'm not referring to the highfalutin' echelon of culinary foams, extrusions, and other foolishness. Rather, it's simply my understanding of what happens when different types of muscles are exposed to different types of heat for different amounts of time under different conditions.

HOW TO COOK

Muscle × Temperature × Time is the basic equation that will make you the envy of all your friends, enemies, and in-laws with your ability to produce juicy and perfectly cooked meat every time. There are other subtle aspects of this equation, such as moisture, but we'll get to those later on.

MUSCLE

The type of muscle (i.e., meat), how it was cut, and the animal it came from is going to influence the choices you make as far as temperature and time.

TEMPERATURE

Temperature has a huge effect on the texture, flavor, and palatability of the meat you cook. Throughout the book, when I refer to cooking at a low temperature, I mean 325°F or below. High heat is above 375°F and, you guessed it, medium heat is between 325° and 375°F. Cheaper, tougher cuts of meat can be made tender and melt-in-your-mouth good if cooked at the right temperature, while prime cuts can be completely ruined with the wrong temperature choice. Cuts like tenderloin, without a lot of connective tissue to seize up and get chewy, can be cooked extremely hot and quick under a broiler or on a grill, even sitting directly on top of burning charcoal. Conversely, cuts with lots of collagen, connective tissue, and/or tendons need low-temperature cooking to ensure that their connective tissue dissolves. Moderately tender items, like whole roasting chickens, are best cooked at medium heat, between 325° and 375°F, because they have a mixture of tender and tougher muscles. Compromise is key to getting a crisp skin and tender meat with a chicken or other bird.

TIME

Depending on the temperature and the type of muscle you're cooking, you will cook something at high heat for a short time or at a lower temperature for a long time. Perhaps the best example of this is the difference between a young 2½-pound chicken, which can be butterflied and grilled in less than 30 minutes over burning grapevine clippings, and a tough old stewing hen, which must be braised for 1½ hours or more. Same animal, different stages of life, different cooking temperatures, radically different cooking times.

If you're interested in learning more about meat science and you do not own a copy of Harold McGee's On Food and Cooking: The Science and Lore of the Kitchen, *you should run, not walk, out the door to buy it and read his chapter on proteins. Any professional cook who claims that his understanding of the hows and whys of meat cookery has not been deeply informed by this book is either lying or stupid.*

GRILLING

Growing up, I thought that all food cooked on a grill was supposed to look and taste like the charcoal briquettes my dad used to make the fire. Unfortunately, it took me years to return to the backyard grill after eating so many incinerated barbecued chicken legs; dry, crumbly burgers; and wooden steaks.

I say unfortunately because a simple grill can be one of the most powerful tools in any cook's arsenal. Its ability to produce vast extremes of BTUs, ranging from hellishly hot to barely above body temperature, is a thing to behold.

Whether you're using gas, hardwood, or charcoal, the primal pleasures of grilling meat over an open flame cannot be replicated by broiler, skillet, or oven. Open fire speaks to us in a language that is older than the savannah where we took our first tentative steps toward becoming *Homo erectus* and satisfies our basest primatologist needs for safety, shelter, and tribe.

Fire was arguably our first great leap forward toward what we now call technology. Scientists like Richard W. Wrangham claim that fire, along with the nutritional benefits of cooking food over it, is hugely responsible for our becoming, well, human. I suggest that you put down the iTablet, turn off the TV, and get back in touch with your hominid roots.

Fuel

The choice of fuel to burn when you grill can be very personal for some people, not unlike the clothes you wear, the car you drive, or where you live. Some people ask themselves, "What does using hickory wood to cook my steak say about me?" while others view what they burn as simply a practical means to an end. Whichever side you fall on, keep an open mind about the fuel and become comfortable with the idea that it is the practice of cooking and the skills built with that practice that are the fundamental building blocks of a good meal; wood, charcoal, and gas are simply choices that have their own merits and issues.

GAS

Every time barbecue weather comes upon us at the shop, we get a throng of enthusiastic but relatively uninformed would-be grillers asking us for advice on how to cook their steaks and sausages. Our first question is always, "What kind of grill do you have?" What follows is usually lowered eyes and a look of shame as they admit that they have a gas grill.

I'm not sure how gas grills got such a bad, unmanly rap, but if it counts for anything, when my wife and I moved into our new apartment, complete with a private deck, I celebrated by buying a gas grill. Why gas and not some sort of byzantine wood-fired grill with adjustable grate heights and a system of pulleys? Simple—I want to use it every night during the summer, not just on special occasions. Gas, while it may not be sexy or cool, is pretty fucking convenient. Ten minutes before you want to grill something, you turn it on and heat up the grill, then you

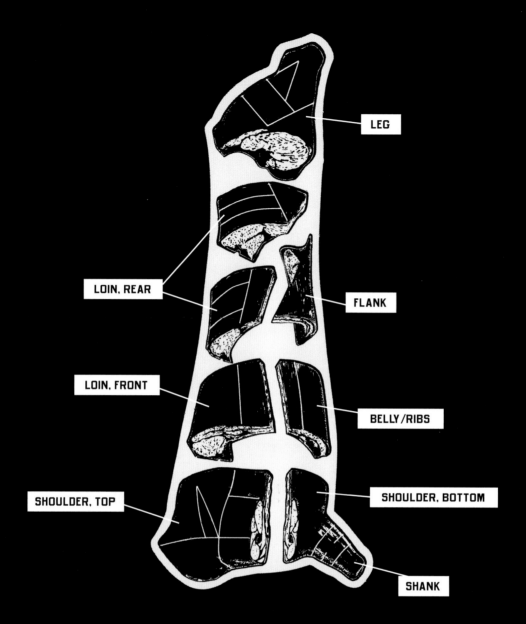

LEG

LOIN, REAR

FLANK

LOIN, FRONT

BELLY/RIBS

SHOULDER, TOP

SHOULDER, BOTTOM

SHANK

GENERAL MEAT COOKING
FOR FOUR-LEGGED ANIMALS

SHANK

The shank is full of all kinds of connective tissue, tendons, and sinews, making it the toughest cut on any animal. Shanks are best braised or stewed for hours over low heat with a good amount of moisture to allow all of those tough rubbery bits to melt away and give your dish a rich, velvety quality.

FLANK

Flank is the original "butcher's cut" (a cut butchers would typically take home for themselves), but home cooks and chefs discovered it as an excellent inexpensive steak masquerading as London broil in the meat cases of the 1960s and '70s. It's lean and has heavily striated muscle fibers that are great for holding onto spices and marinades. Because it's lean, it should be cooked quickly using high heat, under a broiler in a pan, or on the grill, to no more than medium-rare. Make sure to slice it across the muscle fibers when you carve it, or it will be tough and stringy.

SHOULDER, TOP

The top part of the shoulder, while not the most tender cut in the world, can make excellent grilling, smoking, and roasting cuts. For grilling, cutting the shoulder thin and marinating it will help make it more tender. When smoking, keep your temperature at or below 250°F. Roasts from the top of the shoulder should be cooked at or below 325°F to prevent them from drying out and to allow the tougher muscles to break down as much as possible. Slicing them thin across the grain helps too.

SHOULDER, BOTTOM

Referred to as the breast, picnic, or brisket of various species of four-legged animals, this cut is typically fatty and rubbery, with a lot of collagen in the muscle fibers. It's perfect for braising or smoking at or below 225°F for an extended length of time.

LOIN, FRONT

The front portion of the loin is not as tender as the rear portion, but it has much more fat and bone and better lends itself to being cut thicker and grilled or pan-roasted over medium heat. This area of the animal also makes a great slow-roasting joint, as its larger amount of fat helps keep the meat juicy.

LOIN, REAR

The rear part of the loin is the most tender part of the animal (it includes the obviously named tenderloin). Because it's leaner, the rear loin is not as flavorful and juicy as the front, but it is well suited to being quickly cooked in a hot pan or on a grill.

BELLY/RIBS

The belly, or plate, is fairly collagenous and tough, with a good amount of fat. This cut of beef is great smoked or braised at or below 250°F, while the belly and ribs of lamb or pork are great smoked, braised, or roasted below 325°F.

LEG

The leg is made of four major muscles of varying tenderness. In lamb and pork, they're rarely separated and the whole legs are best slow-roasted at around 325°F and crisped up, either at the beginning or the end of cooking, at 450°F. Beef leg, on the other hand, is normally separated into the top round and sirloin tip, as you would with the bottom round and eye of round, it can be tenderized or marinated and used as steaks or slow-roasted below 325°F.

cook your meat and turn it off. No twenty minutes to get the coals going. No carting ashes down the stairs. No expense of wood. My business partner Brent has a fancy Argentinean grill and he once spent $70 on wood that was only enough to fuel three barbecues. He's single and can afford it, I guess, but it's way too rich for my blood.

Another advantage to gas grilling is that it is much easier to modulate the heat output. This is especially useful if you're relatively new to cooking over an open flame. You want high heat on a gas grill? Turn the knob to high. Need to gently roast some half-chickens and sausages on one side of the grill and sear off skirt steaks on the other? No problem: gas does what you tell it to. Just don't forget to get your tank filled, OK?

CHARCOAL

The charcoal grill is the everyman's grill. Despite its stigma as a weekend warrior device serving solely to allow grown men to incinerate barbecued chicken legs on the outside while leaving their interiors dangerous and bloody, the charcoal grill is actually the most powerful cooking tool that the average American has at his disposal. A good old round Weber grill or the like can be called upon to produce insanely high BTUs or to gently smoke a pork shoulder to perfection. It reminds me of a giant beast of an electric drill called the Hole-Hawg that Robert M. Pirsig talks about in one of my favorite books of my troubled teen years, *Zen and the Art of Motorcycle Maintenance*. The charcoal grill, like the massively powerful Hole-Hawg, is a tool so powerful that using it without understanding fully how to cook with it is misguided and a little bit dangerous.

The key to cooking with charcoal is to determine whatever you're going to cook at what point in charcoal's relatively narrow temperature arc. A typical plan would be to grill scallions and veggies when the charcoal is superhot, just after the flames die down, then grill steaks with the less-crazy heat of the coals after they go gray,

and finish with chicken and sausage that do much better over the gentle low heat that comes toward the end of the charcoal's useful life.

The types of charcoal available these days are an embarrassment of riches compared to when I was growing up in the 1980s and the only choice was the familiar white, red, and blue bag of Kingsford, or maybe generic grocery-store stuff. In the age of the Internet, almost everyone has access to exotic Japanese hibachi charcoal that burns hot and produces little smoke, or all manner of hardwood lump charcoal (lump is not briquettes; it looks like wood, but it's charcoal) from hickory to mesquite to maple and everything in between. Unless I'm planning on doing something very specific, like cooking yakitori skewers, I tend to buy lump charcoal on the more inexpensive side; it burns hot and doesn't contain any of the additives that briquettes tend to have, which can give meat a slightly petrochemical smell. Speaking of petrochemical smells, don't buy instant-light charcoal if you can help it—it makes meat taste terrible. Get a $10 chimney starter that uses a few sheets of old newspaper to ignite the charcoal. It is much faster and more environmentally friendly, and your meat will taste better.

WOOD

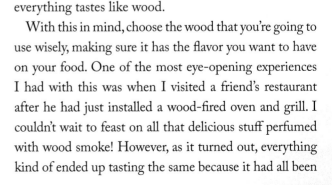

Anything said about charcoal goes double for wood. The pluses of cooking with wood are as follows: everything tastes like wood. The downside: everything tastes like wood.

With this in mind, choose the wood that you're going to use wisely, making sure it has the flavor you want to have on your food. One of the most eye-opening experiences I had with this was when I visited a friend's restaurant after he had just installed a wood-fired oven and grill. I couldn't wait to feast on all that delicious stuff perfumed with wood smoke! However, as it turned out, everything kind of ended up tasting the same because it had all been cooked over the same wood smoke. Because of this sort of monotone flavor situation, I stay away from wood unless I'm smoking meat. A good compromise in strategy is to add wood chunks to your charcoal or gas fire right before you're going to grill the big piece of meat—that way you can have the best of all possible worlds.

Each type of wood will give a different flavor profile to your meat. I lump wood types into the classifications of heavy, fruity, nutty, and other. Keep in mind that there are a lot of different types of the trees we use to cook food out there and that oak or hickory can vary significantly in flavor from one region to another. As always, explore, experiment, and decide for yourself what you like best.

Heavy woods like hickory are among the strongest-flavored woods there are and yield the characteristic aroma and taste that we associate most with the flavor of smoke on meat. If hickory is the archetype of wood-smoke aroma, oak has a similar profile, but without the complexity of hickory, at least in my experience (there are many different types of oak). Mesquite is strong and earthy, with some sweetness. It's great for lamb, beef, chicken, and pork, as long as the spicing is aggressive and sharp:

think black pepper, cumin, coriander, and chiles. It's a heavy flavor and needs heavy flavors to balance it.

Fruity woods, which usually come from fruit-bearing hardwood trees like apple and cherry, have a lighter, sweet, and, well, fruity aroma and flavor. I like to use them for pork, especially if there is any sugar in the rub or cure, as the sweetness of the wood brings out and complements the sweetness in the rub—and helps everything taste vaguely like bacon. These woods can also work well with duck and dark-fleshed game birds.

Nut-tree woods impart a fairly neutral smoke flavor that is neither as sweet and fruity as fruitwoods nor as heavy and resinous as hickory and the like. Chestnut, pecan, and almond are nut-tree woods that work well when cooking delicate meats like chicken and light-fleshed game birds, as well as mild-flavored freshwater fish.

Other types of wood for cooking include olive wood and grapevines, which can add complementary flavors to southern-Mediterranean–style recipes like grilled lamb or goat, or even mackerel. These woods work well with meats flavored with lemon juice, ground sumac, grape leaves, and strong peppery/grassy fresh olive oil.

Grills

Grills are a variable bunch. They can be as primitive as one improvised with a few rocks by the side of the road or controlled by a Skynet-like system of computer-controlled fans, vents, and rack-height-adjustment servos. Most of the grills you'll have access to, though, lie squarely in the mundane middle category of contraptions you can buy at the home-supply or hardware store.

For the sake of simplicity, I just discuss gas and wood/charcoal grills here. If you're into real rare-earth fetish grills, you should move along. I'm only including the grills that mortals can cook over.

GAS GRILLS

As the recent purchaser of a brand-spanking-new gas grill, I can tell you that most of the gas grills available to people like you and me without forking over a car payment are, well, fine. That makes it seem bad, right? Not at all. For 80 percent of what anyone wants to grill, a

bone stock gas grill is great. Requiring little forethought, prep time, or cleanup, a gas grill is perfect for making steaks on a Wednesday night.

Three factors to consider when you are trying to figure out what size grill to buy and the features you want: (1) how much space you have, (2) what kind of stuff you will be cooking, and (3) how many people you will be cooking for at most. I bought a small two-burner number with an attached single-range burner because (a) my deck is small, (b) my wife is from the Northeast and she loves boiled lobsters and steamer clams with her steaks, and (c) the number of people that can fit comfortably on our deck is six to eight. You might have a massive backyard and a lot of Argentinean friends who come over, and who invite their Argentinean friends over as well—in which case you can scrap the range feature and get a huge five-burner for grilling all those crosscut short ribs.

CHARCOAL GRILLS

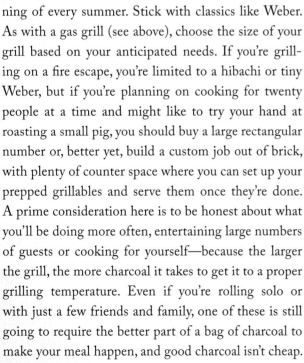

Since they are relatively inexpensive and simple machines, you can't really go wrong with any charcoal grill you buy so long as you stay away from those goofy contraptions often sold at the entrances to grocery stores at the beginning of every summer. Stick with classics like Weber. As with a gas grill (see above), choose the size of your grill based on your anticipated needs. If you're grilling on a fire escape, you're limited to a hibachi or tiny Weber, but if you're planning on cooking for twenty people at a time and might like to try your hand at roasting a small pig, you should buy a large rectangular number or, better yet, build a custom job out of brick, with plenty of counter space where you can set up your prepped grillables and serve them once they're done. A prime consideration here is to be honest about what you'll be doing more often, entertaining large numbers of guests or cooking for yourself—because the larger the grill, the more charcoal it takes to get it to a proper grilling temperature. Even if you're rolling solo or with just a few friends and family, one of these is still going to require the better part of a bag of charcoal to make your meal happen, and good charcoal isn't cheap.

Consider investing in a small personal-sized grill to use when it's just pork chop: party of one.

WOOD GRILLS

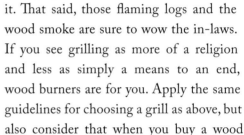

A wood grill is generally *very* expensive, first at purchase and then, more important, in terms of buying the wood to burn in it. That said, those flaming logs and the wood smoke are sure to wow the in-laws. If you see grilling as more of a religion and less as simply a means to an end, wood burners are for you. Apply the same guidelines for choosing a grill as above, but also consider that when you buy a wood grill, you really shouldn't half-ass it. Argentinean-style adjustable-height grills made for wood exclusively are built around all of the issues that come up with wood, such as the ease of adding logs, moving the coals around, and adjusting the grilling surface to match the stage the burning wood has reached. They also feature V-shaped grill rails that drain off the fat that would otherwise cause huge food-blackening flare-ups. See "Fuel" (page 267) for more pros and cons on these bad boys. They're not for everyone.

CERAMIC EGG GRILLS

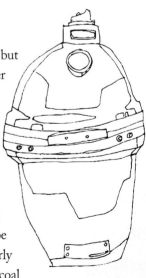

Egg grills are expensive and heavy but luxurious and extremely useful, whether you want to grill at blow-torch temperatures or smoke brisket at 180°F, or anything in between. Don't let the expense of these grills and their cult status scare you off, as they do come in a number of sizes, from tiny to grotesque, and they are versatile and very fuel efficient too, so if you will be using one a lot, it can pay for itself fairly quickly by requiring much less charcoal than a standard grill. This is especially important if you want to use high-end charcoal instead of the grocery-store brand. See "Smoking" (page 282) for a more detailed run-down of these magic eggs and their use as smokers.

Using a Grill

Whether you have a cheaper grill or a top-dollar wood-fired jam, one thing should be made clear: grills don't cook steaks by themselves. How you set up your fire is more important than what kind of fuel you use or the kind of grill you have. You can buy a fancy $5,000 grill, load it up with the most costly Japanese cult charcoal you can find, and completely ruin a lot of expensive meat because you have no idea how to build your fire.

FIRE

OK, so let's go Boy Scout here and talk about building the fire. First, assess your grilling needs: what are you cooking on the grill, and in what order is the food going to be served? Let's say that you're doing a fairly normal weekend party menu with grilled veggies, steaks, chicken, and sausages.

Well, you now know that you'll need two very different heat situations going on with the fire if you want all this stuff to come off the grill at around the same time. This means that you're going to want to build a fire that looks like the one in the illustration. Notice that most of the coals or wood chunks are on one side, with a small amount on the other side.

The two types of fire will allow you to start your chicken and sausage on the high heat side of the grill to get some color on the meat and then move them to the lower-temperature side to cook slowly while you grill your veggies and steaks on the other side.

Or say that you are going straight Neanderthal and are only going to grill up a ton of steaks and chops. You'll need a fire like this:

Notice that this fire is structured so that there are no coals or wood on the right side (reverse this if you're left-handed).

I distinctly remember that my dad had a squirt gun shaped like a mini Uzi submachine gun that he used to try to control flare-ups in the rusty, beaten-down old gas grill that came with our apartment in Orange County, California. Not only did the Uzi do a bad job of quelling the flames of grease fires, it also added a good amount of steam to the mix, which contributed an unwanted flaccid texture to the meat being cooked. Luckily, there is a better way to tame the flames. Because of the fat that is going to be melting and dripping everywhere, you need a part of the grill with no flames under it; this is the place to park your steaks, chops, and chickens and wait it out while the grease burns off when the grill is engulfed in fat-fueled flames. By building a fire in just one side of the grill, you sidestep the whole grease-fire issue. When the flames die down, simply move the meat back to the heat. The grill section without fire is also a good place to let steaks rest before serving or to keep them warm while you whip up a salad, or to allow foods about to be added to the grill to warm up so that they will cook more evenly.

THEORY

Grilling, like all cooking, is the simple act of choosing when, where, and how much heat you will apply to the item you want to stuff in your mouth in a way that yields optimal results.

When you're using a grill, though, things can get a bit more complicated. You'll need to choose (wisely) the type of fuel you're going to burn to achieve the desired results, determine how you are going to structure your fire to give you a range of heat intensity, and manage any flames caused by rendered fat.

A good general strategy for thicker cuts and items like half chickens is to start them off hot, get an acceptable amount of char on them, and then move them to a lower-temperature area to finish. This also works really well if you have guests coming over who don't tend to be punctual when it comes to dinnertime—you can sear your larger items ahead and finish them later, or rewarm said items if some of your buddies roll in after half your friends have already gone home.

However, this setup won't work for quick-cooking thin items like skirt steaks or Korean-style short ribs. For meats that need to take on a char quickly and then get off the grill before they're overcooked, you need extremely high heat. With charcoal or wood grills, you must build one section of your fire closer to the grill grate than the rest of it and plan the arc of your grilling so that these items go on early, when the coals are at their hottest. For gas, you should crank up all your burners to the maximum, close the lid, and walk away from the grill for 20 minutes or more before you open it up again—and only open it when you're ready to throw your thin meats on.

COOKING IN A PAN

As much as we'd like you to believe that we at The Meat Hook do most of our steak cookery outdoors on a wood-fired grill, wearing loincloths and drinking handles of Wild Turkey directly from the bottle, most of the time we're just at home, frying up a little steak, and doing laundry while we catch up on episodes of *Bones*.

Pan-cooking meat is unsexy day-to-day cooking that lacks the bestial punch of grilling, but it is way more practical and versatile, and, if it's done right, just as delicious. Doing right by a piece of meat when you cook it in a pan is pretty straightforward, as long as you have the right pan, the right technique, and the right mind-set. Sixty-four million French people can't be wrong.

Pans

A good pan is a simple machine. It should be thick, heavy, and made of something that can rust. That means no stainless, no nonstick coatings, no copper/aluminum sandwich cores. No bullshit. Luckily, like many of life's most useful items, a great steak pan is also pretty cheap and will last, literally, forever. Here are your options.

CAST IRON

Cast iron is the best, cheapest, and ubiquitous choice. The brand doesn't matter, just make sure the pan is heavy. I bought my main cast-iron pan at Kmart for $13, and it is just as good as any pan four times the price.

CARBON STEEL

If you want to really get fancy, you can get a French-style carbon-steel pan. Be warned: they are more expensive and take much longer to season than cast iron, not to mention that they're a bit of a specialty item and thus it's hard to find one to actually hold in your hands before you decide to take the plunge. The upside is that these pans look way cooler and less "country kitchen" than cast iron. Also, because they're not as porous as cast iron, they are less likely to hold on to strong flavors and aromas (think sketchy fish, ramps, and things like that). Honestly, though, I use my cast-iron pans way more often than my French steel pans simply because my kitchen is really tight and the shorter handles on the cast-iron pans make it easier to get around the stove. But your preference may differ.

CARE AND FEEDING

People make way too big a deal about taking proper care of iron and steel pans. Just don't wash them with dish soap, keep a scrubby around to take off any chunks, and keep the pan "polished."

Clean these pans with hot water while they're still hot; the shock of the water on the hot surface will pop off most of the gunk. Only store them once they're dried thoroughly, and take care not to stack the pans, as moisture can get trapped between them and cause rust rings. If rust happens, just scrub it off with a copper, stainless steel, or steel wool scrubby. Then reseason the pan with some fat, heat it up over a high flame, and wipe off the rusty grease with a paper towel. I usually store my pans in the oven to keep them warm, dry, and rust free.

Fats

The kind of fat you cook your meat in can have a huge effect on its flavor. Be sure to match the profile of the food you're cooking to that of the fat you're cooking it in: for example, use olive oil if you're making a Greek lamb dish, and do not use duck fat to make refried beans. Other fat choices may be a matter of what elements you want to add to the meat you're cooking. Personally, I enjoy hamburgers cooked in bacon fat—but who doesn't? No matter which fat you choose, make sure that you have enough of it in the pan. Fat transfers heat much better than a dry pan alone, so the more fat you have in the pan, the more efficiently and evenly your meat will cook and brown. That said, don't get totally crazy with the fat: you're not frying chicken here. Use three or four tablespoons and call it good. For more specific information about animal fats, see "Fat" (page 251).

OIL AND BUTTER

A classic combo. The butter helps brown the meat faster and the oil raises the smoke point of the butter. The two impart a slightly nutty flavor to most meats, especially beef.

OLIVE OIL

It's not OK to use olive oil for everything! Olive oil is going to lend a viney and vaguely Mediterranean aroma and flavor to your meat, so make sure that is going to work with the other flavors of your meal. When in doubt, use vegetable oils, like peanut.

BUTTER

Butter by itself is as particular as olive oil, so make sure you want the nutty/greasy-spoon flavor baggage that butter imparts when used to cook meat. Making a patty melt or something classically French? Go for it. Trying to wrangle the bold flavors of North Africa into a pan? Perhaps you should rethink using butter.

LARD AND BACON FAT

Our grandmothers knew what they were doing. People say you can make refried beans without lard. Or a piecrust without lard. Those people are fools. Lard and bacon fat are luscious, homey, and packed with flavor, but remember that there is nothing neutral about the flavor of either one. Make sure you want to commit to making whatever you're cooking taste like a pork chop.

SUET OR TALLOW

Suet (rendered beef fat) is great for cooking anything beef or potato related.

DUCK FAT

Duck fat is the lard of the poultry world, and it makes everything delicious. It is a great choice for cooking anything poultry related and excels at cooking other things like potatoes.

SCHMALTZ

Chicken magic! Schmaltz makes anything taste like you sprinkled it with MSG and industrial-strength fake chicken dust. It's also pretty delicious tossed with steamed vegetables.

VEGETABLE OILS

As a rule, I avoid cooking with the sort of vegetable oil commonly found in the grocery store because these oils are yucky. A lot of people really go to bat for grapeseed oil, but I find it unpleasant smelling and not as neutral as people claim it is. Provided you don't have a peanut allergy, I recommend peanut oil as the vegetable oil to go with, as I do, except when I make popcorn.

Heat

Remember the part where we talked about using big, thick, heavy pans? This is where it all starts to make sense. The way that you apply and modulate the heat is a big part of cooking anything right, whether you're talking bacon, Brussels sprouts, or chicken breasts.

The accepted wisdom about cooking in a pan is to get it smoking hot over high heat and then throw down your piece of meat to sear it off as, all the while, your kitchen is filling with a noxious haze and the smoke alarm is going off. This, for lack of a more diplomatic way of putting it, is totally macho, stupid, and wrong.

What dictates the way you cook something in the pan is the nature of the piece of meat you're cooking. Is it thin or thick? Lean or fatty? Tough or tender?

Thin, lean cuts require a high-heat situation, because you need to get that all-important crust on the meat before it overcooks and dries out. For tougher, thicker cuts, or cuts with more fat, which need to be properly rendered to be fully enjoyed, a nice medium-low heat is more desirable.

The best overall approach to cooking anything relatively tender (for tough, collagenous cuts, skip to "Braising," page 279) is to get the pan hot using high heat, then add your fat and, once the fat is as hot as it can get without smoking, toss in your meat or pieces of meat, making sure not to crowd the pan. Once the meat is sizzling along really well, lower your heat to mediumish and let it ride until it needs to be flipped.

"But why the macho high heat?" you ask. Well, that's to help get the pan over the thermal inertia of the colder temperature of the mass of the steak. "Whut?" Just look it up on the Internet. Yes, you can also start with the pan over medium heat, but it just slows everything down, and you also run the risk of the meat steaming more than browning.

Remember that the heavier the pan, the less the thermal inertia of the steak will affect the cooking process and, more important, the browning of your meat.

ROASTING

Roasting, unless it's done over a live wood fire outdoors with wolves howling in the distance, is very home-core and very easy. I wish that there was some sort of breakthrough technique or advice I could give you, but the technique of roasting meat is pretty much the same as it's always been. Here are some of my best tips, but don't overthink this too much. The best roasting cuts are those that are neither too tough (shanks, brisket) nor too lean and tender (tenderloin). Basically, you need fat to keep them juicy for the length of the roasting time and the cuts need to have enough connective tissue to hold them together through the roasting process and allow them to be sliced without falling apart.

Roasting Vessels

Pretty much any heatproof low-sided pan can do double duty as a roasting pan for smaller roasts and whole chickens. I use my medium-sized cast-iron skillet almost exclusively as my roasting pan unless it's around the holidays and I have to break out my turkey roaster. As for what to look for in a roasting pan, it's pretty simple. You want a metal or ceramic vessel that is just slightly bigger than the item to be roasted and has sides that are less than one-third of the height of that item. And if you're not the macho type, make sure the pan doesn't weigh so much that your wrists give out trying to pull the roast out of the oven.

Technique

Sure, roasting is stupid-easy to do well, but there are a few things that can save you some cooking time and make your roasts come out even better.

- **Make sure to season large roasts** (5 pounds or more) at least a day ahead to allow the salt to get in there. Huge roasts like standing rib roasts should be seasoned 3 to 4 days or more ahead.

- **Allow a roast to come to** room temperature before roasting. This will (a) allow the salt to move through the meat better and (b) make the cooking time shorter and keep the meat temperature more even—so that it is perfectly medium-rare all the way through when done. Don't try this with poultry if you're not sure how fresh it is, though, because the hour the chicken spends on the countertop might be just enough time for it to get creepy.

- **For well-marbled and fatty roasts** on the larger side, such as rib roast or pork loin, a lower cooking temperature and a longer cooking time than the recipe specifies will give you better

ROASTING COOKING TIMES

Here's a list of my favorite roasting cuts and how to cook them. Keep in mind that all of these guidelines are for average-sized roasts and the times are calculated assuming that you will brown the meat at 450°F for 15 to 20 minutes prior to roasting.

WHOLE CHICKEN
(3 TO 4 POUNDS)

Cook temp: **325° TO 375°F**

Meat Temp: **165° TO 170°F**

Time per pound: **ABOUT 20 MINUTES**

BONELESS PORK SHOULDER ROAST
(8 TO 10 POUNDS)

Cook temp: **325°F**

Meat Temp: **175° TO 190°F**

Time per pound: **25 TO 35 MINUTES**

PORK LOIN
(5 TO 6 POUNDS)

Cook temp: **325°F**

Meat Temp: **155° TO 160°F**

Time per pound: **30 MINUTES**

WHOLE FRESH HAM
(15 POUNDS)

Cook temp: **225°F**

Meat Temp: **175° TO 180°F**

Time per pound: **ABOUT 30 MINUTES**

LEG OF LAMB OR BONELESS LAMB SHOULDER ROAST
(6 TO 8 POUNDS)

Cook temp: **375° TO 425°F**

Meat Temp: **125° TO 130°F**

Time per pound: **ABOUT 20 MINUTES**

RACK OF LAMB
(2-POUND WHOLE RACK)

Cook temp: **425°F**

Meat Temp: **120° TO 125°F**

Time per pound: **ABOUT 12 MINUTES**

BEEF CHUCK ROLL
(3 TO 4 POUNDS)

Cook temp: **325°F**

Meat Temp: **125° TO 130°F**

Time per pound: **20 TO 30 MINUTES**

BEEF RIB ROAST
(4 BONE)

Cook temp: **250°F**

Meat Temp: **125° TO 135°F**

Time per pound: **ABOUT 40 MINUTES**

WHOLE BEEF TENDERLOIN ROAST
(3 TO 4 POUNDS)

Cook temp: **425°F**

Meat Temp: **120° TO 125°F**

Time per pound: **10 TO 12 MINUTES**

BEEF TOP ROUND ROAST
(6 TO 8 POUNDS)

Cook temp: **250°F**

Meat Temp: **125° TO 130°F**

Time per pound: **ABOUT 30 MINUTES**

results. Letting these items cruise for many hours at 225°F will break down a lot of their connective tissue, deeply render the fat, and just make everything really yummy.

- **Blast the roast with high heat** at the end. Some people say to do this at the beginning, and it's certainly safer to do it that way because you don't run the risk of overcooking your meat, but I prefer to do it at the end since the rendered fat makes the crust crispier. If you're cooking a skin-on pork loin roast, it's the only way to go.

- **Resting is really important. Rest small** and medium roasts (3 to 6 pounds) for 10 minutes, and large roasts for 20 minutes or more. This will ensure that the meat has enough time to relax and redistribute its juices, making the meat moist and tender.

BRAISING

Slow-cooking, or braising, is deceptively elementary. Yes, it's easy to do because it requires very little fussing with while the dish cooks, but you need to front-load the cooking process with more than a little attention to detail if you want your dish to come out right. Just throwing a bunch of stuff in a Crock-Pot is not the same as braising. You're better than that.

THE POT

True, you can use a traditional slow cooker if you don't have an oven or don't have the scratch for a fancy enameled Dutch oven, but don't do it. Number one, it defeats the purpose of a one-pot meal, which should be made, well, in one pot, not a pot and a pan. For your meal to end up right, you need to brown the meat first, and this is something a slow cooker simply cannot do. Number two is a little less cut-and-dried, but here goes: slow cookers make everything taste the same. I have no idea how it happens, but everything that goes into a Crock-Pot tastes like it was cooked in a Crock-Pot—and, to me, doesn't taste good at all.

Now that I've talked you out of that slow-cooker nonsense, get yourself a nice heavy Dutch oven. I bought a cast-iron one at a flea market for $11, so don't cry poverty if you can't get $150 together for a new one. The enameled French ones are nice to have and look really beautiful, but you can get by with regular old black cast iron, as long as you take care of it (see page 274). And your Dutch oven needs a lid that fits snugly.

MEAT

Start by choosing any one or a combination of the tough cuts listed under "General Meat Cooking for Four-Legged Animals" (page 268). Budget about half a pound of meat per person if you want leftovers. Once you've chosen your cut or cuts, start by salting the cut liberally and then browning it off in your Dutch oven over high heat, about 4 minutes per side. Choosing what fat to use when doing this is up to you, but you can reference "Fats" (page 275) to help you decide. Then, once the meat is nice and brown, you can turn off the heat and remove the meat to rest on a waiting plate while you get your act together. Be sure to leave the fat and brown bits in the pot so they can be used to cook and flavor the things that come next.

AROMATICS

Use the usual suspects here: garlic, onions, celery, and carrots. For an example of how much of each to use, check out the Rabbit Ragout recipe (page 233). Yes, it's

BRAISING COOKING TIMES

Here are some of the braising cuts that are favorites in the butcher shop. You can really braising any cut, not just tough and chewy ones, using these guidelines it'll just won't take as long.

BEEF BRISKET
Cook temp: **250° TO 300°F**

Time: **6 TO 8 HOURS**

PORK BELLY
Cook temp: **300° TO 325°F**

Time: **1½ TO 2½ HOURS**

BEEF POT ROAST (BOTTOM ROUND, CHUCK, ETC.)
Cook temp: **300° TO 325°F**

Time: **3 TO 4 HOURS**

LAMB NECK
Cook temp: **300° TO 350°F**

Time: **3 TO 4 HOURS**

BEEF SHORT RIBS
Cook temp: **300° TO 325°F**

Time: **6 TO 8 HOURS**

LAMB SHOULDER
Cook temp: **300° TO 325°F**

Time: **6 TO 8 HOURS**

PORK SHOULDER, BONE-IN
Cook temp: **300° TO 325°F**

Time: **6 TO 8 HOURS**

RABBIT, WHOLE
Cook temp: **300° TO 325°F**

Time: **3 TO 4 HOURS**

PORK SHANK
Cook temp: **300° TO 325°F**

Time: **6 TO 8 HOURS**

DUCK LEG
Cook temp: **275° TO 300°F**

Time: **3 TO 4 HOURS**

a rabbit recipe. No, it doesn't matter if it's rabbit or beef shank—the building blocks are the same. If you have fresh herbs kicking around, feel free to add some of those as well, but step lightly. One sprig of thyme or a few rosemary leaves are all that are needed to add flavor, and if you overdo it, your braise is going to end up tasting like a shot of Jägermeister.

Chop all of your aromatics roughly and get your pot going again over medium heat. Add them and let them sweat (soften) for about 5 minutes. Make sure to scrape up any brown stuff on the bottom of your pot with a spoon and stir it into the aromatics. Now would be a great time to preheat your oven to 250°F, by the way.

LIQUIDS

I find that 1 part Basic Brown Stock (page 243) to 2 parts tomatoes is usually a good place to start. A 28-ounce can of crushed tomatoes is exactly the right amount of tomatoes for a normal-sized braise to feed 4 to 6 people, and you want about half that amount of good stock. Again, when in doubt, reference the Rabbit Ragout recipe (page 233) for specifics, but I'm sure you get the idea. Once the aromatics have had 5 minutes or so in the pot, add your browned meat and then your stock and tomatoes and give everything a good stir. Wish everybody luck, since you won't be seeing these guys for a while. Pop on the lid and put the whole thing in the oven. (Use oven mitts so you don't burn yourself!)

THE WAITING GAME

You had some TV to catch up on, right? Braising times vary, depending on the cut, but the bare minimum should be around 2 hours for chicken and rabbit and up to 8 to 10 hours for really tough cuts of beef like shank or brisket. Read up on whatever cut you're using in its respective chapter to get an idea of how many episodes of *CSI: Miami* you're looking at. And please don't feel compelled to peek at, stir, poke, prod, or generally fuck with your braise until you're about an hour away from go time; it's doing fine without you. If you're the

nervous type, set a timer to remind you about when you're needed, but chances are you'll be able to tell, because your kitchen will smell delicious. At this point, you need to uncover the pot and make a judgment call: is it too wet? Depending on what you're going to do with your braised concoction, you may want it either soupy or more like pulled pork, moisture level–wise. If you want it drier, simply leave the lid off when you place it back in the oven for the last hour, so the liquid will reduce by 20 to 30 percent. Once you've achieved your desired level of liquid, simply replace the lid and call it a day—well, until the last hour is up anyway.

SEASONING AND SERVING

Now that your braise is cooked perfectly, you need to finish it. Notice that I did not mention seasoning the braise earlier beyond salting the meat, and that was on purpose. Remember how you decided to reduce the liquid in the braise an hour ago? If you had seasoned the braise in the beginning, you might have been left with a very salty situation as the water evaporated but the salt stayed. That's why you're just now adding salt. Taste your braise and season it with salt until you like the taste. Are the flavors still not really popping for you? Try adding a small amount of vinegar or a vinegar-based hot sauce and try it again. Magic, right? Serve immediately, with the starch of your choice (I recommend the Drop Dumplings, page 233).

SMOKING

Smoking meat is right up there with cooking meat over a wood campfire as one of the oldest forms of transforming the flesh of animals into food. Unlike grilling over a fire, though, smoking was traditionally used for food preservation, as the combination of salt-curing and complex chemical residues deposited on the meat by the smoldering wood makes it resistant to bugs, bacteria, and other bad actors.

What we know today as American barbecue (not to be confused with grilling, please) is a whole different animal from the sort of smoking-to-preserve-meat type of thing that came over from the Old World and was also preexistent here with some of the native tribes. Rather than trying to keep the bugs off the hams or dry out thin strips of elk, American barbecue is all about cooking large, cheap cuts of meat with smoke at a moderate temperature (around 180° to 225°F) to break down the tough connective tissue and melt the fat until it becomes something else. It's a whole other food group, really. Barbecue has a singular smoky richness unlike that of any cuisine in the world.

AS AMERICAN AS BARBECUE

Like jazz, blues, and the NFL, traditional barbecue is so American it hurts. Southerners will maintain that barbecue is a product of the South, and they're half right. While barbecue might have been born there and was perhaps little known outside the region for years, World War II changed all of that for good. As America mobilized for war in 1942, millions of Southerners of all colors made a mass migration to all corners of the country seeking newly available high-paying manufacturing jobs; others met and mingled in the armed services. After the war was over, many Southerners stayed on in the far-flung cities that had become their homes. More notably for what we're talking about here, many of them then cashed in their war bonds and started barbecue joints. Whether it was out of homesickness or a desire to own a business and turn a profit, those early pioneers of the barbecue diaspora let the genie out of the bottle and forged a truly national cuisine as iconic as that other twentieth-century American standard, the hamburger.

SMOKING COOKING TIMES

The kind of meats that you want to smoke are usually of the tough, fatty, and cheap variety. Here is a magical chart of any and all of the things you can smoke and at what temperature.

BEEF BRISKET
Temperature: **190° TO 220°F**
Time: **10 TO 16 HOURS**

LAMB BREAST
Temperature: **220° TO 250°F**
Time: **6 TO 10 HOURS**

BEEF RIBS
Temperature: **190° TO 220°F**
Time: **8 TO 12 HOURS**

LAMB SHOULDER
Temperature: **220° TO 250°F**
Time: **8 TO 10 HOURS**

BEEF SHOULDER CLOD
Temperature: **190° TO 220°F**
Time: **6 TO 10 HOURS**

CHICKEN, HALVED
Temperature: **290° TO 325°F**
Time: **1 TO 2½ HOURS**

BONE-IN PORK SHOULDER
Temperature: **200° TO 225°F**
Time: **10 TO 12 HOURS**

WHOLE DUCK
Temperature: **275° TO 300°F**
Time: **8 TO 10 HOURS**

PORK RIBS (BABY BACK OR SPARE)
Temperature: **190° TO 220°F**
Time: **6 TO 8 HOURS**

WHOLE TURKEY
Temperature: **290° TO 325°F**
Time: **6 TO 8 HOURS**

PORK BELLY
Temperature: **220°F**
Time: **7 TO 10 HOURS**

Smokers

Smokers range from huge automated carousel smokers that cost as much as a used Porsche to homemade smokers fashioned out of junk from the dump. The smokers discussed here are the kinds that you're most likely to encounter for the home pit master—though keep in mind that a smoker, or "cooker," as people who actually make barbecue for a living call it, can be anything that you can use to smoke meat in successfully (as a trip to any backwoods barbecue place will show you).

OFFSET SMOKERS

This is the most widely available smoker around—you can get one at nearly any big-box home store for around $150. It consists of a chamber for the wood, connected to a larger chamber for the meat, with an air intake valve and an adjustable exhaust on the chimney. Dollar for dollar, an offset smoker is the best bet for a first foray into smoking, but you will have to rotate your meat, as the end closest to the wood chamber will be hotter.

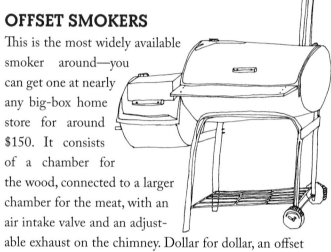

ELECTRIC SMOKERS

Electric smokers come in many shapes and sizes; some include an automated temperature control as well as an automatic wood puck–feeding system so you don't have to trouble yourself with adding more fuel. Those on the lower end look like odd-shaped black trash cans, with a heating element in the bottom that heats up a pan of wood chips, much like the improvised trash-can smoker we have at The Meat Hook (see page 286). My advice is to avoid the cheaper versions of electric smokers and go with an offset one instead, unless you also want to do stuff like smoke fish, sausages, and hams. Fancy automated jobbies like the Bradley smoker work well for those tasks and are pretty acceptable for doing barbecue as well. I personally prefer the romance of burning logs in an offset smoker to the cold practicality of the sawdust-and-puck setups.

EGG SMOKERS

Egg smokers, when used properly, are amazing. If you actually read the instructions thoroughly, you'll find that you can load one of these up with precisely the amount of wood you'll need for smoking your items, and you'll never have to mess with it, aside from swinging by now and then to rotate the meat. Another advantage is that these smokers can also work as kick-ass grills capable of very high heat, and they use very little wood because they are so well insulated and have effective air-flow controls. The downside is that an egg smoker has a steep learning curve; I am still trying to figure out how to use it for all the amazing things that it can do. Plus, it's heavy and expensive. If you won't have to move your egg smoker and you have a thick roll of cash burning a hole in your pocket, go for it.

Wood

Wood is at the heart of smoking, and what wood you choose will have a huge effect on how your meat tastes. My personal preference is cherrywood for pork and hickory or oak for beef, but don't let me influence your choices. From the point of view of traditional barbecue, the right wood is whatever is the cheapest and most available. So if you live in an area with a bunch of apple orchards, you will probably end up with applewood-smoked barbecue, or, if you live in Texas, post oak and mesquite. No matter what wood you choose, just make sure that it is well seasoned—if it's green and/ or wet, it will totally screw up your barbecue. A firewood seller is the best place to find seasoned hardwood; just make sure to ask the guy or lady what kind of wood it is to make sure that you're not getting any pine or other resinous, bad-tasting soft wood.

ONE OTHER THOUGHT ON SMOKING AND BARBECUE

In theory, barbecue is very easy: season meat, stick in smoker at X temperature for X time, and remove when it reads X internal temperature. Well, that is how it is supposed to go, but in reality, every piece of meat is different and cooks in its own particular way. A cut that may be at the proper temperature after smoking for the prescribed amount of time might not actually be ready if you touch it to check for doneness. Other times, the meat you're smoking might take a full hour less than you thought.

What this boils down to is that barbecue is not a formula, it's a feel—which is why there's so much bad barbecue out there, I guess. The real key to doing good barbecue is to experiment, keep records, and, most important, eat lots of good barbecue made by different people. Once you get into the cycle of experimenting and eating excellent barbecue, you will start to figure out what you like and how to make it. Barbecue at its core is (or should be) what the people cooking it love—not what other people tell them they should make.

HOW TO MAKE AN IMPROVISED SMOKER

Once you get the gist of smoking meat, almost anything starts to look like something you can use to make a smoker. Here's one that you can cobble together out of stuff from the hardware store for around $40.

1. Punch a hole in the side of the trash can. It should be about 2 inches above the bottom of the can and big enough for the hot plate cord to pass through. Make sure to smooth the edges of the hole so they don't cut the cord and, well, electrocute you. Place the hot plate inside and set it to high. Do not plug it in yet!

2. Place the cake pan, with about 1 cup of wood chips, on the hot plate heating element. Place the metal rack inside the can, making sure it is level and very firmly in place, as you'll be putting heavy meat on it. I find that a circular rack from a small or medium-sized charcoal grill that has been abandoned works great for this.

3. Place the meat to be smoked on the rack and place the lid loosely on top of the can. If you're using a PID, place the heat sensor on the rack near the meat and send the cord out through the top of the can.

4. Plug the hot plate into the (plugged-in) extension cord, and watch the magic happen! Or, if you're using a PID, plug the hot plate into it and then plug the PID's cord into the extension cord and set the PID to the desired temperature.

Note: You will need to remove the meat and rack periodically to replenish the wood chips. Hey, it's improvised—it's not built for convenience.

SPECIAL EQUIPMENT

Metal trash can with lid
Chisel or other object that can cut through the side of the trash can
Electric hot plate
Cake pan
Wood chips
Round metal rack that fits snugly inside the trash can about a third of the way down
PID setup (optional; for an explanation, see "DIY Sous-Vide," page 291)
Extension cord

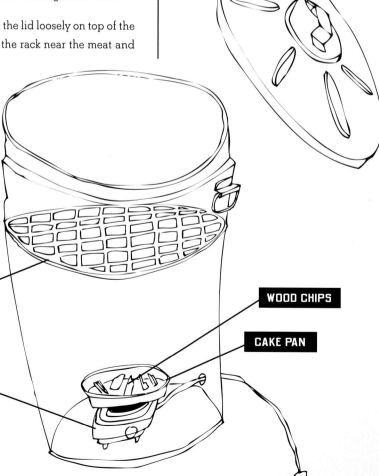

GRATE

WOOD CHIPS

HOT PLATE

CAKE PAN

FRYING

Let's face it: fried food is delicious. I'm not convinced it actually is bad for you, but it tastes so good that it must be. Health considerations aside, it's also pretty damned messy and more than a little dangerous to do at home—all of which makes us at The Meat Hook real fans of frying. Deep-frying works with almost all meats if you prepare them properly, but I think that chicken and tender cuts of pork, like thinly sliced boneless loin, are really where it's at.

Oils and Fats

PEANUT OIL

Peanut oil, unless you are allergic to it, is the king of fryer oils. It has a high smoke point and a fairly neutral taste, and it is easy to find at reasonable prices, especially if you live near a Chinatown.

CORN AND CANOLA OILS

Cheap and ubiquitous corn and canola oils are the most convenient frying oils, but make sure that you're getting one that doesn't get what I can only call the crappy oil smell to it when hot. This aroma will be infused into whatever you're cooking and really downgrade all of the hard work you put into making all that luxurious fried food. Avoid extra-cheap store-brand varieties.

GRAPESEED OIL

Grapeseed oil, as I mentioned earlier, has a high smoke point, but it generally has a weird viney smell. I usually stay away from it, especially since it can cost more than peanut oil, which is totally awesome.

COCONUT OIL

Coconut oil is a great cooking fat for fried sweet things or those with sweet-and-spicy Asian flavors, but it makes everything smell vaguely like tanning oil at the beach.

Dredges and Batters

Deep-frying meat that hasn't been dredged or battered seems kind of silly to me. Following are some of my favorite starches and my favorite batter is on page 290, for your consideration.

CORNSTARCH

This weird, slippery powder makes a batter that is hard, shiny, and nearly glass-like. It's nice to add to a batter or dredge to give extra crunch, but don't go crazy, unless you're looking for that Chinese food crispness.

POTATO STARCH

Similar to cornstarch, but with less glass-like, shiny results. This is a favorite with the Japanese for many fried izakaya items. It's a great additive to any dredge or batter.

TAPIOCA STARCH

Another great blending starch. Use it exactly like potato starch; you'll get a slightly more "cornstarchy" effect of glass-like exteriors.

ALL-PURPOSE FLOUR

AP flour is the standard main ingredient in nearly any dredge or batter. It can get fairly crispy, adds bulk, and gives fried items a nice substantial feel. I like to use about 50 percent all-purpose flour and 50 percent of another starch to get a nice all-around crispy texture.

Brines and Soaks

Putting your meat in a brine or soak before frying helps break down the muscles and make the meat more tender. It also seasons the meat and gives the dredge something extra to stick to. If you like extra-crispy take-out chicken, a brine is the way to go.

Fryers

The simplest frying setup is a Dutch oven with a clip-on thermometer. This is what I usually use, but if you're gadget minded and have a much bigger kitchen than I do, you can get yourself a stand-alone electric fryer pretty cheap on the Internet. These are safer to use since there is no open flame and they allow you to fry outdoors (if you have an electrical outlet outside or feel like snaking an extension cord out the back window), to avoid wiping grease mist off every surface of your kitchen. I like the old-fashioned Fry Daddy types, but if you're having a party, feel free to go nuts and get one of those huge ones that cost $150. I won't stop you.

Temperature

Standard frying temperature is 375°F or thereabouts, but some recipes call for higher or lower temperatures, depending on what you're frying. If you're using a pot full of oil on a range top, heat the oil over high heat until it reaches the desired temperature, then turn the heat down to medium-low to hold the temperature while you get your frying supplies together. Jack the heat up again after you put your items in the oil so that the temperature doesn't dip too low, then turn it down again once the oil has stabilized.

Blanching

No, I'm not thinking about blanching vegetables here. Blanching is how good French fries are made, and Korean fried chicken too. Blanching in oil is simply frying things first at a lower temperature (like 325°F or so) to cook them through and then putting them back into the fryer at the standard 375°F to crisp them up. This works particularly well for fried chicken and anything that has some fat to render or connective tissue to break down.

How to Fry

After all this preamble about starches, dredges, soaks, and whatnot, you'll be pleased to know that the actual frying part is fairly simple. Start by placing a few pieces of your meat at a time into the hot oil. Absolutely do not try to crowd in a lot of pieces! This will cause the oil to be too cold for too long and the result will be soggy, greasy fried meat. Once you've added these items, leave them alone for a few minutes before turning them with your tongs or chopsticks or what have you so that they fry evenly. Continue turning the pieces until they are a nice golden color and the meat is cooked through. Remove a piece to test if in doubt as to their doneness. Once you're satisfied with the color and doneness, transfer the pieces to a rack or paper-towel-lined plate to drain. Serve hot.

FRYER SAFETY

Before you get all liquored up and decide to beer-batter a bunch of bacon strips and dip them in maple syrup (not that we have ever done this), you need to understand that frying is a dangerous business and you must observe a few safety measures.

- Never fry without a fire extinguisher made for grease fires close at hand. Hot oil is very flammable and grease fires are really tough to put out.

- Do not overfill your fryer or pot with oil, as it can overflow when the food is added, leading to a grease fire. Half- to two-thirds full is about as high as you want

- Don't fry frozen things other than onion rings and French fries.

- Keep some burn spray handy. Oil burns aren't as bad as sugar burns, but they're not fun either.

BASIC DREDGE

Think of this dredge recipe as a starting point, not something chiseled in stone. If you want more crunch, reduce the all-purpose flour and use more cornstarch or potato starch (or tapioca). If what you're frying is on the bland side, you may want to increase the salt or spices or add other spices that complement the flavors of the end dish.   **MAKES 1¼ CUPS**

In a small bowl, combine all the ingredients, whisking them together very well and taking care not to let the spices and salt fall to the bottom of the bowl. It's a good idea to rewhisk before using the dredge if it sits for long, as it may resettle.

1 cup all-purpose flour
¼ cup cornstarch or potato starch
1 teaspoon kosher salt
1 teaspoon hot smoked paprika or pimentón
½ teaspoon freshly ground black pepper
¼ teaspoon onion powder
¼ teaspoon garlic powder

BASIC BEER BATTER

Take the Basic Dredge and whisk in beer, about 1 cup, until it reaches a consistency that coats the whisk well but isn't gloppy. Keep in mind that all beers are not equal—stay away from those with flavors that may not complement the food you are frying. Avoid extremely hoppy or bitter ales; try a lager or amber ale instead. Dip your protein of choice—or almost anything, really—into the batter and then transfer it gently to your fryer oil.

MAKES ABOUT 2 CUPS

MEAT HOOK CHICKEN SOAK

Your chicken will like hanging out in this buttermilk-and-hot-sauce soak before getting dredged or battered.   **MAKES ABOUT 6½ CUPS, ENOUGH FOR 2 CHICKENS, CUT INTO 8 PIECES EACH**

Mix all the ingredients together thoroughly in a large bowl. Add the chicken pieces and toss and turn them well, making sure all the pieces are fully coated. Cover the bowl with two or three layers of plastic wrap, place the chicken on the bottom shelf of the refrigerator, and let soak for at least 24 hours and up to 48 hours.

1 quart buttermilk
¼ cup hot sauce, such as Texas Pete
2 cups water
2 tablespoons kosher salt
1 tablespoon sugar

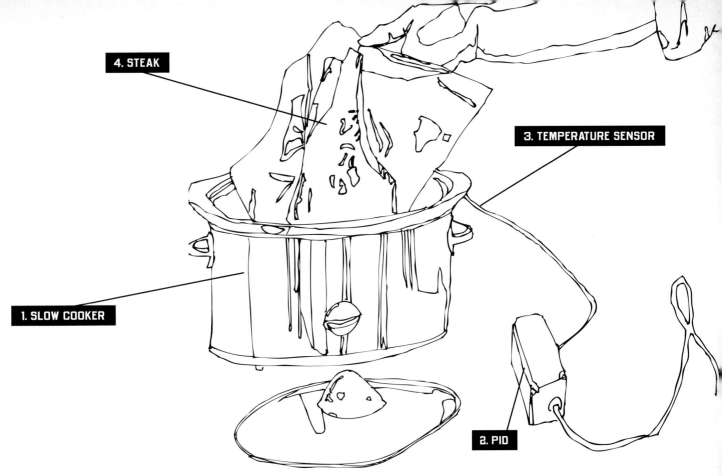

4. STEAK

3. TEMPERATURE SENSOR

1. SLOW COOKER

2. PID

DIY SOUS-VIDE

Sous vide **is the French way** of saying you're going to cook (in this case meat) in a vacuum-sealed bag that's submerged in hot water. If you're a curious human being, you may want to dabble in this whole sous-vide thing without shelling out $4,000 for an immersion circulator and a vacuum sealer. While the setup described here is not the most professional, it will get the job done if your goal is to explore the world of sous vide before taking a significant financial plunge. Bonus points for already owning a slow cooker.

This budget sous-vide system is based on a PID controller that you can buy online for less than a hundred bucks, resealable plastic bags, and a slow cooker full of water. What is a PID? Well, basically, it's a thermostat that is hooked up to a power control unit that modulates the heating device of the slow cooker by allowing electricity to go to the plug of the cooker or not. You follow? Yeah, me neither. It might be better if I just showed you a picture of it.

1. This is the main event, the electric slow cooker where the meat is cooked in plastic bags submerged in the water.

2. This is what the slow cooker is plugged into, which, in turn, is plugged into the wall socket. Here's where you set the time and temperature. It controls the heat of the water by turning the element on or off based on the readings from the temperature probe.

3. The temperature sensor is placed in the water bath and cues the PID to turn the heat on or off to maintain the temperature of the water.

4. A sous-vide bag improvised from a vaccum-sealed bag or Ziploc bag.

So, how does it work? Basically, you choose a cut of meat you want cooked perfectly to temperature, and you want it to reach the temperature over the course of a few hours, instead of the usual few minutes or so, to render it more tender (i.e., there's more time for connective tissue to dissolve) and more evenly cooked. Then a final sear is achieved via a brief visit to the grill, since the steak is already cooked through.

You need to be careful when cooking sous vide for a number of reasons, but mostly you want to make sure that you're not using the technique with creepy meat, as the "danger-zone" temperatures of typical sous vide (danger zone equals 41° to 140°F) will cause bacteria to multiply (think dirty hot tub). The best meat to use is pastured meat that has not been Cryovacced (i.e., wet-aged), because it will have fewer harmful bacteria versus good bacteria due to its general health and lower water activity (a fancy way of saying it is drier). I'm not going to pay your medical bills if you don't follow my suggestions for clean meat, so don't try at-home sous vide on the cheap, OK?

SOUS-VIDE RIB STEAK

For much more extensive advice and ideas on sous vide, see *Modernist Cuisine* by Nathan Myhrvold. Since you spent significantly less money buying this book, though, I'll give you a recipe to illustrate a small portion of what this technology is capable of and to furnish a starting point for future experiments. **SERVES 2 TO 3**

One 2-inch-thick dry-aged, grass-fed rib-eye steak from the shoulder end (about 3 pounds)
Kosher salt

SPECIAL EQUIPMENT
DIY sous-vide setup (see page 291)
A gallon-sized Ziploc bag

1. Fill your slow cooker with water. Set your temperature (115°F) in the PID and allow 1 hour for the water to come to temperature. Next, salt the rib eye liberally and insert it into the plastic bag. Seal it and press out the air completely. When the water is at temperature, add the bagged steak and allow it to cook for about 1$^{1}/_{2}$ hours. Then pull it out of the water and the bag and allow it to rest, dry, and cool on a plate in the refrigerator for 1 hour.

2. While the steak rests, heat your grill/pan/broiler until it is as hot as it can get. Place the steak in/on said cooking surface for just a few minutes, until it has achieved some color or char on one side, then flip and repeat on the other side. Once the steak has acquired the color you want, allow it to rest on a plate and carryover cook for 5 minutes before slicing and serving.

Salt

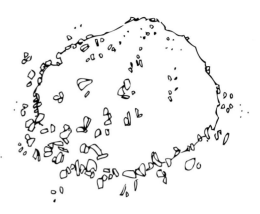

Salt is *the* key ingredient to making meat taste the way it should. While the recipes in this book call for kosher salt because it is by far the most ubiquitous and easy-to-use good-quality salt, that doesn't mean it's the only game in town. There are as many types of salt as there are cuisines on earth, if not more. If you get a present of an exotic black volcanic salt from Fiji, experiment with it first on a small scale, then move on to larger recipes. Here's a brief rundown of the commonly available salts out there and what they're useful for.

KOSHER SALT

Kosher salt is neutral, contains no iodine, and has big flakes that stick well to food in general and meat in particular. It's easy to portion intuitively with pinched fingers.

FINE SEA SALT

Fine sea salt contains less sodium than kosher salt, but it has more trace mineral salts that are good for you. You can use less salt than with regular table salt. The salt may contain natural color-fixing nitrates. One downside is that it clumps and is hard to sprinkle evenly on meat.

COARSE SEA SALT

Coarse sea salt is chunky and easy to sprinkle compared to fine sea salt, which means it's great for seasoning large roasts or curing salt pork, hams, and prosciutto.

SICILIAN SEA SALT

Sicilian sea salt has all the qualities of the sea salts above plus a good amount of natural nitrate-related mineral salts. It is good for seasoning things when using olive oil and resinous herb flavors, and it goes well with fish. It is the go-to salt for curing ham without pink salt. Experiment before trying out major recipes, as this tastes much saltier than the same volume of kosher salt.

MALDON SALT

Maldon is a beautiful-looking and extremely clean-tasting sea salt that is extracted via a special evaporation process that gives it its snowflake-meets-diamonds look. It's too pricey to use every day, but it does make a great finishing salt to sprinkle on a big steak.

SEL GRIS AND FLEUR DE SEL

These salts are naturally precipitated in large ponds in southern France. Sel gris is very briny tasting and may have bits of seaweed and sand in it. I find that it sometimes gives a slightly fishy flavor to dry-aged, grass-fed beef. Fleur de sel comes from these same ponds, but it is the light, delicate crystals that form and float on the top of the water rather than underneath the water, like sel gris. These crystals are gently scooped off the surface by hand and are much less seaweedy in flavor, as they never touch the bottom.

HIMALAYAN PINK SEA SALT

Himalayan salt has a slightly different mineral content than other sea salts and a much lower water content, because it is a fossil salt that was buried underground for millions of years.

RED, BLACK, GREEN, AND OTHER COLORED SALTS

Colored salts are usually tinted by the local clay, or they may contain other minerals that give them color and also reduce the salinity-to-volume ratio, making them taste less salty. Colored salts can be great, but usually they're more of a gimmick than anything else. Black salt, though, is extremely heavy metal.

FARMING

Farms are the heart and soul of The Meat Hook. Without them, we'd be just another bunch of idiots listening to hair metal and cutting pork chops. When we were opening the shop, we decided to simply work with only the five farms we loved working with at our previous butchering gigs. These are farms that have the consistent high quality we were by now looking for. I say that "we were by now looking for" because in our early days as butchers, we didn't really know good from bad stuff. As long as the farm had all the proper feel-good adjectives attached to its farming practices, we ordered up and waited to see what we were going to get. Nothing will show you the quality of meat that you want more than getting a whole lot of stuff that you don't want.

Working with a lot of farms, talking with the farmers, and visiting them as often as we could taught us that simply buying in to buzzwords and breed names is not the way to source meat. Learning to tell the difference between a farmer who knows what he's doing and a guy going through the motions taught us more about farming and animal husbandry than any of us ever thought we would know. Our relationships with our farmers go beyond riding around in a truck, looking at animals grazing in beautiful pastoral landscapes, and patting ourselves on the back for being such good human beings. We are now part of the evolution of our farms. We are in a constant conversation with our farms, asking questions, giving feedback, and anteing up our hard-won dollars to engage in experiments with our farmers.

I also began to read a lot about farming. Sometimes too much. During a particular period of obsessive farm research, I am quite sure I annoyed the hell out of our farmers by pestering them with wacky ideas I had gotten from a Greg Judy book or from watching a farm conference lecture. Part of what I have learned from our farmers is the difference between what can theoretically be done on a farm and what is practical. With that humbling experience in mind, I'd like to give you just enough information about pasture-based farming to bemuse and, OK, perhaps irritate the next farmer you chat up at the market.

GENETICS

Genetics is the single most important element of animal husbandry when it comes to the quality of the meat. Wait, you say, I thought we were talking about beef, not Franken-corn! Relax, I'm not referring to engineering a glow-in-the-dark heifer that produces its own pesticides and craps gold coins and superconductors. Animals have been naturally bred for thousands of years to do all kinds of things. Whether we're talking about a teacup poodle or a Clydesdale, various breeds have been bred to be able to perform a specific task, and meat animals are no exception. For an animal to fatten up well in the universe outside of feedlots and other concentrated feed operations, a farmer needs to start with animals that have genes that enable them not just to survive on but also to excel on pasture.

Most people who have skimmed a Michael Pollan book or read a profile of Joel Salatin in the newspaper would likely be hollering about grass at this point and how grass (or pasture management, really) *is* important. However, all the amazing pastureland in the world is not enough to turn a poorly bred animal into a source of prime meat. Unfortunately, we've spent the last seventy years or more breeding out the genetic traits that allow animals to flourish on pasture. But what it takes for an animal to truly do well outside an industrial meat operation is not uncomplicated.

Grazers like sheep and beef have to have short, stocky, wide frames and girthy bellies with large rumens (stomachs) to convert all of that grass into muscle and fat. Pigs need sturdy feet and aggressive foraging abilities to get around on uneven ground and find delicious grubs hidden under logs. Poultry has to be hardy enough to weather cold nights that would have their battery-raised relatives dropping dead. All pastured animals must be low-maintenance, docile, and fertile and have good mothering abilities.

Years of selecting and breeding animals that efficiently convert forage into well-marbled tender meat, reproduce well, and are all but impervious to parasites and disease are required to raise meat that compares to that of animals plied with corn, hormones, and antibiotics. Luckily for us, not all of those genetic traits have been lost, and through the magic of artificial insemination, these days ensuring that animals have the proper traits can be only a phone call or a mouse click away. While artificial insemination (AI in the business) is neither cheap nor easy, it does allow for the possibility of the genes of all but extinct breeds to make a comeback, and for the results of decades of selective breeding on, say, some remote farm on the other side of the world to spread to bull breeders and local farms much more quickly than if they had to start from scratch.

Linear Measurement

I realize that I'm pushing it here by trying to sneak a section called Linear Measurement (LM) into a pop butchering book, so I'll keep it short. LM is about the ratios and relationships among the various measurements of a given animal and how those predict how it will perform on breeding, mothering ability, performance on pasture, and taste. It's not unlike a smaller version of the master code to the universe from the movie *Pi*.

The measurements involved are much like those of bust, arm length, and waist size on people. Once you take these measurements for a given animal, you can do the math, which will tell you if the animal is desirable for breeding, putting on pasture, or merely sending off to market. What ratios are desirable in grass-fed animals? Well, basically what we've been discussing: those that translate into short, stocky, wide animals. This also extends to symmetrical udders or testicles.

GROWING GRASS

After genetics, the growing or, really, the management of pasture is what separates a grass-based farm enterprise that has fat, happy animals from one that is just getting by. Grass is a strange kind of permaculture that, once established, either by Mother Nature or by seeding, continues to evolve day by day, season by season, and year by year, reflecting how it is treated. Whether it becomes lush, with deep layers of microbe-rich humus, or thin and dry has a lot to do with what the animals eating it are, well, eating.

GEARLD FRY

Not many people know who Gearld Fry is, and that is just a damned shame. Gearld is the grand old man of pasture-raised beef—and he is singlehandedly responsible for most of what I have learned about beef before it gets to our breaking table. Of the many things I gleaned from Gearld during my brief time with him on a hot day in 2007 was that weaning and selection are far more important to the end product than I would have ever guessed. He taught me that calves need to fully wean from their mothers. This process may take as long as ten or eleven months, and because it requires so much time, many people skimp on it and pull the animals out to pasture before they are ready. The result of incomplete weaning isn't cattle with mommy complexes, but rather cattle with underdeveloped gastrointestinal tracts, which means that they can't do as complete or efficient a job of converting grass, hay, or baleage to bone, fat, and muscle. Not good. Second, a good farmer needs to recognize which of his young animals have the best genetics to pass on to the next generation, judging them on the hoof and selecting tomorrow's bulls and heifers by looking

Managed Grazing and Mob Grazing

While our romantic ideas of the American West might lead us to believe that the best beef in the world is derived from free-roaming steers dotting the sides of hills on the open range while the shadows of lazy clouds slide by, it's simply not true. For pastureland to be at its best, it must be grazed in a way that works with the "grassness" of the land and not against it. If this seems like complete hippie bullshit, let me explain what I mean.

If you could transport yourself back in time to the vast primordial grasslands of the Midwest and Africa, you would notice that the animals that ate those grasses were not traveling across them in the broad, spread-out herds that you would see today in Montana or Texas. Rather, because of the prodigious numbers of natural predators, the herds of wild grazers stayed in very densely packed units to help protect themselves from being picked

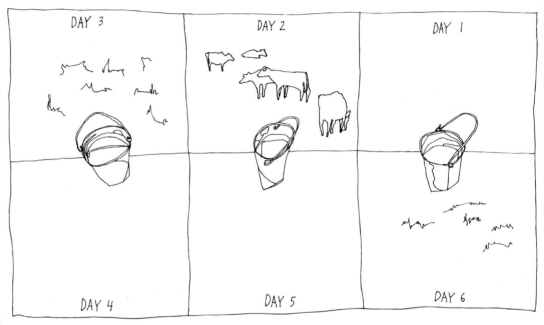

off one at a time. This sort of strength-in-numbers survival strategy had a strange effect on the ancient swards as the plants and herbivores coexisted over time.

In the same way that fire, drought, and seasonal weather changes influenced the growth and dormancy of savannah flora, so did the intensive herd grazing of animals. Once a mob had chewed up, stomped down, and pooped all over the grasses and moved on, the symbiotic community would be spurred into action. Insects, fungi, and microbes brought the nutrients from the dung, urine, and trampled vegetation down into the humus. The plants, fired up by the activity in the humus and by their natural tendency not to be shaded out by other grasses, started to grow at a rapid rate. It was a process that increased the vitality of the plants and the soil while building up the humus that would make the soil more drought resistant.

What it boils down to is that managed intensive grazing (MIG—there are many different schools of thought about which styles are best) is a good thing for the pasture and soil, and it's also good for the herbivores that eat that grass, not just because the quality of the forage improves after each graze. A large part of keeping animals stress-free and healthy is making sure that they're free of parasites. One of the natural side benefits to rotational grazing is that it interrupts the life cycle of those nasty little bastards, because by the time they're ready to do their thing, the herd has left the paddock and won't be back for weeks or even months.

SLAUGHTERHOUSES

Once a farmer has produced a jewel of a beast, it must be sent off to slaughter before it can be turned into case-ready cuts. If you feel yet another catch coming, your instincts are correct. First you have to find a slaughterhouse, or abattoir, which is more difficult than you might expect. Over the past thirty years or so, small family-operated slaughterhouses across the United States have been closing at an alarming rate, and very few new ones have opened to take their place. Where a farmer a generation or two ago would have had no trouble finding a "kill slot" at a small local slaughterhouse, today a farmer might be unable to find a slot at a slaughterhouse in his own state, or even a neighboring state! Many farmers in the Northeast have to drive for the better part of a day to get their animals to slaughter and then the slaughterhouse may not have a kill slot available, throwing off the farmer's rotation and depriving his customers of beef.

On a hopeful note, we may be on the edge of a new spate of small slaughterhouses opening because of the rise in demand for local meat and the corresponding increase in demand for more small- and medium-sized local abattoirs. Most of the slaughterhouses we use at The Meat Hook have opened in the last five years, and we couldn't do what we do without them.

Killing, Chilling, and Rigor

What is the slaughter process for large animals? Typically the animal (steer, hog, sheep, or goat) is led from its holding pen into what is called the kill chute, where it is held in place by some

GREG JUDY

The world of pasture-based agriculture is full of what might be called farmer-guru types. The most well known of these may be Joel Salatin of Polyface Farms, but I consider Greg Judy the most radical, and in the world of farmer-preachers, that is saying something indeed.

Greg's farming techniques are based on both his own experience and the work and theories of Ian Mitchell-Innes, the South African pioneer of mob grazing. Greg's style of attacking conformity and conservatism in the grass-based farming community and beyond through his simple, easy-to-understand books and lectures is becoming legend. And his techniques of longer resting periods between grazes, stockpiling hay without cutting or baling, and running massive herds of multiple species at once (like cattle, sheep, goats, and pigs) stand out in their fearless experimentation.

I am not a farmer and I am not a farming expert, so save your tomatoes for someone else. But I am suggesting that Greg Judy might be a guy you want to look up on the Internet and search for on YouTube. At this critical tipping point, the farming world could use a few more good preachers like him.

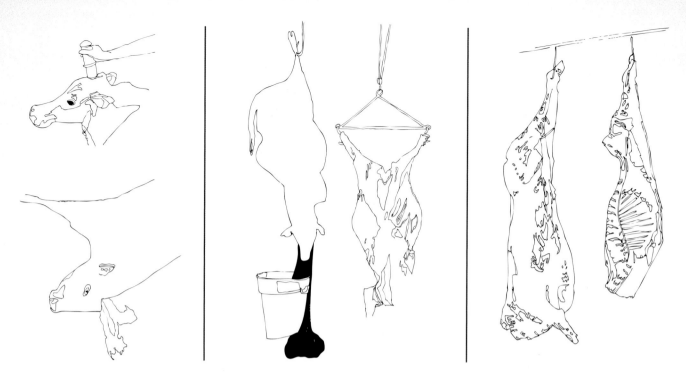

sort of restraint and stunned by means of either electric shock to the brain or a bolt gun. Once the animal is stunned ("stunned" is code for becoming unconscious and unaware of pain or what is happening), it is hauled up by its hind legs, its throat is cut, and it is left to bleed out through its cut jugular veins.

After the animal is killed and bled, it is eviscerated and, in the case of animals with hides like sheep and cattle, skinned. Hogs have their bristles removed by the means of a scalding tank that softens the bristles, and then the hair is scraped off. All animals are then washed, inspected, and taken off to chilling rooms, where fans blast them with cold air.

As I write this, I am fully aware of how grisly it all sounds, but I have no intention of softening any of the edges of slaughter. It is what it is: killing a living thing. To lie about it is the worst kind of treason against the truth. Everyone who eats meat should know where their meat comes from and what is involved at every step of the way in the slaughter process so they can make their own decision to be a carnivore or not based on their conscience. In the spirit of full disclosure, after I killed a pig for the first time and processed it, I nearly returned to my previous state of vegetarianism and quit butchering altogether. But I didn't. Instead, I saw past the brutal reality of slaughtering animals and realized that all animals die (human beings included), and what is really important is how they live. In fact, the act of killing that pig might have been the moment the Meat Hook mission, to support farmers raising animals in a humane manner, was born. Anyway, it's heavy stuff, and don't let anyone tell you different.

Slaughter, processing, or whatever you want to call it makes or breaks the quality of an animal's meat. A beautiful grass-fed steer can be ruined if it is not killed properly. The meat will be tough and spoil relatively quickly. Until recently, little was known about the whats, whys, and hows of the difference between a "good" and "bad" kill at the slaughterhouse outside of meat-sci programs at agricultural universities. Luckily for us, the amazing Nathan Myhrvold wrote *Modernist Cuisine,* and anyone who can beg, borrow, or steal a copy of his *Animals and Plants* volume can now access this once-esoteric information. The well-written but dense account from *Modernist Cuisine* can be summed up as follows: If an animal is sick, tired, stressed out, scared, cold, having an adrenaline reaction, or in any other way abused before slaughter, bad things don't just happen to the animal while it's alive, they happen to the flesh it leaves behind on the mortal plane.

When an animal is healthy, relaxed, properly handled, and killed well, the symphony of biological and chemical reactions that occurs after its death results in tender, flavorful meat with a good texture and a long keeping time. If not, the way the muscles transform themselves during the process of rigor mortis will have a negative result.

Rigor, for lack of another way to describe it, is the final act for the animal's muscles as it dies and becomes meat. What causes the stiffening of a carcass, or a body, probably does not have to be explained in depth in this age of procedural crime dramas, but here goes: once an animal dies, the muscles pull against each other (remember that all skeletal/muscle situations are based on a push/pull-lever model), and the tension on either side of each skeletal lever renders it stiff.

Once the muscles have gone into rigor, the systems that once regulated enzymes and movement are suddenly in a lawless environment, free to break down muscle fibers and proteins at will, resulting in the relaxation of the muscles and their inevitable breakdown into flavorful amino acids. How long the rigor process lasts depends on the makeup of the animal's muscles. Beef, for example, are high in myosin (the muscle protein that makes red meat red), which greatly affects rigor; they can take up to fourteen days to go through rigor, while chickens may take only a matter of hours.

LARRY ALTHISER

We have amazing relationships with the people at all of our slaughterhouses. We can call them up and make butcher jokes that no one "back home" would understand, ask them about upstate agricultural gossip, and generally shoot the shit in a laid-back way that seems so human and civil compared to the dog-eat-dog world of New York City.

However, among all the sweethearts we deal with (underneath their gruff exteriors, the guys at the slaughterhouses are sweethearts—well, most of them, at least), Larry, the owner of Larry's Custom Meats, just around the corner from the Baseball Hall of Fame in Cooperstown, New York, stands out. There are few people in the slaughter business who care more or know more and are willing to open their kill floor to cameras, unending questions, and even videographers. Every time we visit our slaughterhouses (about twice a year, sometimes more), we learn all sorts of new things. Some of the other slaughterhouse guys play their knowledge close to the vest, but Larry goes out of his way to share his lifetime of hard-won knowledge—not just with me and my partners, but also with interns and random regular customers we talk into coming along on our farm trips. (Did I mention that Larry is handsome and has the world's best handshake?)

PASTURE BREEDS I THINK ARE PRETTY AWESOME

So what breeds thrive on grass? Honestly, any breed can be bred to do really well on grass, and one hundred years ago, that's how all animals were raised. The only exceptions were semiwild cattle like Florida Crackers and Texas Longhorns, the hardiest of herds, which were selected by nature to do well in the wild. That said, in terms of good meat on the dinner plate, here are a few of the best.

Cattle

LOWLINE ANGUS

Lowlines are a sub-breed of Black Angus that was developed at an experimental cattle station in Australia during the 1970s. There they took two identical Angus herds and selected smaller cattle, the low line, and larger cattle, the high line. The results of the experiment showed that the low line (smaller, stockier cattle) did much better and produced more meat per acre than the high line (Angus that were bred larger and longer). Angus in general, and lowline Angus in particular, produce some of the most consistently tender and delicious meat. The fat is buttery and there is generally less gristle in the loin muscles than in that of other breeds.

ROTOKAWA RED DEVON

These guys are a sub-breed of a remote closed herd in New Zealand that was discovered by Gearld Fry (see page 297). Red Devons, or Southern Devons as they are sometimes called, are the result of the superior breeding practices originally introduced in Great Britain by Robert Bakewell, the inventor of modern line breeding.

HEREFORD

Of the common American breeds, Herefords seem to have been the least screwed up by the twentieth century. I'd like to think that their docile behavior and handsome looks caused ranchers to treat them differently, but in reality, I'm about 100 percent sure Herefords remained relatively unchanged because they didn't become a commodity brand name, like Black Angus.

SCOTTISH HIGHLAND

Scottish Highlands are cattle that look like pets. They're adorable and goofy like sheepdogs. They're also the best beef animal to put on really rough, marginal land and still get good meat from. Just make sure that your local slaughterhouse guy is cool with processing them before you buy them. Many places won't take beef with horns as big as those of the Scottish Highlands, because the processing is more dangerous.

Sheep

KATAHDIN AND DORPER

I'm putting the Katahdin and Dorper breeds together because they're the gold standard in grass-fed lamb and mutton production in the United States. Both breeds are hair sheep, which means that they don't grow wool as we know it and thus don't have to be wrangled off pasture several times a year to be shorn (which can be a real pain in the ass). Because they don't produce wool, their meat is milder tasting and less gamy in older, well-marbled animals, which is why we use these breeds exclusively.

Pigs

I know pigs aren't true pasture animals and most people feed them grain. However, I've included them here because when pigs get loose and run into the woods, they do just fine without someone bringing them a bucket of flaked corn every day. Some farmers, like Greg Judy (see page 299), even raise their Tamworths exclusively on grass and run them with their beef.

TAMWORTH

Tamworths are the standard pastured pig breed in our neck of the woods, because they are very aggressive foragers. Sometimes too aggressive—keep them away from your toes, kneecaps, and children; they can nip you!

BERKSHIRE

Most of the pork we sell in the shop on any given day is Berkshire, which we have raised for us by our two pig farmers. This breed came screaming back in the 1990s, and its name is pretty much code for good pork in the same way that "Angus" is synonymous with good beef. Berks live up to the hype flavorwise, without the ridiculous amount of fat that most heritage breeds put on. Plus, they are less likely to try to chew your boots off.

OSSABAWS

There's a lot of shit being talked these days about one pig breed being more delicious tasting than another. There's even a touring chef competition based on breed-tastiness shit talking. Listen up: what pigs eat is *way* more important than what breed they are. Feed a regular industrial white pig acorns during the last two months before slaughter, and you'll freak out over the taste. However, some breeds are hands-down better tasting than others, and for me, one such breed is the Ossabaw Island pig from coastal Georgia and its crosses. These pigs remind me of Pigpen from *Peanuts*. They have tiny (think glass slipper) feet, a mile of back fat, and a very small loin, but they're the best-tasting pork you can get this side of the exorbitantly expensive, exotic Euro breeds like Mangalitsa. Unfortunately, they're too fatty to work in our shop unless we're willing to throw out a lot of fat every week (no one buys that much lardo), so we stick to Berkshires.

OLD SPOTS

Old Spots are a real treasure. They're good foragers and have the temperament of a sweet sheepdog, and their meat is tender and delicious. Just be careful if you buy one of these pigs—you may end up with a pet instead of pork chop sandwiches.

FINAL THOUGHTS AND FURTHER READING

While I have tried to make this book as complete as possible on the topic of meat, the subjects of butchering, cooking, and charcuterie are vast. If this book has given you the itch to learn more (and I hope it has), the following books are great resources and solid starting points for further study.

The River Cottage Cookbook

by Hugh Fearnley-Whittingstall

This is the book that really started it all for me. Fearnley-Whittingstall's neo-back-to-the-land treatise on the pleasures of growing and eating your own food is as inspirational as it is fun to read. While you're probably not going to move to the country to start your own small holding farm, the well-written text and excellent, simple recipes might make you consider it.

Home Production of Quality Meats and Sausages

by Stanley Marianski and Adam Marianski

If you're interested in sausage making and advanced charcuterie, this book is an indispensable resource. The Marianskis merge hard-core meat science with the culinary capabilities of the average Joe, explaining all the hows and whys of sausage making, ham curing, smoking, and beyond. The best twenty bucks you'll ever spend.

Reproduction and Animal Health: How to Select, Breed, and Manage a Herd for Health and Performance on Grass

by Charles Walters and Gearld Fry

If you want to really nerd out on grass-fed cattle raising, this book, despite its cryptic and clinical title, is a good read and will fill in almost every possible blank when it comes to what makes good beef cattle great.

The Pig: A British History

by Julian Wiseman

If the Baconers and Lard Pigs sidebar in this book (page 121) gave you a taste for porcine history, Wiseman's history of the British pig is a fascinating account of how the pork we eat became what it is. Chock-full of historical documents and pig-breed esoterica for the heritage-breed-pig nerd.

You Can Farm: The Entrepreneur's Guide to Start and Succeed in a Farming Enterprise

by Joel Salatin

Written back when local food and pastured meat were most certainly not considered cool, this is farming and economics 101 by the master himself. If you really want to understand how farming works, this book will teach you in a single volume.

RESOURCES

Ambrosi Cutlery

Tel: 914-617-8444

www.ambrosicutlery.com

Mail-order knife sharpening service

Anson Mills

Tel: 803-467-4122

www.ansonmills.com

Coarse grits

Asian Supermarket 365

Tel: 888-822-8910

www.asiansupermarket365.com

Asian groceries, including longan honey and Chinese egg noodles (ramen)

Beecher's Handmade Cheese

Tel: 877-907-1644

www.beechershandmadecheese.com

Retail locations in New York City and Seattle

Fresh cheese curds

Butcher-Packer

Tel: 248-583-1250

www.butcher-packer.com

Digital scales, sausage-making supplies, cut-resistant cloth gloves, burger presses, collagen casings, high-quality grinders with size #22 plate

Chef Depot

Tel: 630-739-5200

www.chefdepot.net

Stainless steel chain-mail apron

D'Artagnan, Inc.

Tel: 800-327-8246

www.dartagnan.com

Frozen rabbits for online order

Dorkfood

www.dorkfood.com

Sous-vide supplies

Heritage Foods USA

Tel: 718-389-0985

www.heritagefoodsusa.com

Pork caul fat, Red Wattle bone-shoulder chops, small pigs (pigs larger than 20 pounds cannot be purchased online—seek out your local butcher or farmer)

Hudson Valley Foie Gras

Tel: 845-292-2500

www.hudsonvalleyfoiegras.com

Foie gras, duck hearts, duck fat

Mound Tool

Tel: 314-968-3991

www.moundtool.com

Butchering tools and supplies

The Sausage Maker, Inc.

Tel: 716-824-5814 or 888-490-8525

www.sausagemaker.com

Sausage casings, hog casings, small piston stuffers, high-quality grinder with size #22 plate

Soap.com

Tel: 800-762-7123

www.soap.com

1-gallon-sized vacuum bag and hand pump, bonito flakes

The Spice House

Tel: 847-328-3711

www.thespicehouse.com

Retail locations in Illinois and Wisconsin

Spices (including French 4-spice) and curing salts

And if you're looking for us:

The Meat Hook
100 Frost Street
Brooklyn, NY 11211
Tel: 718-349-5033
www.the-meathook.com

ACKNOWLEDGMENTS

First I would like to thank my business partners, Brent Young, Ben Turley, and Harry Rosenblum; our general manager, Sara Bigelow; and, of course, my wife, Annaliese Griffin. Without them there would be no Meat Hook.

I'd also like to thank the following (in no particular order) for guidance, inspiration, and good times: Nina Lalli, Jordana Rothman, Francis Mallmann, Hugh Fearnley-Whittingstall, Ted Allen, Fergus Henderson, Peter Kaminsky, Greg Morabito, Chloe Brownstein, MattyDeathBro, Matthew Jennings, Matt Greene, Corby Kummer, Ben Hudson, Joe Garden, Joe and Kat Randazzo and all of the people from the Onion-verse, Fred Morin, Martin Picard, Andrew Dorsey, Julie Powell, Kelly Geary, Sherri Wasserman, Kate Bonner, Sasha Davies, Francis Lam, Caroline Fidanza, Mike Odea, Carolyn Bane, Dennis Spina, Jean Adamson, Liza Queen, Edoardo Mantelli, CP, Brandon, Carlo, and the whole Roberta's crew, Bud and Jane Young, Lee Tiernan, Zak Pelaccio, Josh Applestone, Mark Firth, Andrew Tarlow and all Diner/Marlow alumni, Sean Rembold, Dave Gould (I really love picking thyme now; thank you!), Aaron Lenz, Eric Sherman, Millicent Souris, Anna Dunn, Stephen Tanner, Jose Soto, Holly Howard, Andrew Field, Zeb Stuart, Santiago Arango, Big Sexy and the La Fama crew in Bogotá, Alicia and Tuffet NYC (where this book was written), Judy Pray and everyone at Artisan, Jenni Ferrari-Adler, The East River Bar, Homer Murray, Lon Koontz and the Koontz family, Northwood Pizza, Jake Loiko, Lauren Griffin, the Ambrosi family, Evelyn Little, Danzig, Whiskey, the Couteau d'Argent crew, Keens, Sake Bar Hagi, the Richardson, Andy and Mateo Kehler, Rob Kaufelt (I still owe you $1,000), Anne Saxelby, Patrick Martins, Hugue Dufour, Ariane Daguin, Quino Baca and the Brooklyn Star crew, Joey Toes, Mikey Sideburns, Shanna Pacifico, Peter Hoffman, Kev Pemoulie, Brady Lowe, Noah Wall, Mike Fusco (our amazing designer!), Emma Straub, and, most of all, everyone we've ever worked with at The Meat Hook. Thank you so much for making it what it is.

INDEX

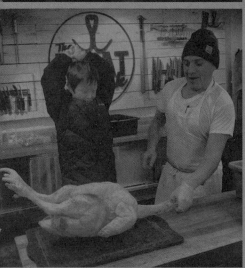

Local
Sustainable
Meat

RULE
#1
DONT BE
A DICK!